IMAGES
of America

MOUNT LAUREL

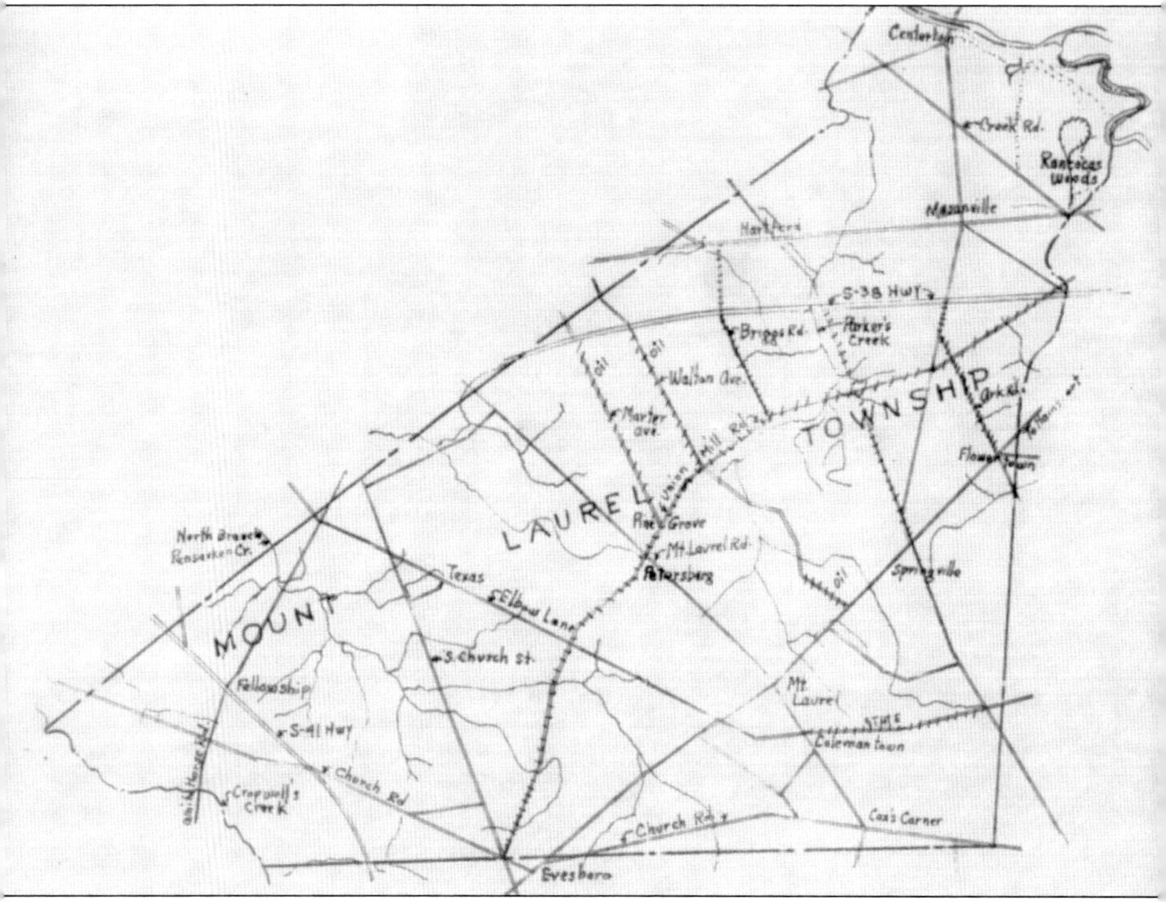

This simplified map of Mount Laurel shows not only the borders and streets, but also indicates where the various waterways, villages, and schools were located. (Courtesy of Robert E. DeBolt.)

On the Cover: Ned Comfort, age 11, and Nancy Comfort, 9, are shown in 1931 with their horse, Tilly. The horse pulled the lawn mower around the Comfort farm on Ark Road, where Bretton Way, Bedford Walk, and Woodlark developments are today. The Comfort family lost their home during the Depression after two fruit freezes. The bank was unable to lend the family any more money. (Courtesy of Nancy Jones.)

IMAGES
of America

MOUNT LAUREL

Stephanie Marks Sawyer

ARCADIA
PUBLISHING

ISBN 978-1-4671-2162-0

Published by Arcadia Publishing
Charleston, South Carolina

Printed in the United States of America

Library of Congress Control Number: 2013951301

For all general information, please contact Arcadia Publishing:
Telephone 843-853-2070
Fax 843-853-0044
E-mail sales@arcadiapublishing.com
For customer service and orders:
Toll-Free 1-888-313-2665

Visit us on the Internet at www.arcadiapublishing.com

This book is dedicated to my amazing daughters, Janna and Jadyn; my husband, Steve; and my parents, Darlene and Dennis, who discovered a wonderful community in 1978.

Contents

ACKNOWLEDGMENTS

I would like to acknowledge so many people who generously offered their time, stories, photographs, connections, and knowledge. First and foremost, I must thank Marie Reynolds, whose Browns Mills book inspired me to consider writing this history, and who then convinced me that I was the right person to do it. I am indebted to historian Paul W. Schopp, who altruistically edited everything for accuracy and flow. From the Mount Laurel Historical Society, I thank Fran Daily, who was happy to allow me to rummage through and photograph everything in Farmer's Hall and who answered my questions on numerous occasions.

Thank you to members, both past and present, of the Mount Laurel community who allowed me access to their family history, memories, and photograph collections: Pat DeBolt Noble, Maurice "Buddy" Rudderow, Hank Rudderow, Judith Monte, Debbie Monte Callahan, Gail Greenberg, Marian and Jim Hartshorne, Aubrey Haines, Calvin Forvour, Nancy Comfort Jones, Meg Burkhardt Ellis, Lucy Beard and the Alice Paul Institute, Shirley Clevenger Bootsma, Keith Carmelia, Charles Kester, Robbie Godfrey, Geoffrey Hall, police chief Dennis Cribben, Jim Ruhle, Dorothy Rudderow, the Fellowship Fire Company, Larry Sclaroff, Herb Diamond, Tony Trotter, and especially Annetta Havers Verner and Jarry Jones, who were undeniably invaluable. I hope I have done you all proud in retelling your stories and sharing the past through your personal photographs and recollections.

Richard Tremper, from the Masonville Fire Company, not only allowed me access to hundreds of photographs that he has been collecting over the years, but he helped identify people, apparatus, and locations. A big thank-you to James Morel from Second Time Books and to the fabulous librarians at the Mount Laurel Library who helped spread the word about my project and answered countless questions.

Additionally, a long-distance thank-you goes to nonresidents of Mount Laurel who made significant contributions: Jim Megee, Dr. O. Kirk Spurr, HistoricAerials.com, the *Burlington County Times*, Dennis McDonald, the Delaware State Archives, the Free Library of Philadelphia, Ruth Bogutz, and Russell T. Sharp via the goodness of Bill Gwodz.

Lastly, I thank Holly Troilo, who picked up the Fleetwood PTO slack when my attention was solely on Mount Laurel.

INTRODUCTION

Mount Laurel Township, located 17 miles outside of Philadelphia in historic Burlington County, is a thriving community. Originally part of Evesham Township, Mount Laurel comprises approximately 22 square miles and contains a population, as of 2010, of about 42,000 residents. In the late 1800s, the township had just over 1,000 residents, but the 1960s ushered in a large increase in population with the building of large housing developments, including Ramblewood and Larchmont.

Although Mount Laurel is sometimes associated with the significant "Mount Laurel" court decisions requiring towns to offer affordable housing, the town is also amazingly rich in history. The colonizers of this township can be traced back to Welsh and English Quaker immigrants who settled here in 1688. The William Evans Jr. family purchased 300 acres of land, including the "mount," and this is the earliest recorded land transaction in the township. The Evans family lived in an excavated depression, or "cave," on the side of the mount until they completed a cabin in 1694. Their dwelling stood at the intersection of two Native American trails at the base of the mount. Today, descendants of the Evans family still live in Mount Laurel, neighboring Evesham, and nearby towns.

After holding Sunday worship meetings in private homes, the local Quakers constructed a meetinghouse in 1698 on the east side of the mount. In 1717, the Evans family deeded just over one acre to the Society of Friends for meetings and to have "a place to bury their dead forever." The Friends completed a new meetinghouse in 1717, using Jersey sandstone quarried from the mount. In 1758, application was made to the Haddonfield Monthly Meeting to establish an official meeting at Evesham, which was granted in 1760. A school constructed in 1783 stood across Moorestown–Mount Laurel Road from the meetinghouse. Northwest of the meeting, the members constructed a schoolmaster's house in 1795, which later became the caretaker's house. The Friends' meetinghouse underwent other changes, observed in the stone pattern, which included additions in 1760 and 1798. The latter work included the demolition of the 1717 meeting and the reuse of the materials.

In 1760, the Quakers built the first schoolhouse in Mount Laurel, which was part of the Friends' meeting until 1828. As of 1880, there were five school districts in the township, and each had its own schoolteacher, property, and registered students. The school's medical needs were met by a member of the Moorestown Visiting Nurse Association, who spent one day a week in the Mount Laurel Schools. Nearly all of these schools were moved and then renovated, some multiple times, throughout the years. In 1918, the schools were consolidated and all of the small schoolhouses were closed over the next few years. Mount Laurel School No. 3 was moved to Mount Laurel Road and became the "colored" school, currently the Mount Laurel Schools Transportation Center. The other two schools were Masonville School, currently the offices of the grounds and maintenance department, and Mount Laurel School No. 1, currently the Hattie Britt Administration Building.

New Jersey played an important role in the Revolutionary War. In June 1778, the British Army and Hessian mercenaries evacuated Philadelphia for an overland march to Sandy Hook, where waiting ships would carry the forces to New York. Gen. Henry Clinton arrived in Mount Laurel with his soldiers, and the Friends' meetinghouse became provisional barracks for the troops, while Clinton used a nearby tavern as his personal headquarters and as a temporary hospital. Finding the local residents hostile to the military's presence, the British forces destroyed two houses by fire.

Prior to 1849, people referred to the mount as Evesham Mount, Mount Pray, Evans Mount, and even Penny Hill. In 1849, the US Post Office Department established the Mount Laurel Post Office in Mount Laurel Village. The New Jersey State Legislature used this name when it erected a new township out of Evesham Township's landmass in 1872. The new township included the small communities that had developed within the territory that would become Mount Laurel, including settlements named Centerton, Masonville, Hartford, Mount Laurel Village, and Fellowship, along with the African American enclave of Colemantown, Petersburg, and Little Texas.

The village of Centerton grew near the Rancocas Creek and contained a tavern and a lumber and coal yard. Just above Centerton, at a location known as "Texas," a phosphorus factory called Rancocas Chemical Works was established that also produced phosphates and sulfuric acids. In 1899, the Diamond Match Company purchased the plant and demolished it. The Centerton area also yielded molding sand used in the iron and steel industry. It was here that a bridge was built across the Rancocas Creek and also a wharf, where the steamboats and freight ships docked.

In 1867, the Camden & Burlington County Railroad completed its route between Camden and Mount Holly. The railroad's presence aided in community development, including Hartford village, which was established along the Mount Holly–Moorestown Turnpike, now known as Marne Highway, prior to the railroad's arrival. The village contained a general store, a post office, blacksmiths, and wheelwrights. Hartford had a public schoolhouse that was also used for visiting preachers; every few weeks, a different denomination would worship. Built in 1881 along Hartford Road, near the current turnpike access road, the Hartford Creamery Company processed 15,000 pounds of milk daily, fueled by steam. There are still active farms in the Hartford section of Mount Laurel.

Masonville, first known as Five Points, was another small village in Mount Laurel Township, located east of Hartford along Marne Highway, four miles from the county seat of Mount Holly. This settlement had a post office, established in 1868 due to the railroad's presence, a general store, a Methodist church, and a schoolhouse. There was also a foundry located near the railroad's passenger and freight depots.

Mount Laurel Village stood near the mount, centrally located in the township. The community featured a library, stagecoach stop, general store, and post office, which received mail daily by stagecoach from Philadelphia. The town also had the standard blacksmith and wheelwright shops. The Darnell family owned much of the land in this area. PAWS farm, a modern nature center, is located on the Darnells' historic homestead property, which dates to the early 1700s. This property also contains a cemetery where members of the Darnell family are buried.

Another section of Mount Laurel, called Fellowship, is located near what is now Route 73, formerly Route S-41. Fellowship had general stores, a wagon shop, a shoe shop, mechanics' shops, and a Catholic congregation that met on the second floor of the blacksmith shop. This area was an agricultural community and had various farms raising chickens and producing milk, vegetables, and other goods. Farm produce was shipped via a variety of routes to their marketplaces, including the Rancocas Creek, the Moorestown–Mount Holly Turnpike, the Moorestown–Mount Laurel Turnpike, and, in later years, the railroad. Although many of the farms no longer exist, they formed the foundation for a growing community. Most of the farms in old Mount Laurel have been razed to create large developments of single-family homes, townhouses, or apartments.

Colemantown once existed down the road from the mount on Elbo Lane. It featured 10 to 12 houses, a store, a tollhouse, and a carpenter shop. The Colemantown Colored Cemetery, located behind Jacob's Chapel, contains the graves of black Civil War soldiers. James Still, an herbalist doctor without formal training and known as the "Black Doctor of the Pines," is also buried at the cemetery. Colemantown served as a stop on the Underground Railroad.

A famous Quaker, suffragette Alice Stokes Paul, lived in Mount Laurel throughout her childhood. When she reached school age, Alice walked a mile to the Moorestown Friends' School. Alice Paul dedicated her life to obtaining equal rights, including that of voting, for women. In 1923, she authored an Equal Rights Amendment to the US Constitution that the US Senate finally approved in 1972, but the required number of states failed to approve the amendment on a timely basis. "Paulsdale" still stands off Hooten Road in Mount Laurel and is now home to the Alice Paul Institute, where work continues to advance equality and rights for women.

Although Mount Laurel has changed throughout the years, with housing developments taking over nearly all of the farmland that was once prevalent, there are still families in the township descended from early residents. Many landmarks can still be found and are a tribute to the people who established the fine community that Mount Laurel Township is today.

One

The Early Days and Foundations of Mount Laurel

The Rancocas Creek was an important waterway for the early inhabitants in the Mount Laurel area. Early watercraft included Native American dugout canoes, flatboats, and small sailing vessels. During the early 19th century, boats powered by horses, and then steamboats, navigated the creek, along with various types of rigged commercial boats, including sailing barges. Places in Mount Laurel that used vessels to transport goods included the Rancocas Chemical Works and the Huelings Lumberyard at Centerton. The chemical works manufactured phosphates, fertilizers, and sulfuric acid and had 35 employees in 1886. The Diamond Match Company purchased the works in 1899, razed the buildings, and sold the land.

During the Revolutionary War, present-day Mount Laurel Township was in the crosshairs when Gen. Henry Clinton led British and Hessian troops through the area on the night of June 19, 1778, during their retreat from Philadelphia. Most of the force encamped around the Friends' meetinghouse at the base of the mount, while Clinton and his senior officers used Abraham Matlack's farmhouse on Hainesport–Mount Laurel Road as an overnight headquarters. Some ill and wounded soldiers also received treatment here.

Mount Laurel, at 450 feet above sea level, is the highest point in Burlington County. It has had many names through the years, including Evans' Mount, Mount Pray, and Evesham Mount. Nearby, the Friends' meetinghouse carried the name "Evesham." Hannah Gillingham, a teacher at the school near the mount, named Mount Laurel for the profuse stands of laurel growing nearby. The US Post Office Department formalized the name when officials established the Mount Laurel Post Office in 1849. At the base of the mount sits Farmer's Hall, constructed in 1866 for the Mount Laurel Farmer's Club, which had 102 stockholders. At different points throughout the years, it housed the town hall, the Mount Laurel Pursuing & Detective Company, and the Mount Laurel Police Department.

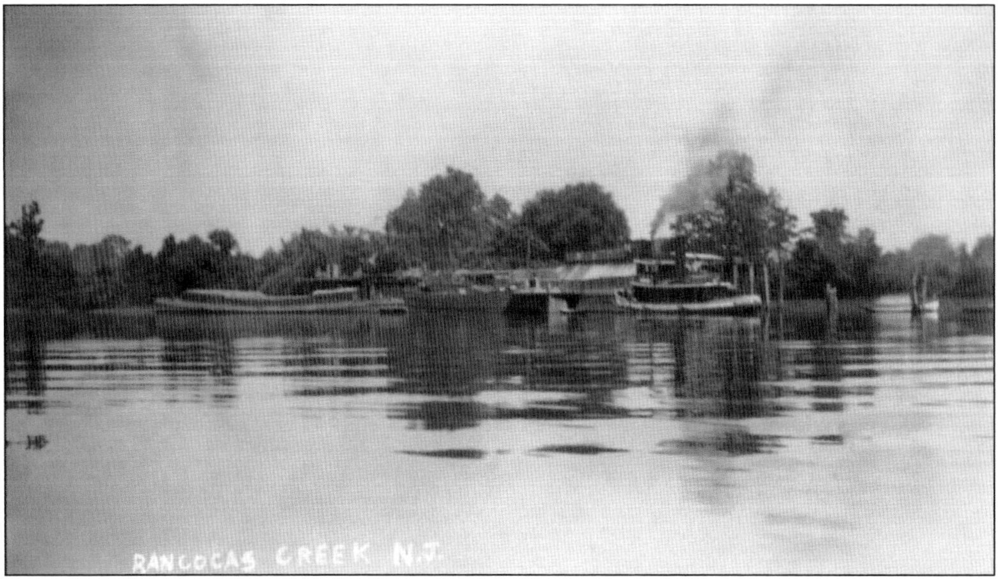

The banks of the Rancocas Creek featured numerous deposits of various types of sand, including foundry molding sand. In this 1907 photograph, J.W. Paxson's tugboat *Minerva* waits to transport sand-filled barges to Philadelphia, to the company's depot at Pier 45 North. The wharf seen here, with the narrow gauge sand train on top, stood between the Centreton Bridge and the New Turnpike Bridge over the creek on the south bank. (Courtesy of the Paul W. Schopp Collection.)

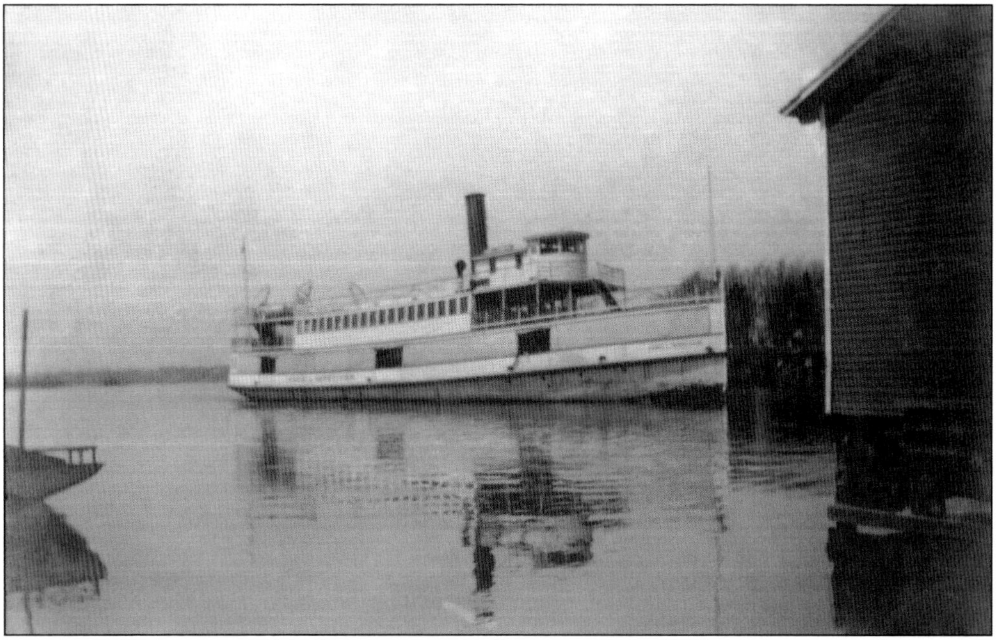

Constructed in 1904 at the Dialogue Shipyard at Kaighn's Point, Camden, New Jersey, at a cost of $42,000, Capt. Vansciver's second *Annie L. Vansciver* was the desire of every moonlight cruise on the Rancocas. She cut through the creek's currents for only three years before the company sold her to the North River Line of Albemarle Sound in North Carolina. Here, she is waiting by the Gibbs family boathouse while a Mr. Johnson uses the large key to open Centreton Bridge. (Courtesy of the Paul W. Schopp Collection.)

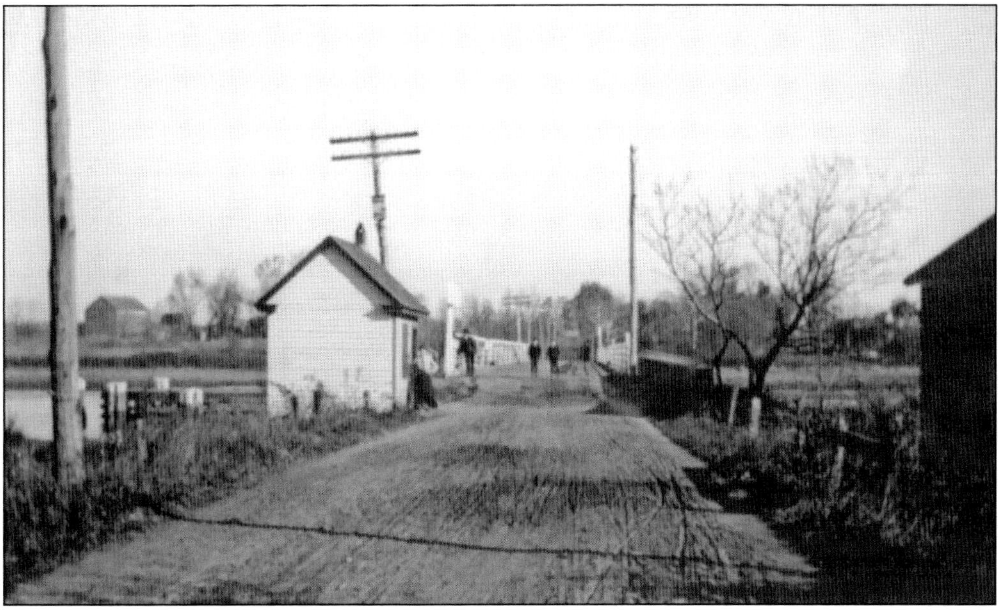

Centerton Bridge is seen here about 1910. In 1832, the Board of Chosen Freeholders completed the first bridge at this crossing, joining Centerton with Willingboro over the Rancocas Creek at a cost of $8,000. In this view of the third bridge built here, a dirt road leads past the tollgate house, shown to the left of the bridge. The keeper was Everett Johnson's grandfather. (Courtesy of Robert E. DeBolt.)

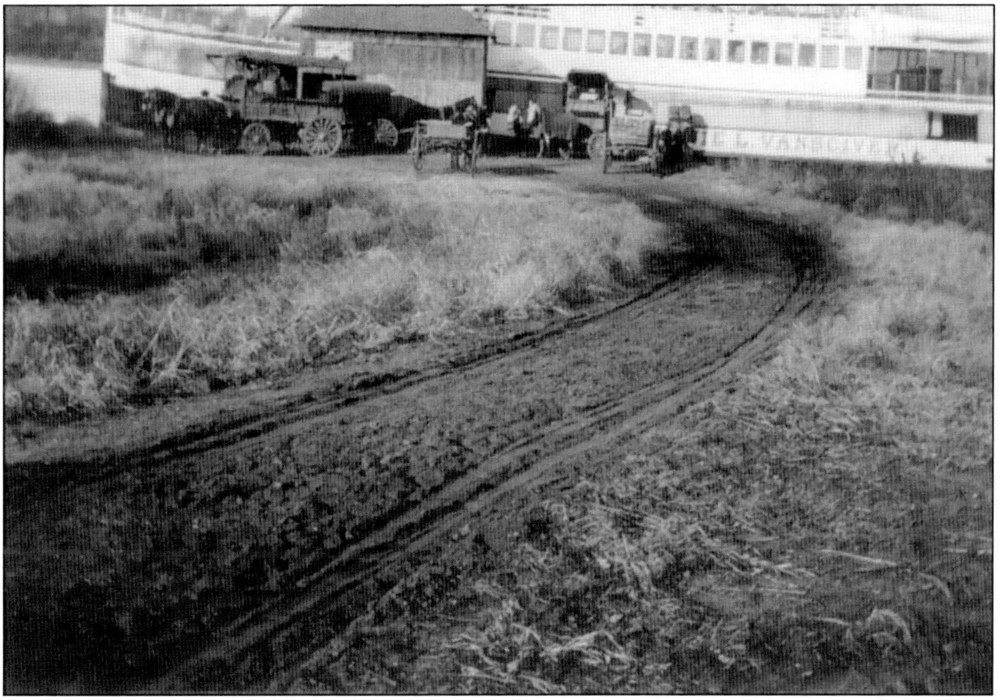

This photograph shows the steamer *Annie L. Vansciver* being loaded with freight at the wharf above the Centerton Road Bridge. This steamer also took many excursions along the Rancocas Creek up to Hainesport and on the Delaware River. (Courtesy of Robert E. DeBolt.)

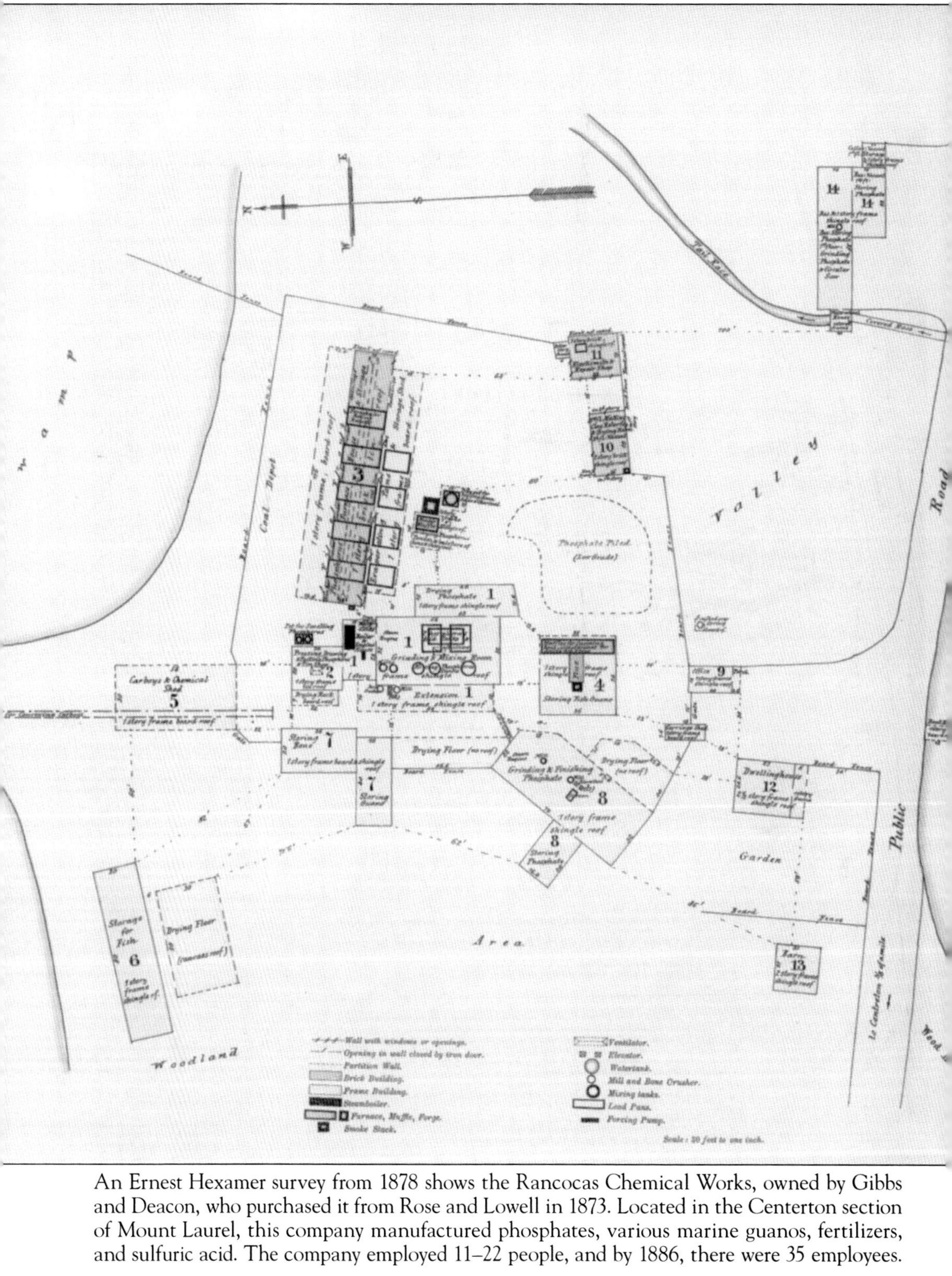

An Ernest Hexamer survey from 1878 shows the Rancocas Chemical Works, owned by Gibbs and Deacon, who purchased it from Rose and Lowell in 1873. Located in the Centerton section of Mount Laurel, this company manufactured phosphates, various marine guanos, fertilizers, and sulfuric acid. The company employed 11–22 people, and by 1886, there were 35 employees.

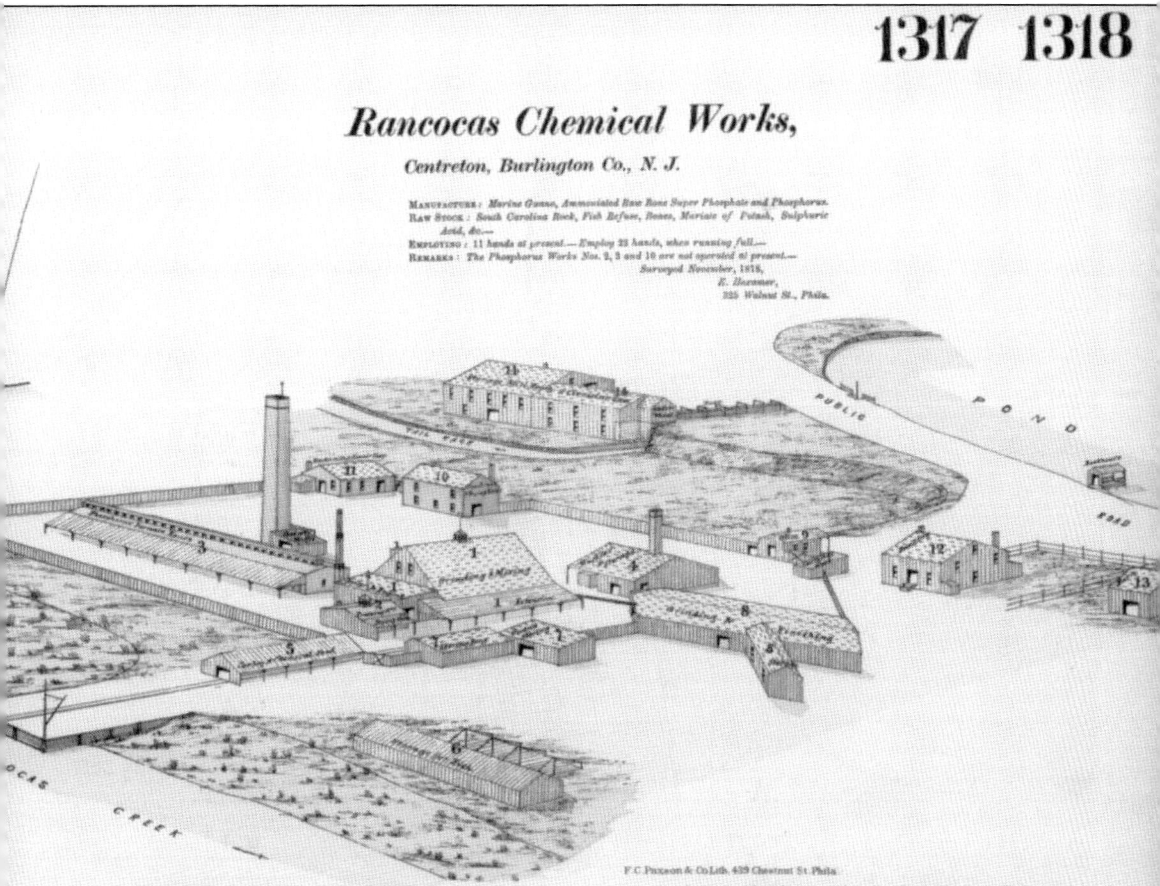

1317 1318

Rancocas Chemical Works,

Centreton, Burlington Co., N. J.

MANUFACTURE: *Marine Guano, Ammoniated Raw Bone Super Phosphate and Phosphorus.*
RAW STOCK: *South Carolina Rock, Fish Refuse, Bones, Muriate of Potash, Sulphuric Acid, &c.—*
EMPLOYING: 11 *hands at present.—Employ* 22 *hands, when running full.—*
REMARKS: *The Phosphorus Works Nos.* 2, 3 *and* 10 *are not operated at present.—*

Surveyed November, 1878,
E. Hexamer,
325 *Walnut St., Phila.*

F.C. Paxson & Co.Lith. 429 Chestnut St. Phila.

OWNERS: *Property owned by Gibbs and Deacon.—Materials for manufacturing phosphates owned by J. J. Allen's Sons.—*
SUPERINTENDED: *by the owners.—*
NAME: *Rancocas Chemical Works.—*
LOCATION: *Situated on the Rancocas Creek, near Centreton, Burlington Co., N. J.,* 1½ *miles from Masonville Station, Penna. R. R.—*
AGE: *Buildings erected* 1871.—*Age of No.* 14 *unknown.—*
CONSTRUCTION: *Good.—No.* 6 *and No.* 14 *in bad condition.—No.* 6 *now undergoing repairs.—*
COMMUNICATIONS: *Iron doors on furnace house No.* 3, *communicating with extensions North and South.—*
POWER: *steam.—Use waterpower in No.* 14.—
HEIGHT: *Main building No.*1, 14' *and* 30'.—*Boiler and Engine house No.* 1, 16' *and* 24'. —*Phosphate drying room No.* 1, 10'.—*No.* 2, 10'.—*No.* 3, 11' *and* 14'.—*No.* 4, 7' *and* 14'.—*No.* 5, 5' *and* 16'.—*No.* 6, 9' *and* 18'.—*No.* 7, 7' *and* 12'.—*No.* 8, 10' *and* 16'.—*No.* 9, 9'.—*No.* 10, 9'—6' *and* 12'.—*No.* 11, 10' *and* 18'.—*No.* 14, 10'—9' *and* 16'.—
LENGTH: *see plan.—*
WALLS: *No.* 3, 13".—*No.* 10, 9"—9".—*No.* 11, 9".—*Part of basement of No.* 14, 18" *stone walls.—*
CEILINGS: *in office No.* 9, *mill room No.* 14, *and phosphate drying room No.* 1, *lathed and plastered.—Others not finished.—*
ROOF: *as per diagram.—*
GUTTERS: *none.—Wooden gutter on north side of No.* 10.—
CORNICE: *of wood.—*
SCUTTLE: *none.—*
TOWER: *none.—*
LADDERS: *None permanent.—Some wooden movable ladders kept, reaching to the roofs.—*
LIGHTNING ROD: *with one point on smoke stock, none on buildings.—*
FLOORS: *Brick floor in boiler and engine house No.* 1, *in No.* 2, *No.* 3 *and No.* 4.—*Brick and wood flooring in main building No.* 1.—*Iron flooring in drying room No.* 1. —*Cement flooring in* 1*st story of No.* 10.—*Ground floors in Nos.* 5 *and* 11.—
WINDOWS: *as per plan and view.—*
STAIRWAY: *none.—*
ELEVATORS: *two belt and bucket elevators* (a *and* b) *in Nos.* 1 *and* 8, *for conveying phosphate from mills to top of screens.—*
HATCHWAY: *none.—*
MACHINE SHOP: *none.—Repairing done in No.* 11.—
FORGE: 1 *brick forge in No.* 11, *built on ground floor.—*

WOOD SHAVINGS: *only made in case of repairs.—Use occasionally one circular saw in No.* 14 *for cutting lumber.—*
HEATING: *Works warmed by natural heat of manufacturing fires.—*
STOVES: 1 *cast iron stove in No.* 2 *and* 1 *in No.* 9, *well secured.—*
STOVEPIPES: *sound and in good order, entering brick chimneys built from the ground.—*
LIGHTED: *No lights used.—*1 *enclosed kerosine lantern for night watchman.—*
WATCHMAN: *night watchman on the premises.—*
WATCHCLOCK: *none.—*
FUEL: *Anthracite and Bituminous Coal.—*
BOILER: *located as per plan, enclosed by brick walls, in proper distance of wood works.—*
BOILER CHIMNEY: *of brick, plastered inside, rising* 42 *feet above the ground.—*
STEAM ENGINES: *three,* 50—10—10 *horsepower.—*
STILLS: *none.—*
RETORTS, FURNACES AND PANS: *of brick, iron and lead, well constructed, located as per plan.*
SMOKE STACK: *of furnaces in No.* 3, *of brick, plastered inside, rising* 80 *feet above the ground.—Underground flues leading from furnaces to smoke stack.—*
DRYING: *Phosphate drying in No.* 1, *iron plates floor, plastered walls and plastered ceiling, heated by steampipes resting on iron.—Bone and fish dried at present on muffles in No.* 4.—*Phosphate rock dried outside of No.* 2 *by exhaust steampipes from engine.—Drying done by open atmospheric air on drying floors outside of No.* 6 *and* 8.—*Clay retorts dried in* 1*st story of No.* 10 *on brick flue with iron plate running around the building at the foot of walls.—Phosphorus powder (a mixture of ground bone, charcoal and sulphuric acid) dried in muffle outside of No.* 2.—
ACIDS: *Keep on average* 1000 *to* 1200 *carboys of Sulphuric acid in No.* 5.—
OCCUPANCY: *as per plan.—*
PROVISIONS FOR EXTINGUISHING FIRE:
PUMP: *Knowles' steam pump* (c) *in boiler and engine house No.* 1, *with* 1" *hose connection.—Pump used for supplying boiler.—*
HOSE: 125 *feet* 1" *rubber hose kept attached to pump.—*
WATER TANKS: *Two iron water tanks in boiler room, supplied by underground iron waterpipes from the pond.—Water tanks for supplying boiler.—*
STEAM FIRE COMPANY: *Nearest one in Mount Holly, within four miles, can be summoned by steam whistle.—Volunteer Fire Department in Mount Holly.—*
CARE IN MANAGEMENT: *Fair.—*
GENERAL CONDITION OF THE PROPERTY: *Good; except No.* 6 *and* 14.—
EXTERNAL EXPOSURES: *none.—*
MACHINERY: 6 *grinding mills* (5 *by steam and* 1 *by waterpower).—*1 *crusher.—*3 *mixers.—*1 *six foot revolving screen.—*2 *elevators with* 24 5" *iron buckets and* 50 *feet rubber belt.—*1 *steamboiler.—*3 *steam engines.—*2 *steam pumps (only one used).—*1 *circular saw.—*1 *hydraulic press.*

There was housing on location for the workers. Rancocas Chemical Works was located where the Timbercrest development is today. This area was eventually bought by the Diamond Match Company, which razed the facilities. (Courtesy of the Free Library of Philadelphia.)

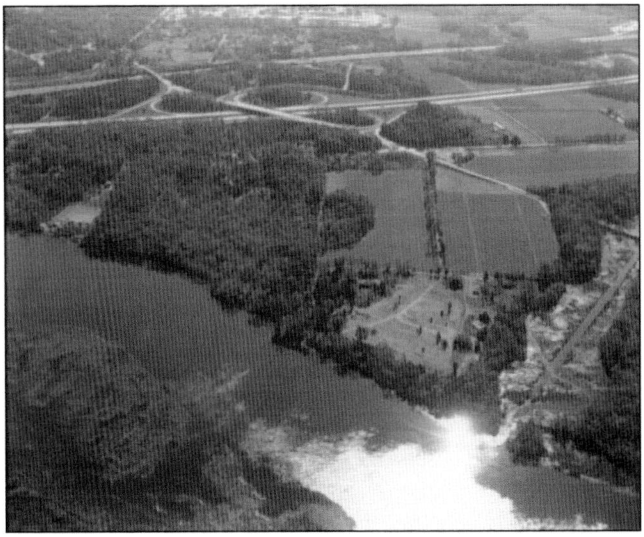

This aerial photograph of the Rancocas Creek and Centerton shows Buzby's Farm. The Wheeler sisters, schoolteachers, originally owned the property, including the house, which dated to the mid-to-late 1800s. They sold the property to a former mayor of Willingboro, Thomas Buzby, and his wife, Betty. The Buzby family subdivided the farm and sold it to a man named Loux, who conveyed the old farmhouse to William E. Carmelia and his partner, Lawrence J. Babb, in 1974. (Courtesy of Keith Carmelia.)

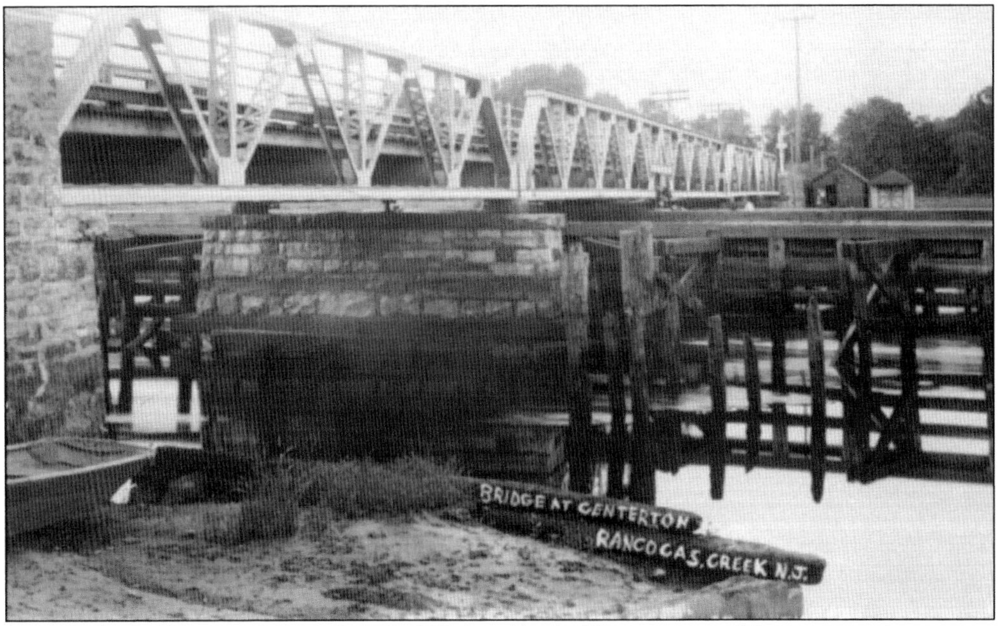

In 1907, the Burlington County Board of Chosen Freeholders contracted for a new bridge to cross the Rancocas at Centreton. The third span erected at this creek crossing remains in place today, now over 100 years old. A large key inserted into a gear would open the swing span. Today, the county has welded the bridge closed. (Courtesy of the Paul W. Schopp Collection.)

Danley's Cigar Store, located at the corner of Masonville Road and Woolman Street, was built in 1870. From the signs, it looks like the store also sold grocery items. Mr. Danley would burn his trash in his yard and, in one incident, suffered severe burns, forcing him to close the store. It is a private residence today. (Courtesy of Harry Herring.)

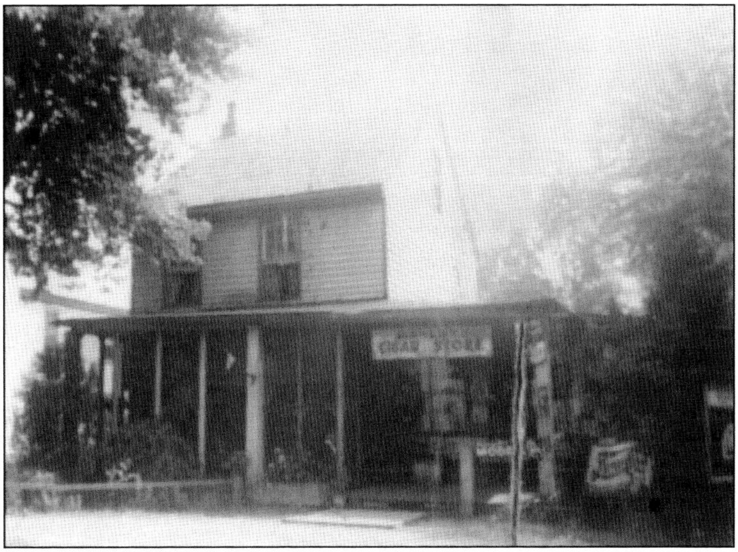

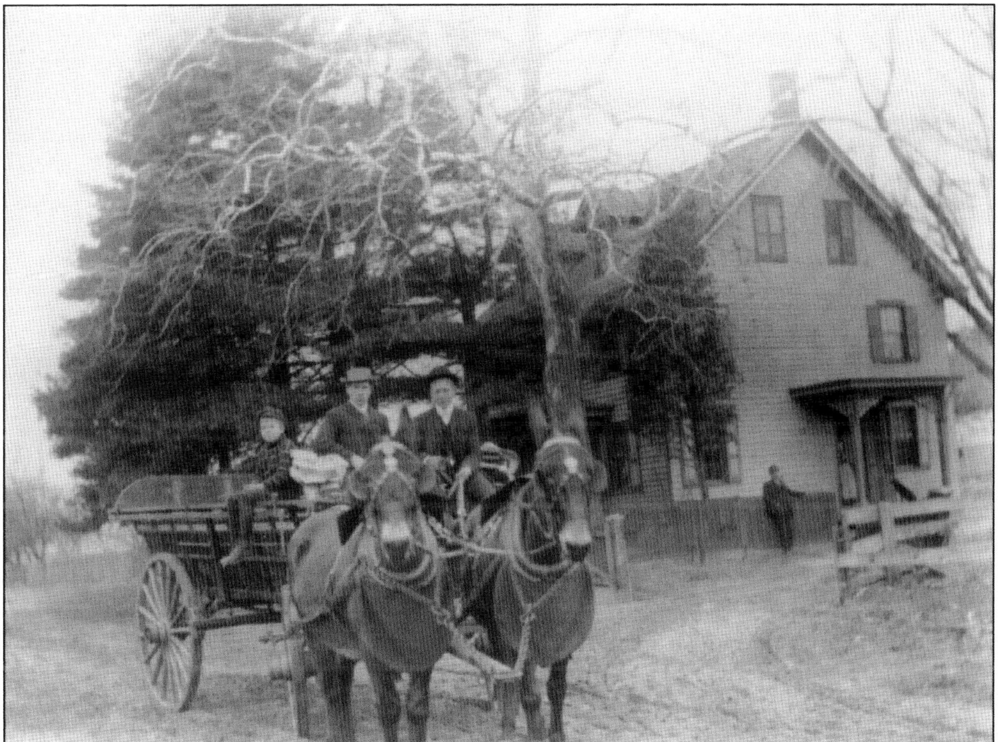

This home still stands today, directly behind the Benjamin Moore paint store, formerly Melcer's Grocery. The photograph is undated, but it was taken when Masonville Road was a still a dirt thoroughfare. Today, all of the trees in this photograph are no longer standing. The people shown here are unidentified. (Courtesy of Richard Tremper and the Masonville Fire Company.)

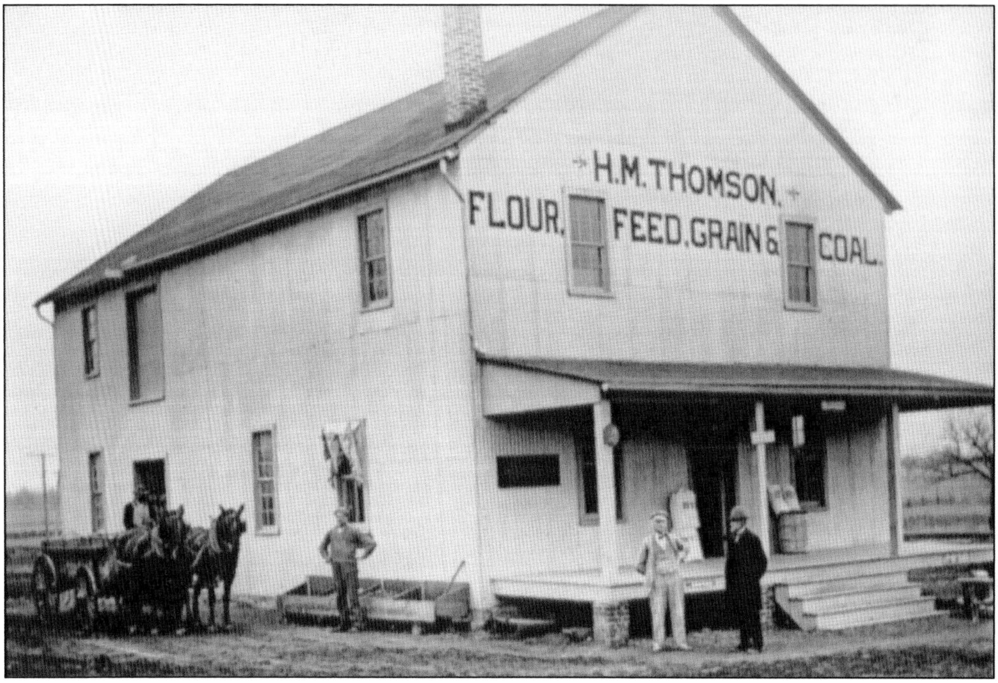

This late-1920s photograph shows Thomson's feed and grain store, built in the early 1890s near the Masonville train station. In front of the store, H.M. Thomson (second from right) is talking to Mark Buzby, one of Mount Laurel's first town council members. On the left, Ellis Forvour, driving the horses, has his cart weighed by Dennis, a helper at the mill. This building currently stands next to where the Masonville depots were at the corner of Ark Road and Marne Highway. (Courtesy of Robert E. DeBolt.)

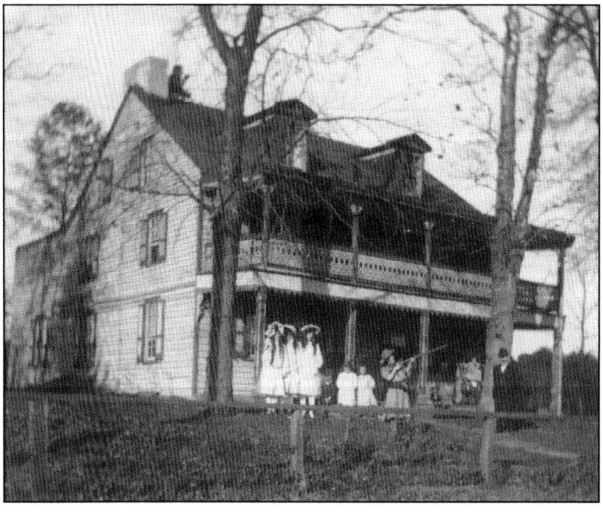

Caleb Lane appears to be the first tavern keeper at the Bull's Head Tavern, which stood on the site now occupied by the Cater2U establishment. Lane opened the tavern in 1802. Other tavern keepers included Solomon Mason (1818), Joseph Tallman (1819–1820), John Hackney (1821–1823), John Davis (1824), and Joseph Nixon (1825–1830), who called the tavern the Farmer's Hotel. In this 1907 photograph, a young woman dressed like Annie Oakley appears to be protecting a group of girls dressed in white. (Courtesy of the Paul W. Schopp Collection.)

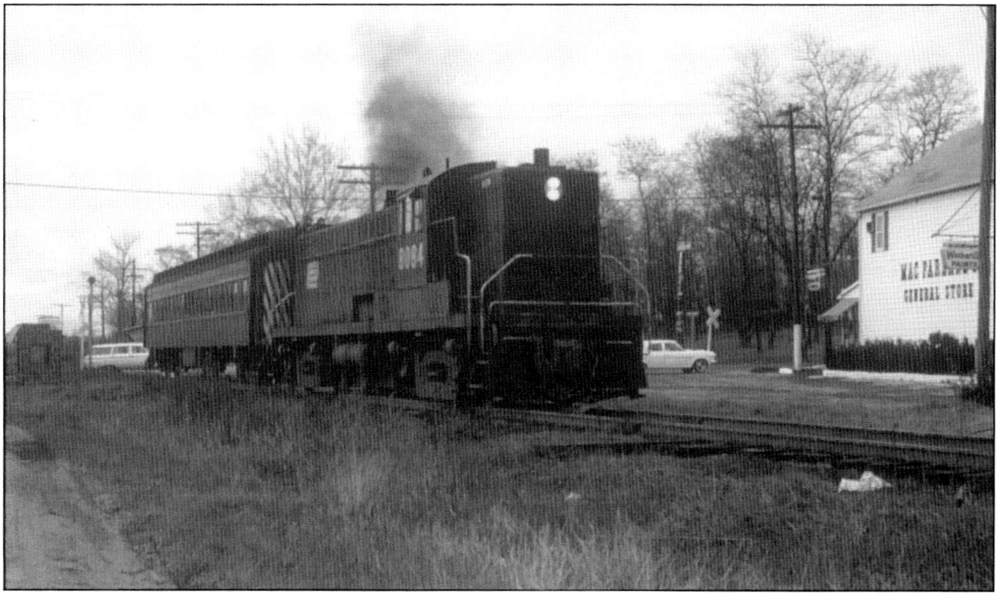

This photograph from April 1969 shows the Pennsylvania Railroad's train No. 988 heading toward Camden. Masonville and Hartford had freight depots as well as passenger stations, where people could catch the Camden & Burlington County Railroad. Visible in the distance, right of center, is the Boy Scout's totem pole; it was taken down in the 1980s. On the right, H.M. Thompson's feed and grain store had become MacFarland's General Store. In 1981, it became J&J Hardware. Siding was installed over the corrugated tin, which is still there today. (Courtesy of Russell T. Sharp.)

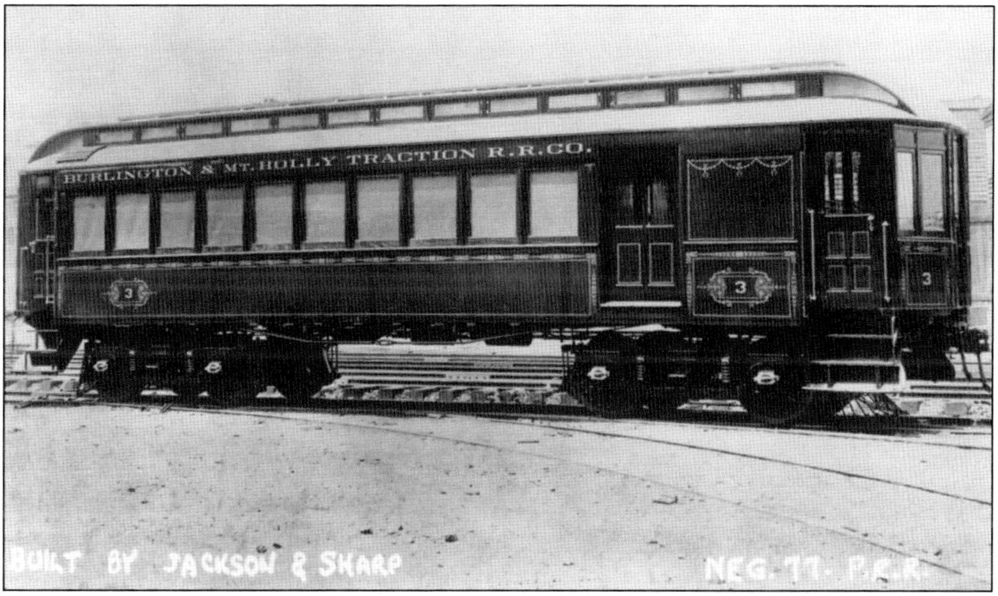

This photograph shows the type of passenger train car that ran on the local railroads in the late 1800s and early 1900s. With trains running between Camden and Mount Holly, there were railroad stations in Mount Laurel at Hartford and Masonville. The Pennsylvania Railroad continued to operate regular routes between Camden and Pemberton through the 1960s. (Courtesy of the Delaware State Archives.)

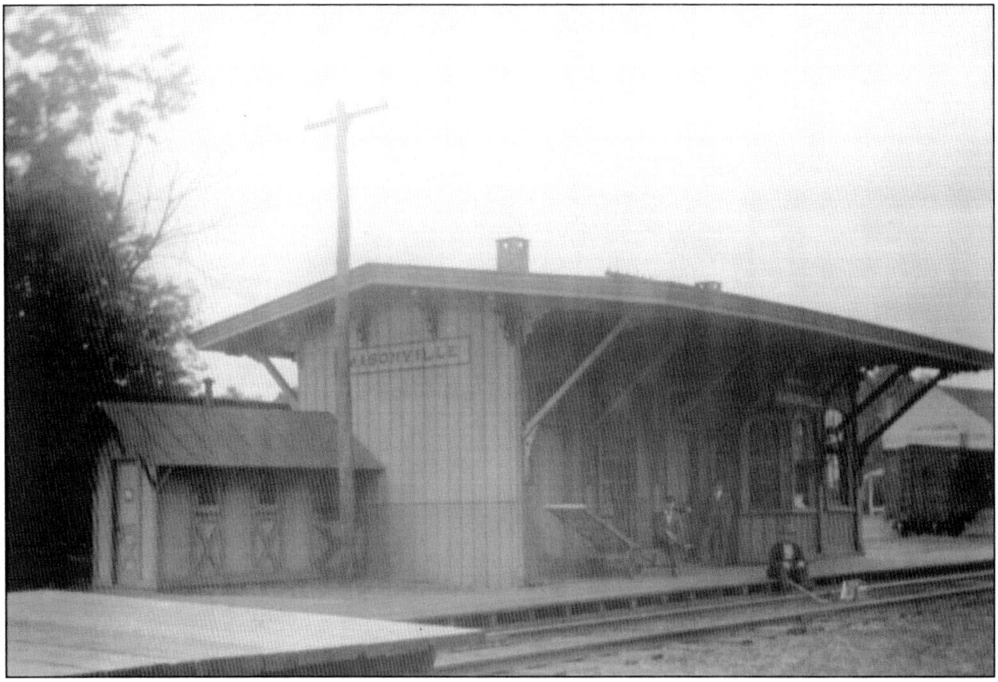

The Pennsylvania Railroad's Masonville train station stood along Marne Highway near Ark Road. Shown sitting on the platform is the trackwalker, whose job included not only keeping the tracks free of debris, but also checking the joints and looking for broken rails. Also on the platform, sitting on the baggage cart, is Carl Devis. (Courtesy of Robert E. DeBolt.)

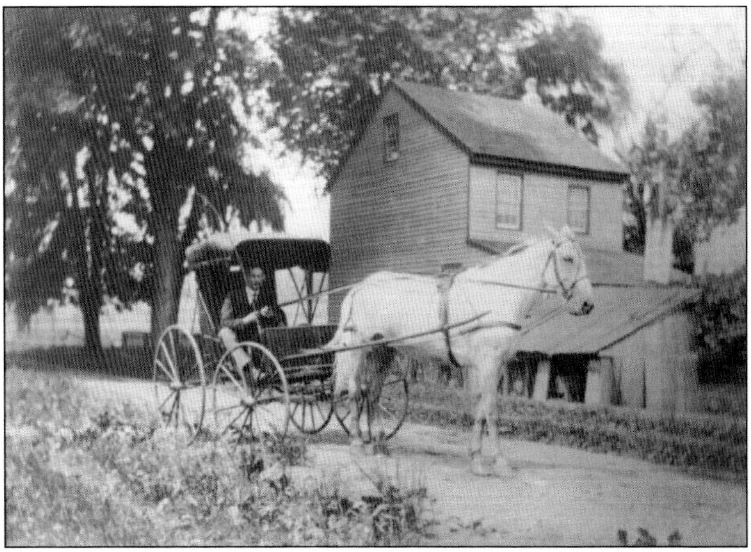

This c. 1910 photograph, looking toward Masonville Road, shows Ed Proud with his horse and buggy on Woolman Street. Proud, the Masonville truant officer for the schools, lived on Masonville Road next to the Masonville Methodist Church. (Courtesy of Harry Herring.)

According to the 1876 *Scott's Atlas*, the I.W. Heulings' Sons company had a coal yard and a lumberyard in Centerton, built in 1870, near the Phosphorus Works of Gibbs and Deacon (Rancocas Chemical Works). Also nearby was the Centreton Hotel and the steamboat wharf. Vessels brought lumber from Maine via the Delaware River to the Rancocas, to be offloaded at the lumberyard. (Courtesy of the author.)

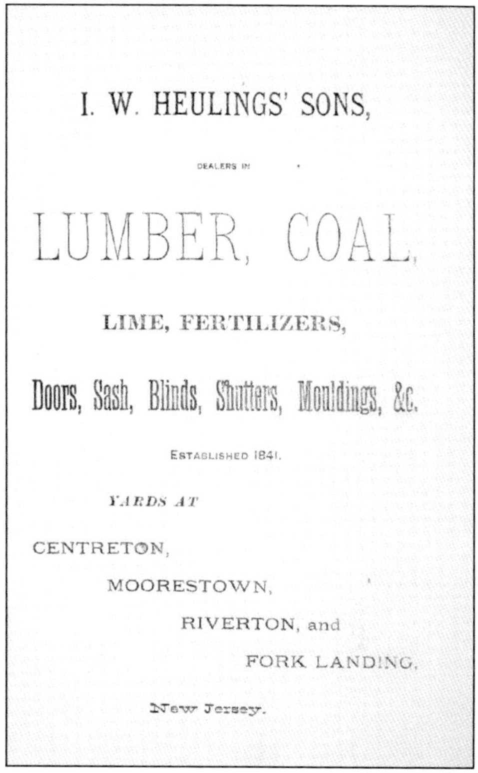

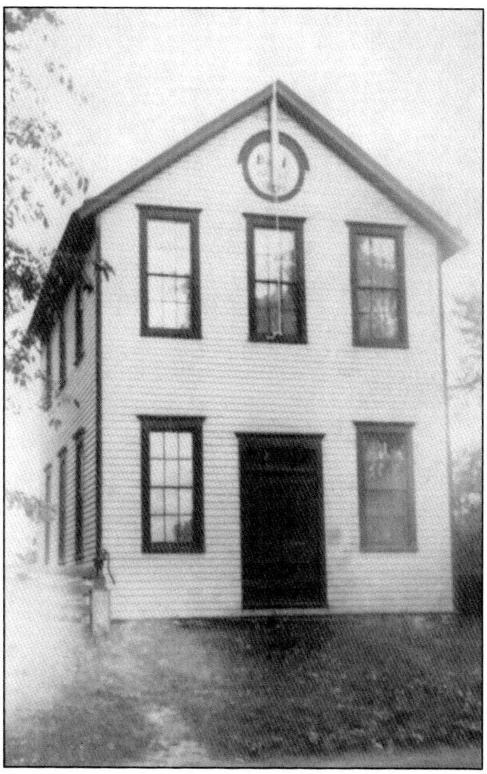

This hall, which stood near the church on Masonville Road, housed the fraternal organization Brotherhood of America. The Masonville Glee Club and other forms of entertainment used this location as well. A water pump is visible near the front door, and the sign at the top of the hall shows a date of 1836. (Courtesy of Robert E. DeBolt.)

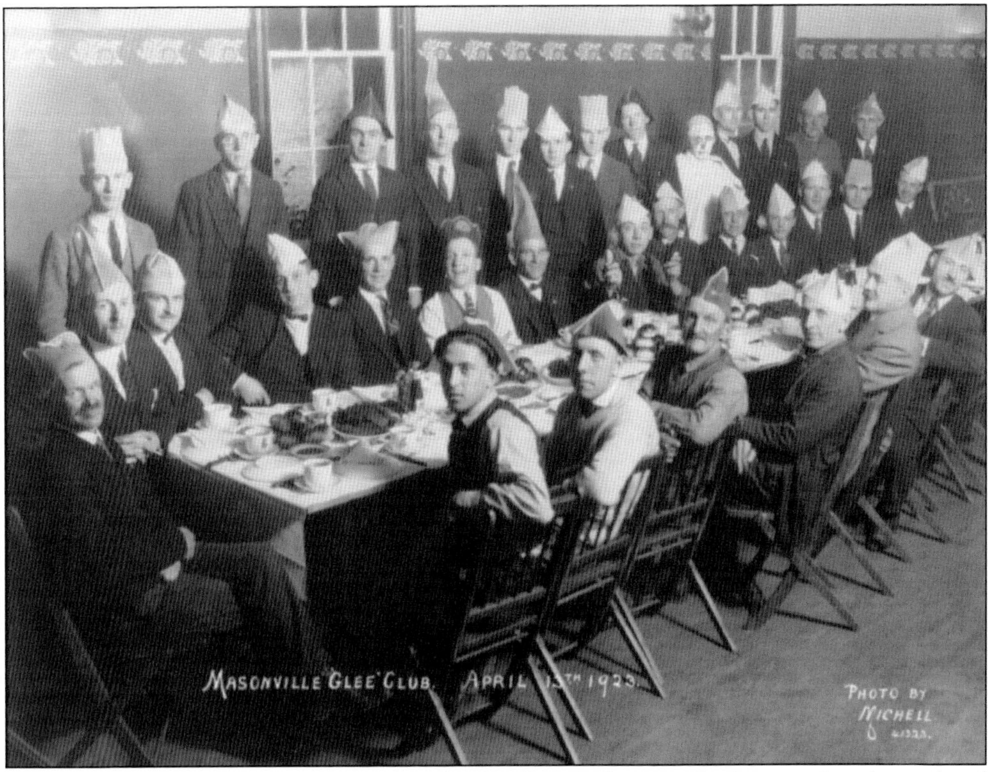

The Masonville Glee Club is pictured in the April 1923 photograph above and in the undated photograph below. The club put on musical performances and minstrel shows, and it helped out in the community. When the Masonville United Methodist Church needed a pipeless heater, the men of the Masonville Glee Club volunteered to dig a basement beneath the existing building to aid in its installation. (Courtesy of Richard Tremper and the Masonville Fire Company.)

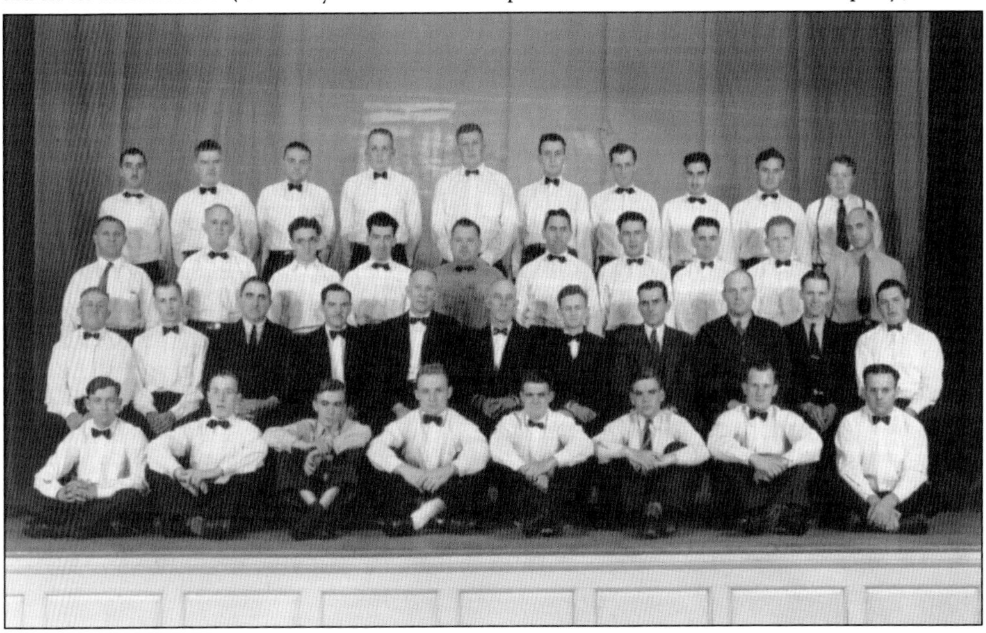

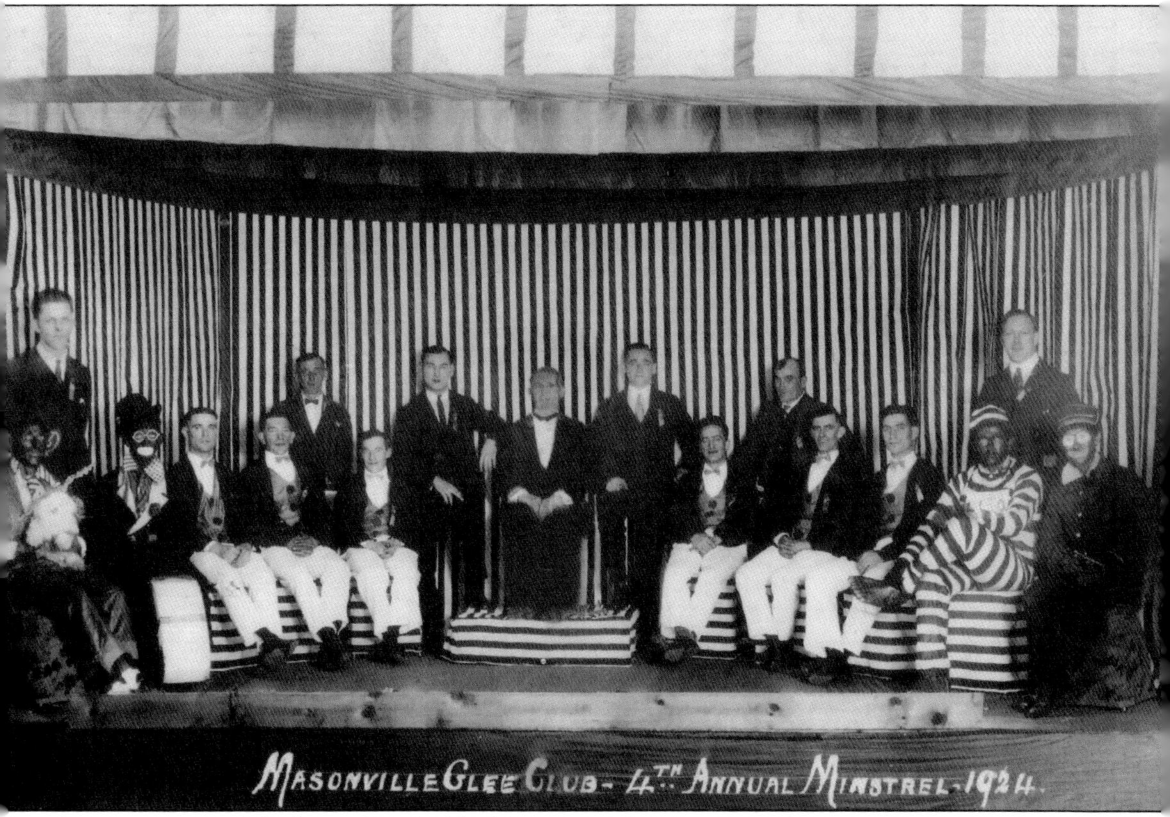

Beginning around the late 1830s, the blackface minstrel act was a popular form of entertainment. In this highly racist depiction of African Americans, white men attempted to caricature or imitate their perceptions of black people. Unfortunately, many people assumed that those characterizations really reflected black culture, and it had a detrimental effect on societal views of blacks. Minstrel shows had different sets of acts, but each had a variety section, which was a precursor to vaudeville. The Masonville Glee Club participated in these types of shows, as seen in this photograph from 1924. (Courtesy of the author.)

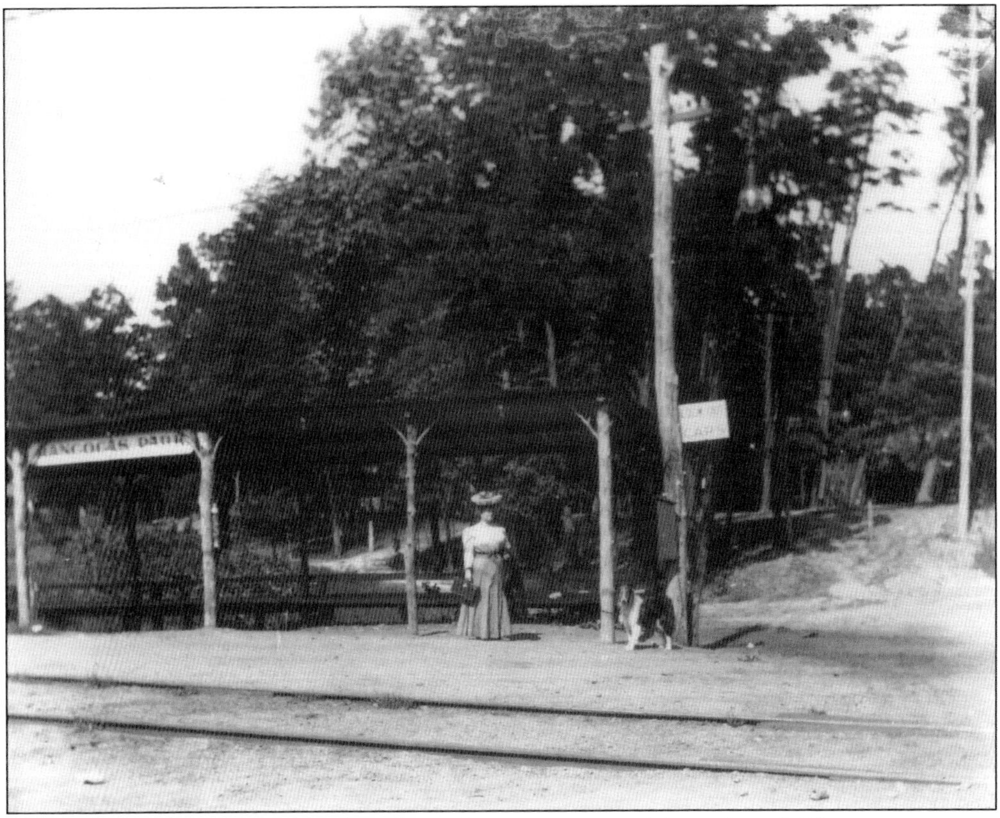

Rancocas Woods was one of the first planned communities in Mount Laurel. This area was once an amuseument park, complete with a lake, which ice-skaters used in the winter. Mrs. Stephen Dunn is seen standing at the trolley stop in front of the entrance to Rancocas Lake Park. Mrs. Stephen Dunn stands at the trolley stop at the entrance to Rancocas Park near the lake, created by damming Mason's Run at its confluence with the Rancocas. The trolley tracks are visible in the foreground. Mimicking Medford Lakes, the homes that replaced the amusements in the 1930s were log cabins. (Courtesy of Richard Tremper and the Masonville Fire Company.)

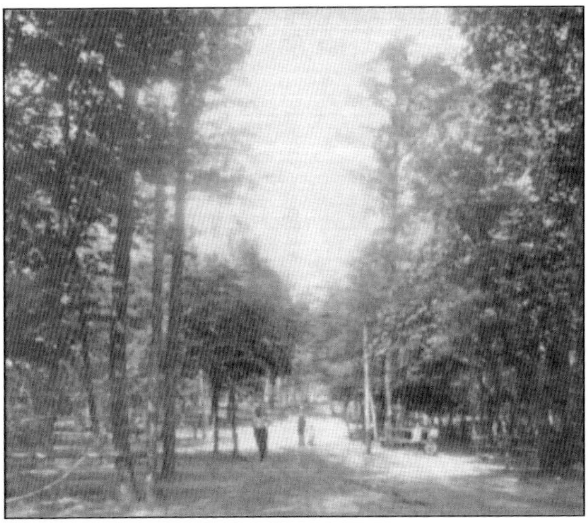

When the Burlington County Traction Company began trolley operations along Marne Highway between Mount Holly and Moorestown in 1904, George Potts, an entrepreneur, opened Rancocas Park on the bluff overlooking Mason's Creek. Potts offered picnic groves, a dance pavilion, a boating lake, a carousel and other amusement rides, a midway with games of chance and skill, and an array of food vendors. The park remained very popular through World War I, but it fell out of favor during the 1920s. (Courtesy of the Paul W. Schopp Collection.)

Park owner George Potts offered his summer revelers a full range of amenities, including food and ice-cream concessions. Here, ladies and children garbed in summer white attire enjoy a sylvan day at the park. (Courtesy of the Paul W. Schopp Collection.)

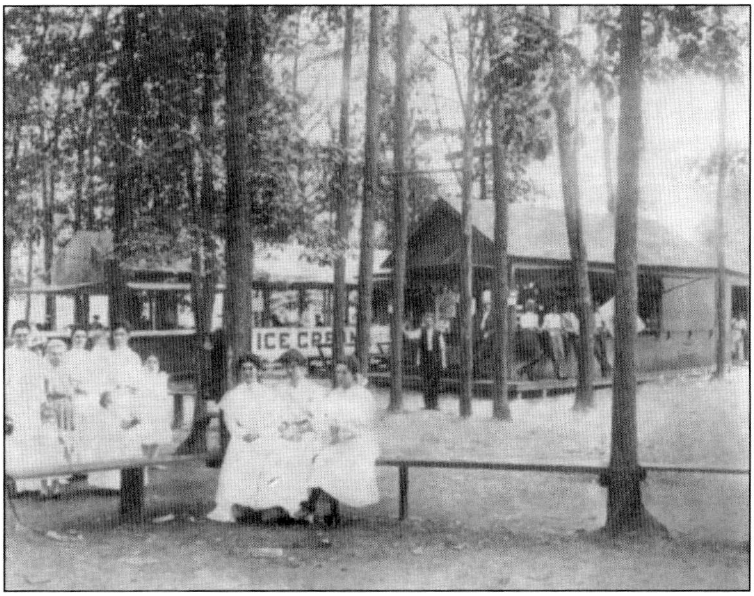

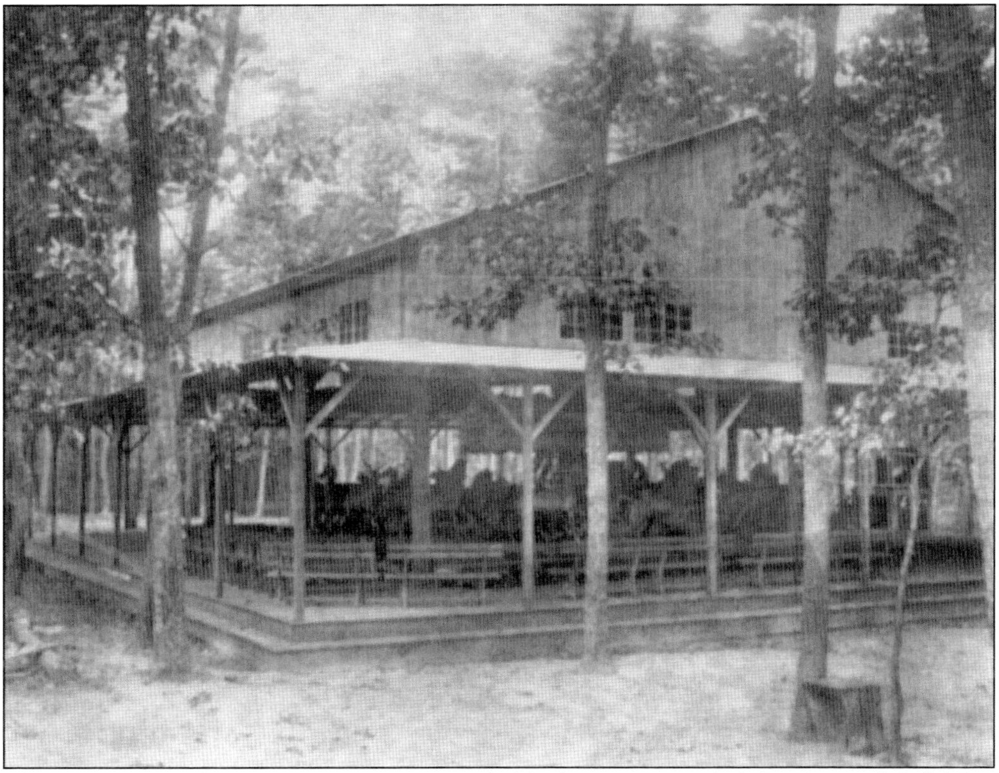

The amusement rides that George Potts provided for his visitors included a classic Philadelphia carousel. Housed in its own building to protect its fine appointments and menagerie of carved animals, the carousel brought joy to young and old alike, as riders traveled to the tunes of a Wurlitzer bandmaster organ. (Courtesy of the Paul W. Schopp Collection.)

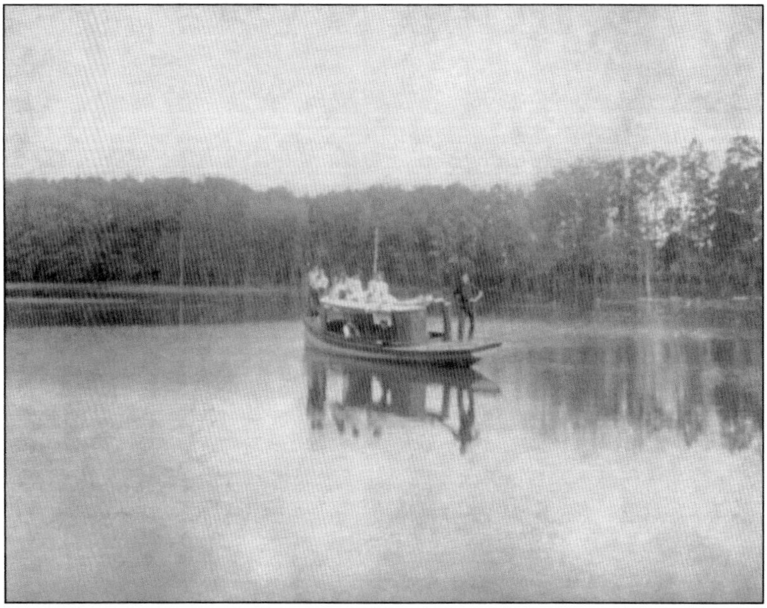

Rancocas Park offered a lake for boating during the summer months and ice-skating in the winter. The lake was created by constructing two dams on Mason's Creek. During the park's history, several drownings occurred in this lake. (Courtesy of the Paul W. Schopp Collection.)

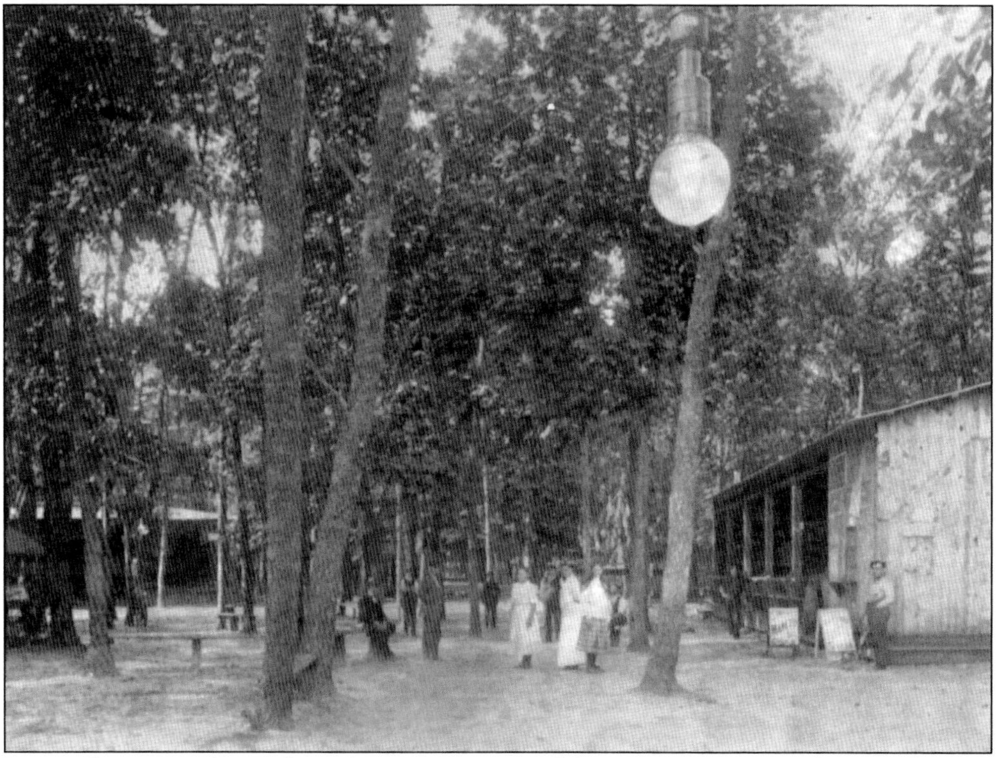

Men and women gather in the park grove near some of the amusements. A nearby sign advertises "Maneto 5¢ Cigars." In the background on the left is the carousel pavilion. In a move to generate more revenue from his rides, George Potts relocated a number of his mechanical amusements to Burlington Island for several years, but then returned them to his own park when management on the island purchased larger and better rides for their visitors. Potts's rides lost popularity among Burlington Island revelers. (Courtesy of the Paul W. Schopp Collection.)

George Risdon's Mount Laurel tax notice for 1877 shows that the bulk of the payment was a $1 poll tax. Personal property made up the rest of the taxes, consisting of state, county, and township taxes and school tax, amounting to 50¢. There was also a dog tax, which did not apply to Risdon. A 12-percent interest was applied per year for unpaid taxes. The tax collector, Clayton H. Dudley, who was located in the Fellowship area of the township, went to the Laurance Hotel in Centreton, Farmer's Hall, and his own residence to collect the taxes in December 1877. The appeals court was to be held in the Farmer's Hall, on the second floor, in the area used for court proceedings. (Courtesy of the Mount Laurel Historical Society.)

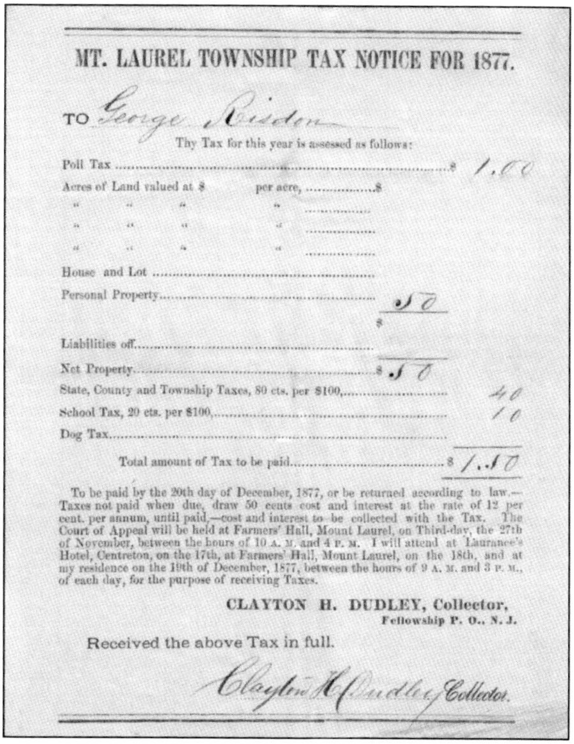

MT. LAUREL TOWNSHIP TAX NOTICE FOR 1877.

TO George Risdon

Thy Tax for this year is assessed as follows:

Poll Tax .... $ 1.00

Acres of Land valued at $ per acre, ... $

House and Lot ....

Personal Property 50

Liabilities off ....

Net Property .... $ 50

State, County and Township Taxes, 80 cts. per $100, ... 40

School Tax, 20 cts. per $100, ... 10

Dog Tax ....

Total amount of Tax to be paid .... $ 1.50

To be paid by the 20th day of December, 1877, or be returned according to law.—Taxes not paid when due, draw 50 cents cost and interest at the rate of 12 per cent. per annum, until paid,—cost and interest to be collected with the Tax. The Court of Appeal will be held at Farmers' Hall, Mount Laurel, on Third-day, the 27th of November, between the hours of 10 A. M. and 4 P. M. I will attend at Laurance's Hotel, Centreton, on the 17th, at Farmers' Hall, Mount Laurel, on the 18th, and at my residence on the 19th of December, 1877, between the hours of 9 A. M. and 3 P. M., of each day, for the purpose of receiving Taxes.

CLAYTON H. DUDLEY, Collector,
Fellowship P. O., N. J.

Received the above Tax in full.

Clayton H. Dudley Collector.

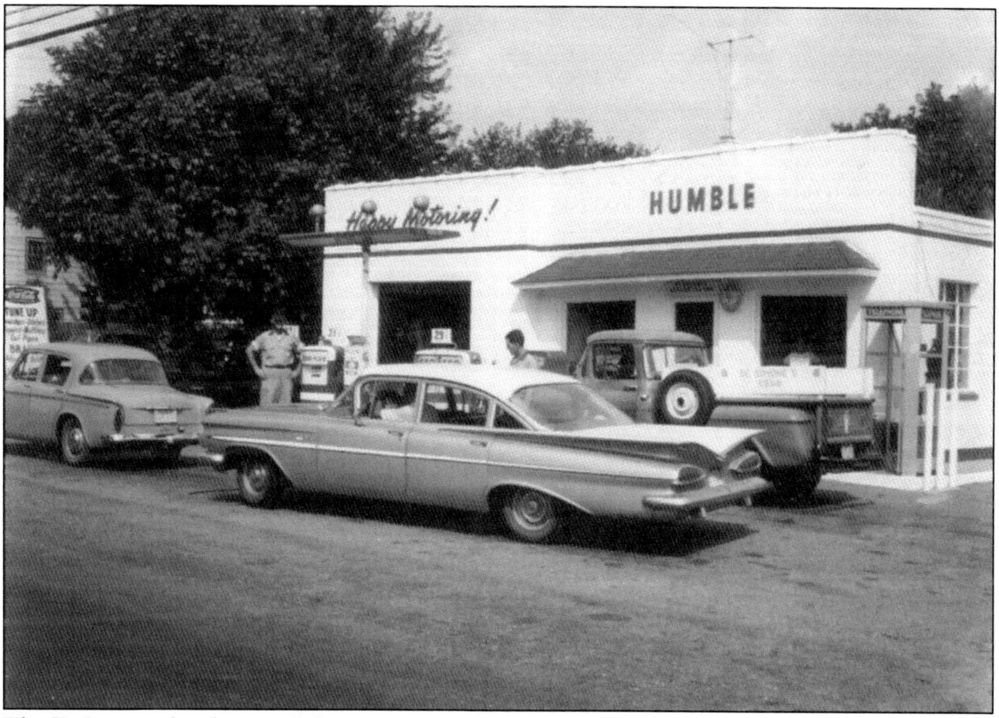

The DeSimone family owned this gas station at the corner of Hartford Road and Marne Highway. It stood for many years on this corner, changing names during its existence. The facility was razed for a road expansion project that never came to fruition. (Courtesy of Judith Monte.)

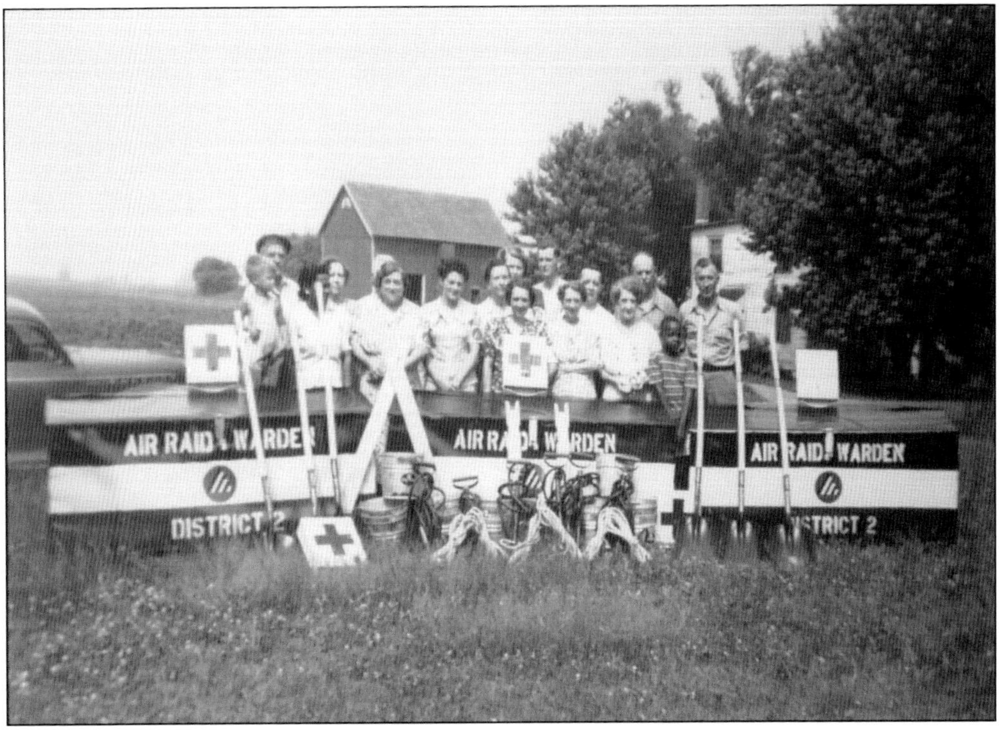

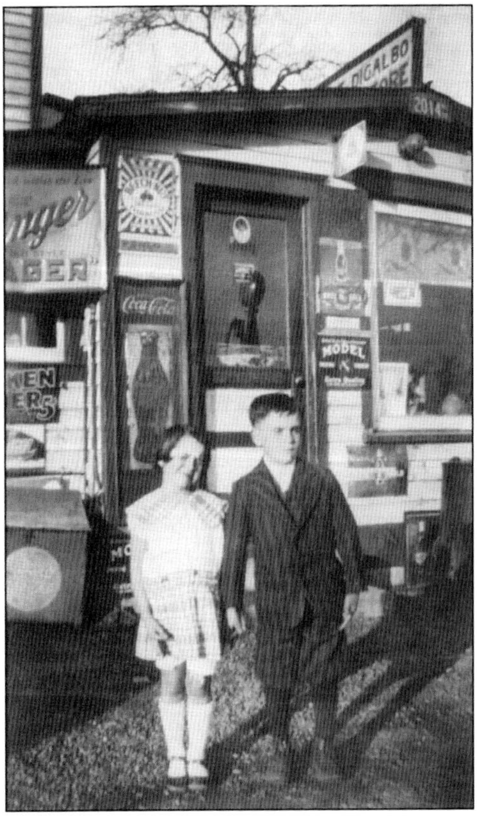

The 1943 Hartford Civic Association is shown near the schoolhouse on Hartford Road at the current Route 295. Pictured here are, from left to right, the following: (first row) Gordon Lenher (grandson), Anna Hill, Mrs. Lenher (grandmother), Gladys Spruill, Phyllis Spruill, Mrs. Lenher (mother), Florence Brown, and Mr. Hill; (second row) Mrs. Perry, Mae Plasket, Edna Perry, Betty Bingham, Ed Spruill, Dave Lenher, Ed Spruill Sr., and Howard Tull. The group is shown with equipment and banners of the Air Raid Warden of District 2. (Courtesy of the Mount Laurel Historical Society.)

Paul and Anna DiGalbo stand in front of their grandmother's home, which had a store in the front, located two buildings down from DeSimone's Gas Station. Paul and Anna lived with their parents and their grandmother, Mary DeSimone Moscatello, from the late 1920s to the 1940s while their parents worked in the store. Paul and Fran DiGalbos later opened their own store at the corner of Hartford Road and Marne Highway. (Courtesy of Judith Monte.)

This photograph shows a page from the family Bible of Samuel and Elizabeth Roberts, who lived in the Hartford village where Samuel was a tailor. The Bible was given to them by their mother, Rebecca Shute, in 1791. The birth dates and death dates are listed for their family members. (Courtesy of Charles Kester.)

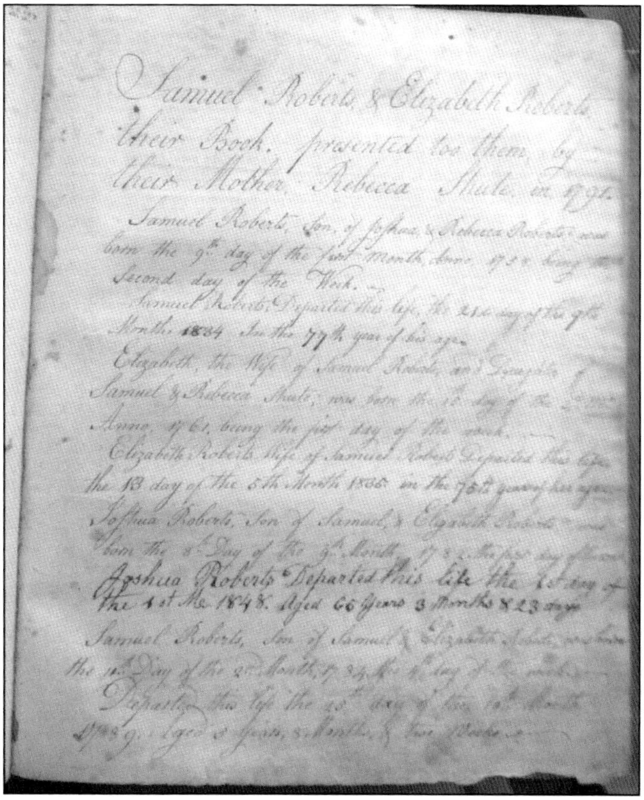

Samuel Roberts & Elizabeth Roberts
their Book. presented to them by
their Mother Rebecca Shute in 1791.

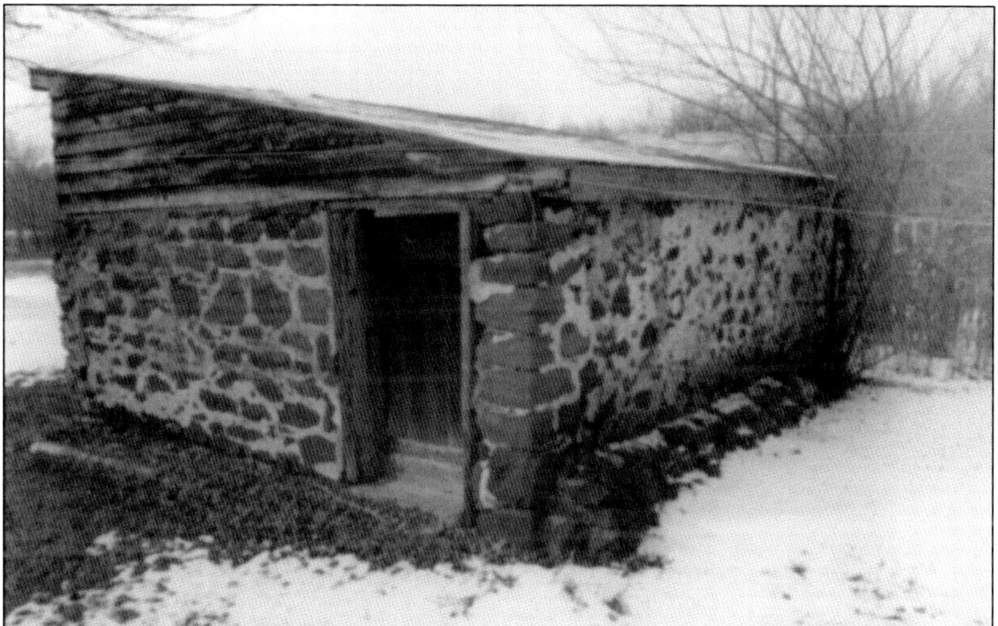

Shown at the Darnell homestead, this typical icehouse, constructed of local ironstone, provided the means to store perishables. Large blocks of ice, used for keeping the icehouse cold, were insulated with hay or sawdust. (Courtesy of the Mount Laurel Historical Society.)

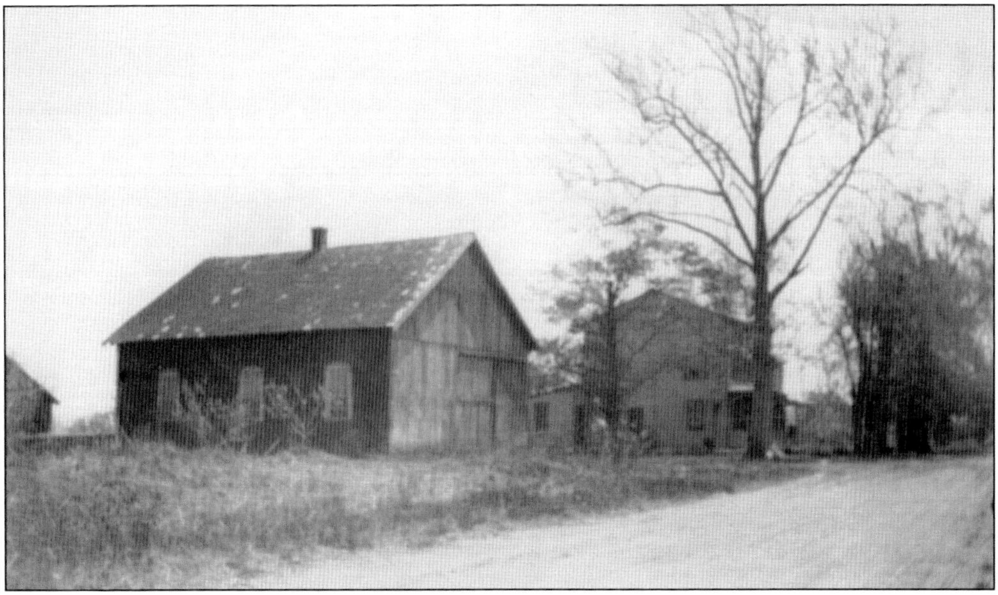

This undated photograph shows Green's Blacksmith Shop in the Fellowship section of Mount Laurel. It was upstairs at this shop that the first Catholic congregation in Mount Laurel held worship services, starting in 1849. (Courtesy of Meg Ellis.)

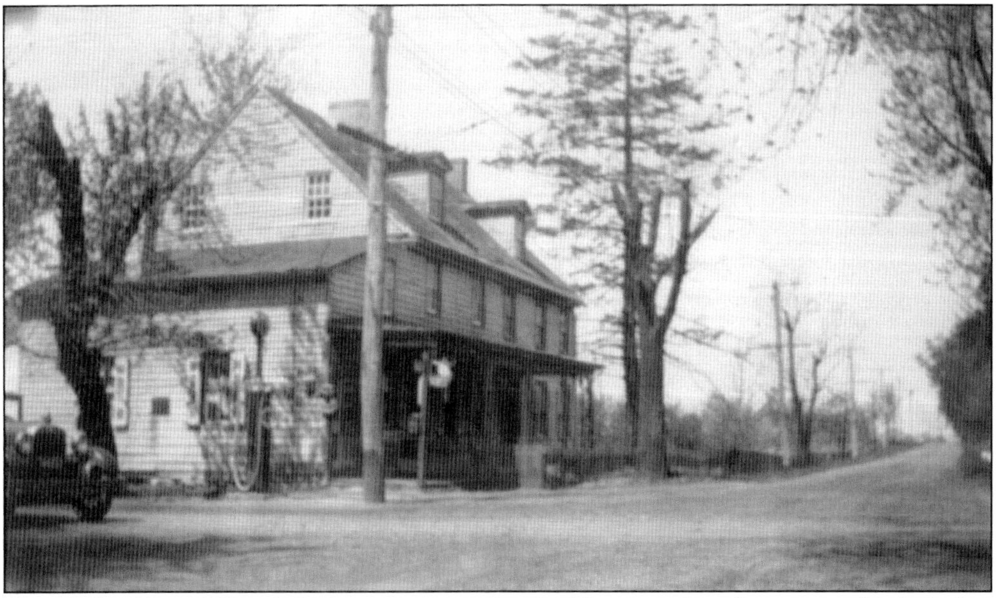

Identified as Susie O'Brien's little corner store, this building stood on the corner of S-41, before it became Route 73, and Fellowship Road. Marian Rudderow Hartshorne remembers that the store sold ice cream and candy. The New Jersey Highway Department razed this building during the construction of Route 73. Today, a Bob Evans restaurant stands at this location. (Courtesy of Meg Ellis.)

Two

Historic Homes, Prominent Farms, and the Hamlets of Mount Laurel

When Mount Laurel became a separate township, a number of small hamlets and crossroad villages already existed across the landscape, including Centreton, Masonville, Hartford, Colemantown, Fellowship, and Mount Laurel Village. Being an agrarian township, many farms surrounded each of these settlements.

In 1867, the Camden & Burlington County Railroad Company completed its line, which brought new people and industry to Mount Laurel. Centreton, near Moorestown, also flourished because of its wharf, lumber and coal yard, phosphorus factory, tavern, and the Centreton Hotel. The Centreton area had become a popular vacation spot for families from Philadelphia seeking the serenity of the countryside in the summer.

Located east of Moorestown, Masonville grew after surveyors laid out the New Road to Philadelphia around 1792, later known as the Moorestown–Mount Holly Turnpike. Today, the route is known as Marne Highway (CR 537). Masonville is still a small, viable community today. The village derives its name from the James Mason Plantation. In 1882, it contained about 100 people, an iron factory, facing mill, a railroad freight and passenger depot, and Darnell's Grist and Sawmill (Union Mills). Masonville is located on a portion of an 1,800-acre tract surveyed to John Borton in 1716. The home of the late senator C. William Haines Jr. and his wife, Sally, still stands along Marne Highway on the foundation of the original house, built by his ancestor, John Borton.

On the western side of the township, the community of Fellowship developed on land owned by George Roberts, a well-known Quaker. The Fellowship area was the most developed of all the villages that comprised Mount Laurel Township at that time, and many of the farms surrounding the village lasted well into the middle of the 20th century. The village included two general stores, a wagon shop, a shoe shop, a blacksmith shop, mechanics shops, and a boarding school. By 1849, Fellowship had a Roman Catholic congregation meeting in the second floor of the blacksmith shop, and a post office.

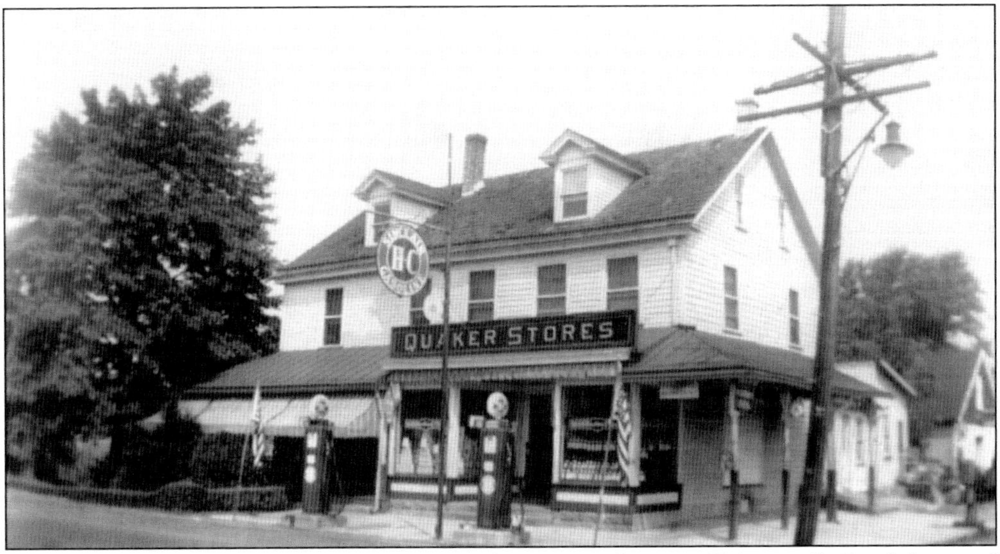

A.A. Zelly's Quaker Store stood at the corner of Marne Highway and Masonville Road. It served as the Masonville Post Office at one time. The family lived upstairs. It was later razed, and the Burlington County Trust Company constructed a bank in its place, which later became a hobby shop. It is now a Dunkin' Donuts. (Courtesy of Harry Herring.)

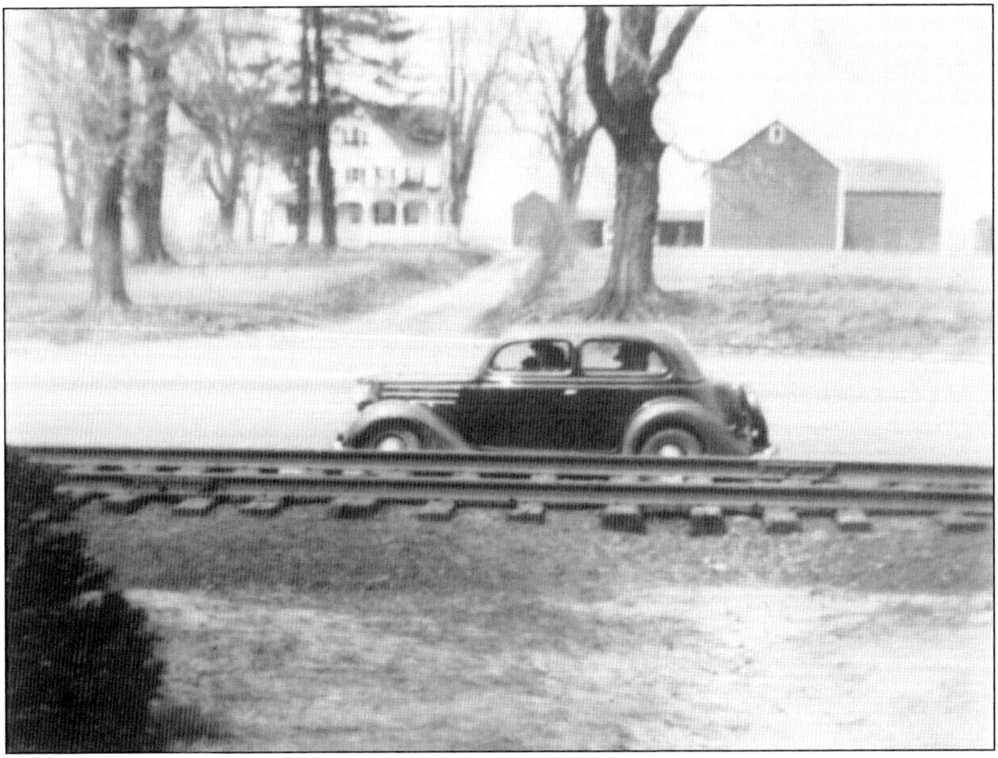

This 1942 photograph faces the Montes' Lakeside Farm in Hartford on Marne Highway. The railroad tracks, which run parallel to Marne Highway, are still in use today, although passenger service no longer operates and only freight trains run on the line between Camden and Mount Holly. (Courtesy of Judith Monte.)

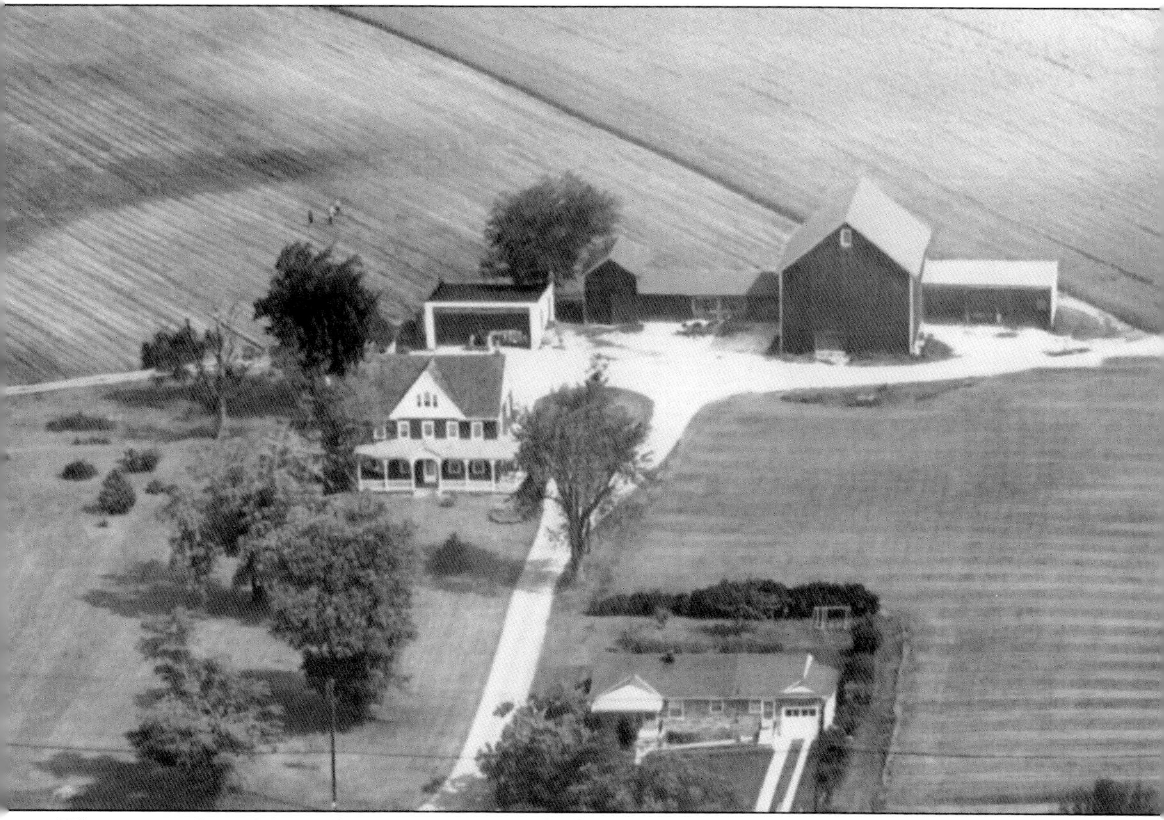

There were three Monte farms; one on Hartford Road and two farms on Marne Highway in Hartford. The farm on Hartford Road, where the Le Club development is located today, was owned by John and Virginia Monte until a major flood in 1938 and a chimney fire in 1942 caused them to sell the property and purchase the Marne Highway farm. John and Virginia Monte purchased the 133-acre farm on Marne Highway in 1942, shown in the photograph. In 1946, the couple sold this farm to their son and his wife, Michael and Mary Monte, who farmed fruits and vegetables that they sold at a roadside stand. They also made their produce available to locals, to the Philadelphia and New York markets, and to the Campbell Soup Company. Across the street was another Monte farm, owned by Carmen Monte, son of John and brother to Mike Monte. Mike called his farm "Lakeside Estates," while Carmen called his "Vita Green Farm." The Monte daughters, Judy, Diann, Shirl, and Debbie, are the current owners of the Lakeside Estates property. (Courtesy of Judith Monte.)

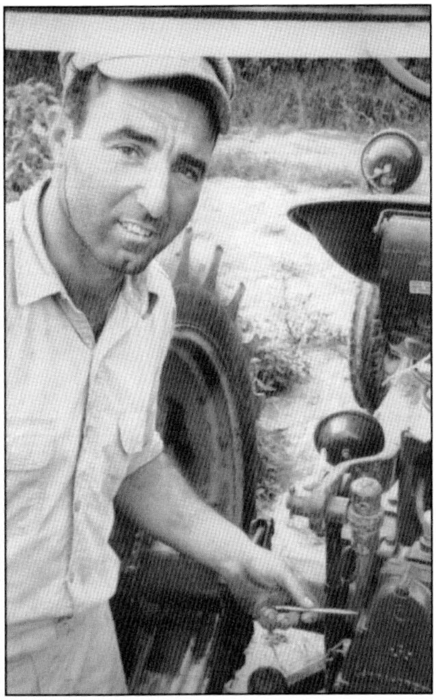

Michael Monte repairs his tractor in the 1950s. Owning a farm required knowledge in various areas. One needed to be a mechanic, welder, accountant, manager, weather forecaster, and farmer. The Monte children participated in running the farm. One important task was to let their father know if they heard a bad weather forecast for that day, so he would know whether to irrigate or harvest a crop sooner. (Courtesy of Judith Monte.)

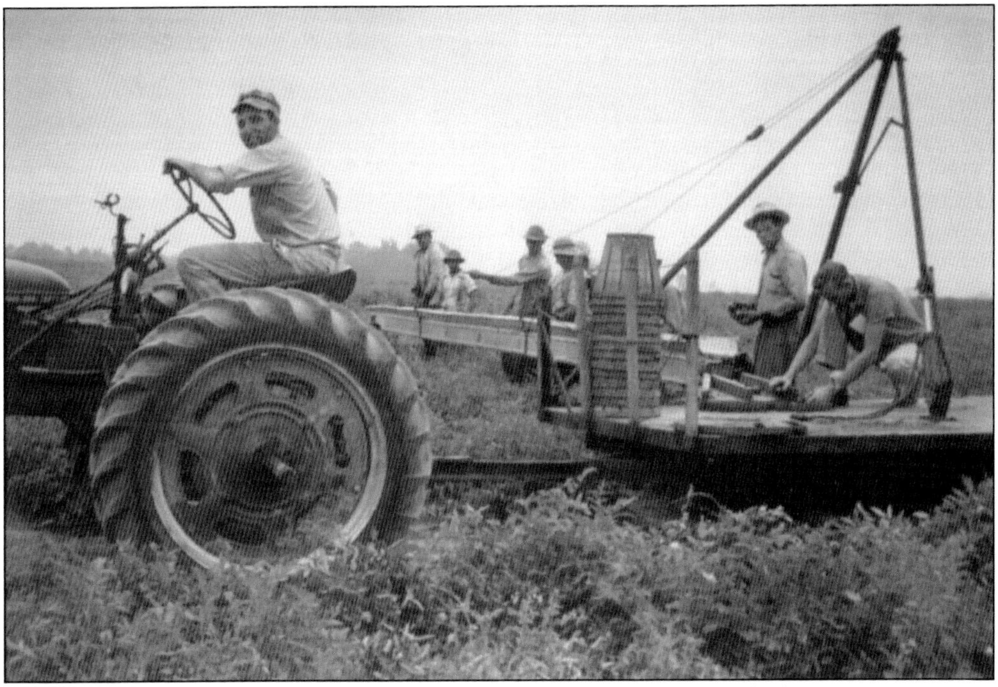

Michael Monte is shown doing experimental harvesting of tomatoes with the county extension officer and Puerto Rican laborers in the late 1950s. The Monte family produced asparagus, strawberries, sweet corn, tomatoes, carrots, and wheat on the farm as well as on two other farms that they leased, totaling over 300 acres of farmland producing crops each summer. The produce was sold at the family's roadside stand and to local retailers. It was also delivered to the Campbell Soup Company in Camden, Hightstown, and the Philadelphia and New York markets. (Courtesy of Judith Monte.)

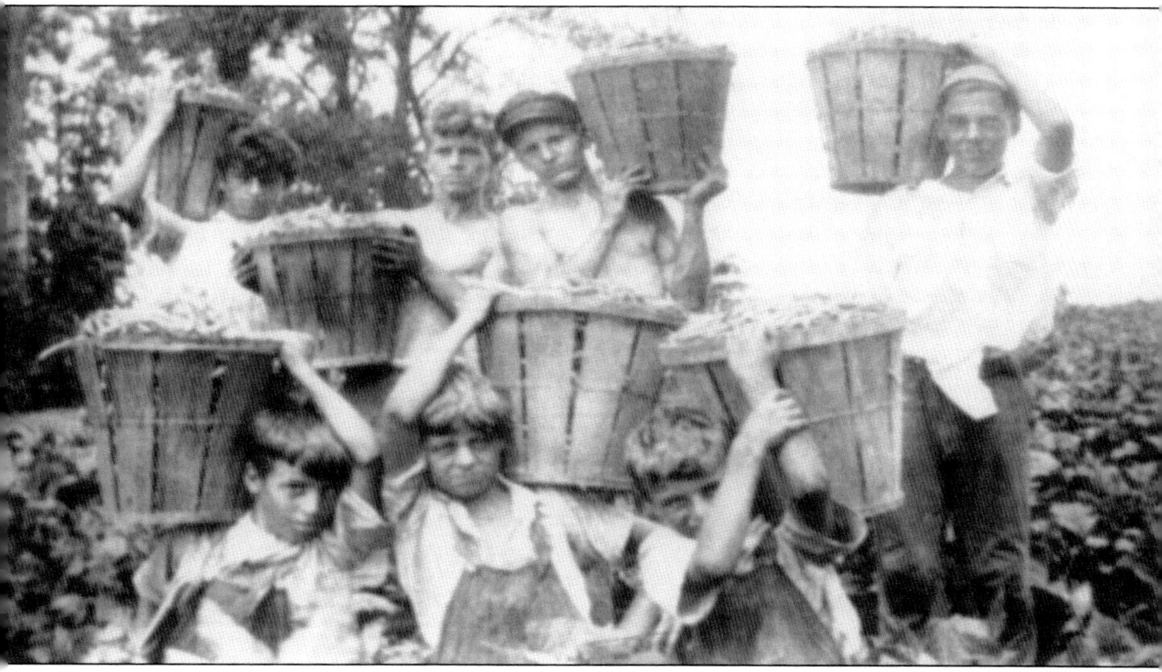

These tomato pickers on the Monte farm did "piece" work. Some of the laborers were family members, and others were hired Puerto Rican hands who returned year after year. Workers would put a ticket on the tomato or strawberry basket with their unique number on it. The farmer would collect the tickets and count them, and the worker would get paid based on the number of baskets/flats they had picked. These aluminum tickets were used from the 1950s through the 1970s. John Monte and Michael Monte made these tickets and punched the numbers onto each ticket by hand. Paul DiGalbo, on the bottom left, was the future son-in-law of John and Virginia Monte. This farm also grew asparagus, strawberries, sweet corn, tomatoes, carrots, and some wheat. (Courtesy of Judith Monte.)

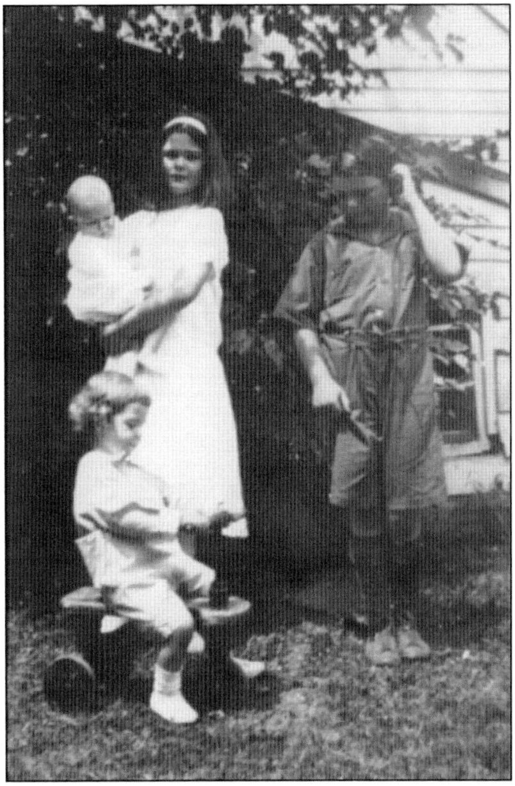

The Comfort family's children pose for a photograph around 1922. Shown here from left to right are Ned (on the bike), Betty (holding Nancy), and Bob. The Comfort farm produced fruits, such as peaches and apples, and vegetables, such as corn, potatoes, and asparagus. The family also grew tomatoes for the Campbell Soup Company in Camden. (Courtesy of Nancy Jones.)

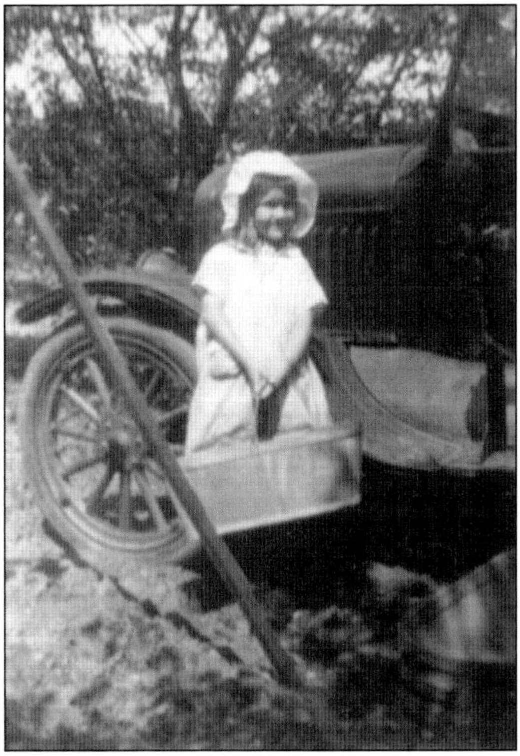

Nancy Comfort stands in front of the family's automobile after picking cherries in June 1929. Nancy's father, Edward M. Comfort, was the township clerk for many years. The family was related to the Coles family, which settled in present-day Cherry Hill in the 17th century. (Courtesy of Nancy Jones.)

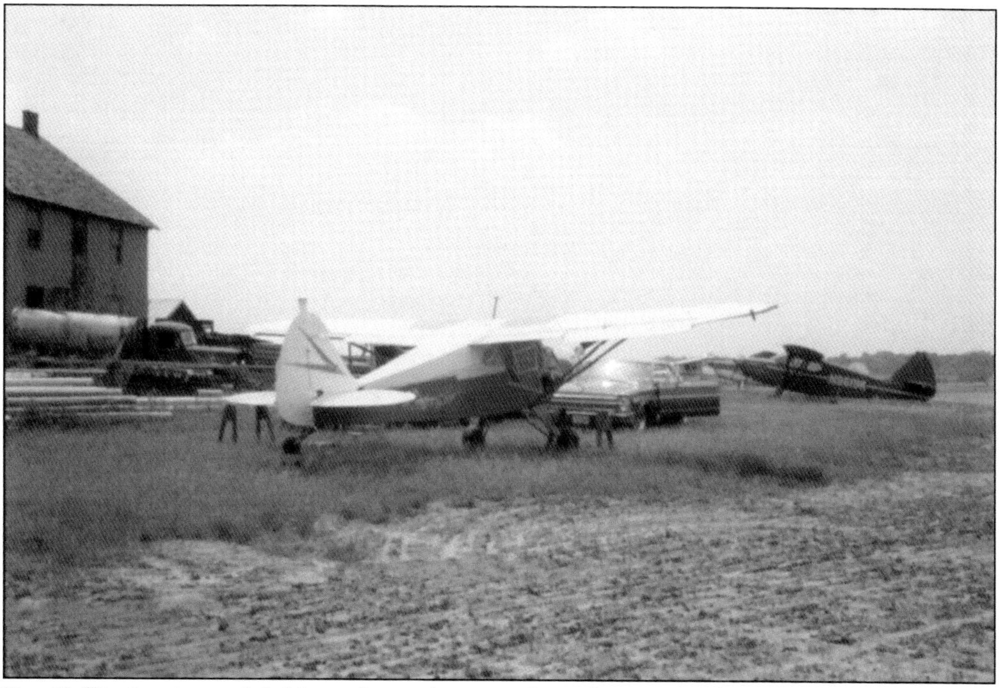

Roy Collins's private airfield was located next to Interchange 40 of present-day I-295. Collins was an airframe and power-plant mechanic who owned an airstrip on his farm that ran parallel to Route 295 on the southbound side. The house and barn stood near the off-ramp. The runway was located at the current site of the stores of the Centerton Square shopping center. (Courtesy of Jim Megee.)

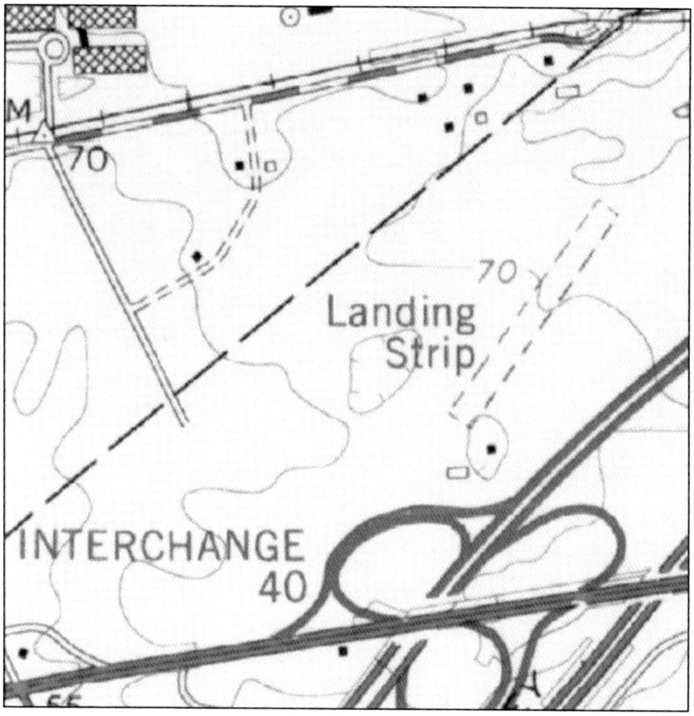

This topographic map shows the location of the landing strip for the Collins Airfield. The airstrip is where the current Centerton Square shopping center is now located. Route 295 went right through the farm. (Courtesy of HistoricAerials.com.)

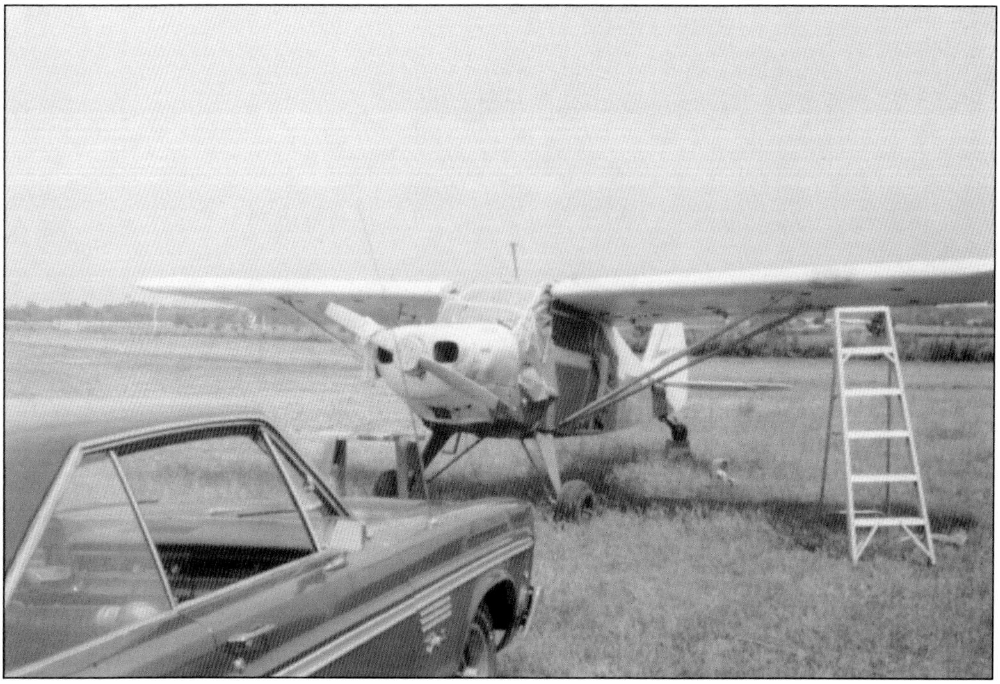

This 1950 Piper Pacer, a high-wing light aircraft, is shown being painted in 1975 at Roy Collins's airfield. Collins established the airfield around 1944–1949, and it featured an unpaved runway of approximately 2,600 feet. (Courtesy of Jim Megee.)

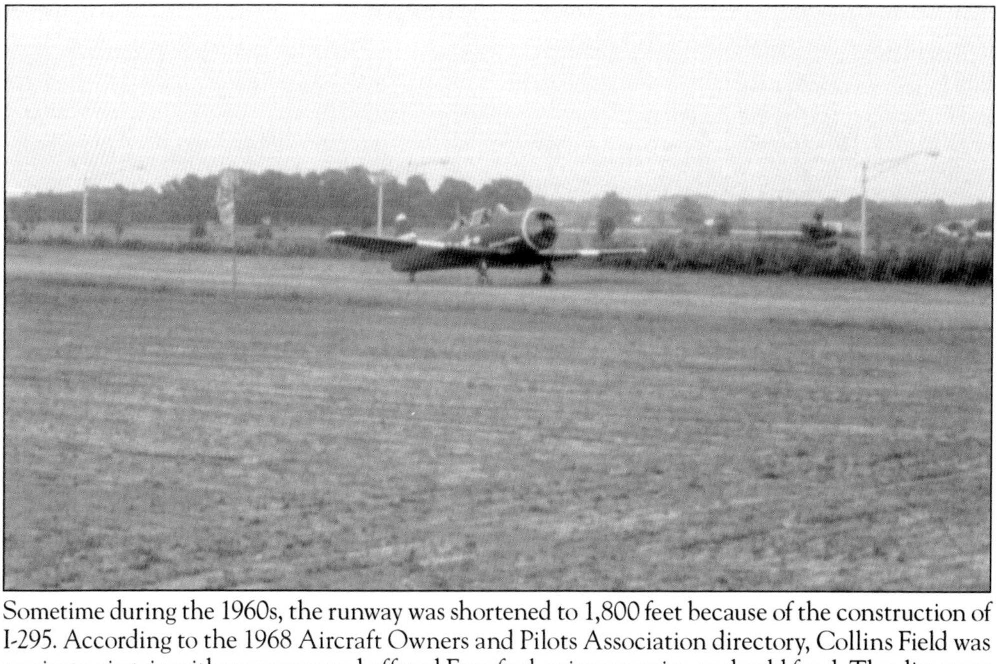

Sometime during the 1960s, the runway was shortened to 1,800 feet because of the construction of I-295. According to the 1968 Aircraft Owners and Pilots Association directory, Collins Field was a private airstrip with a runway and offered Esso fuel, minor repairs, and cold food. The directory also indicated that there was a power-line obstruction at the south end. This airstrip appeared on the Washington sectional chart of airports. (Courtesy of Jim Megee.)

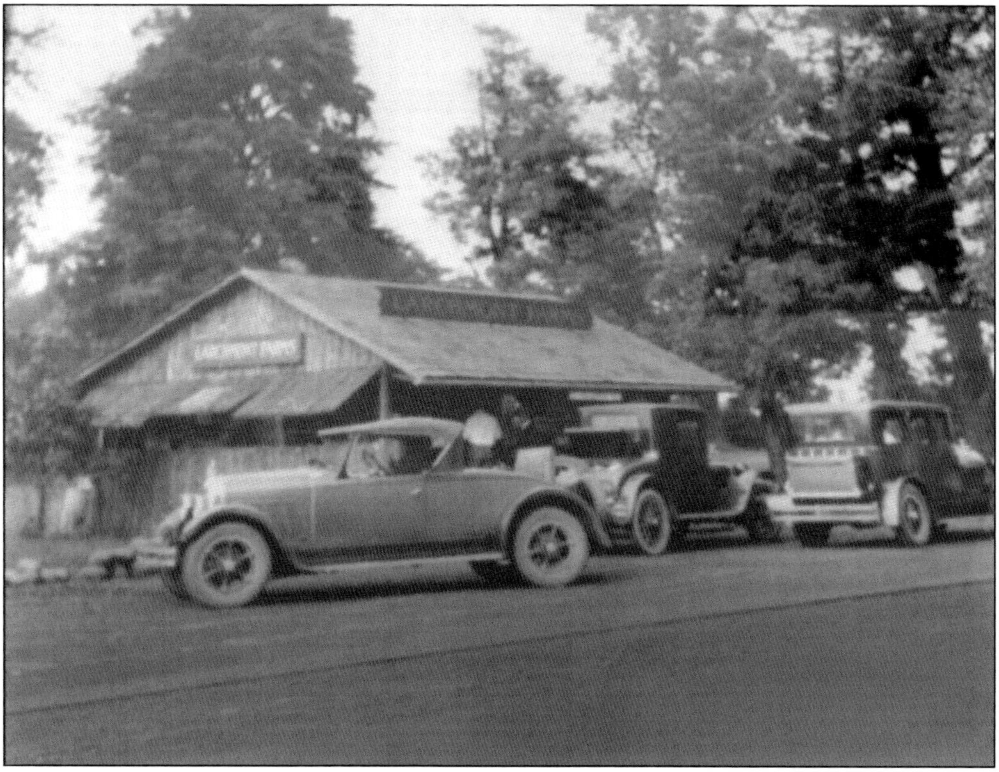

Larchmont Farm, located on Marne Highway between Masonville and Hartford, operated a road stand from which the Haines family sold apples, peaches, and other produce. In later years, they also sold stick candy and apple-cherry slushes. C. William "Bill" Haines was the mayor of Mount Laurel in 1970. He became a New Jersey state assemblyman and then a state senator until he passed away in the 1990s. (Courtesy of the Haines family.)

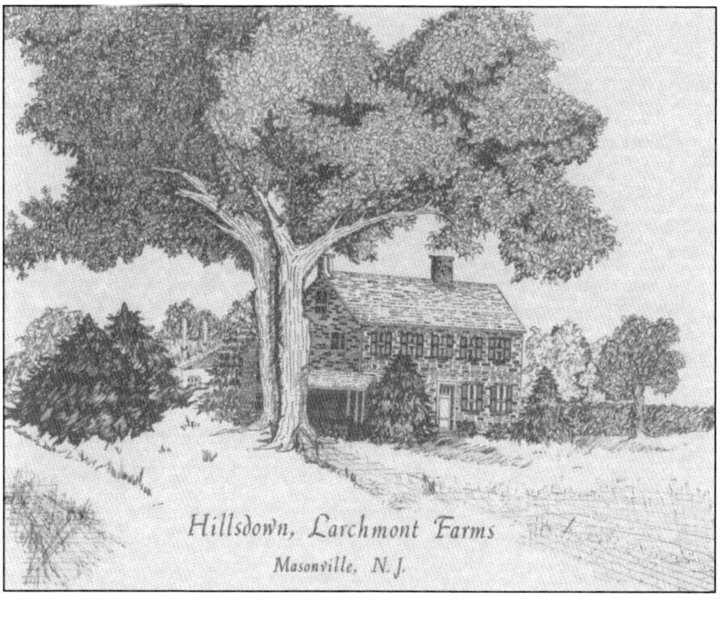

There are only two buildings that remain of the original Larchmont farm: the Haines house on Dickens Lane, which the Devonshire development absorbed; and the Borton Haines House, also called Hillsdown, shown in this sketch. (Courtesy of the author.)

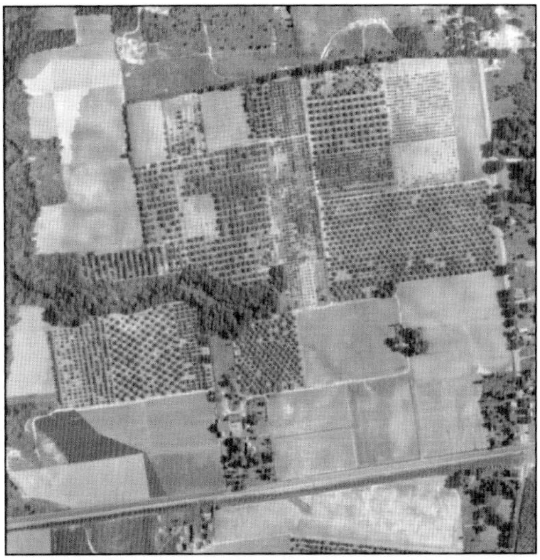

Larchmont Farm stood in the Masonville section of Mount Laurel and was known for its vast apple and peach orchards. These aerial photographs show a thriving farm in 1940 (above) and, in 2007, long after demolition of the orchards and farm, part of one of the largest planned developments in Mount Laurel, called Larchmont. The development comprises single-family homes, townhouses, condominiums, and apartments along with recreation facilities and a swim club. (Both images courtesy of HistoricAerials.com.)

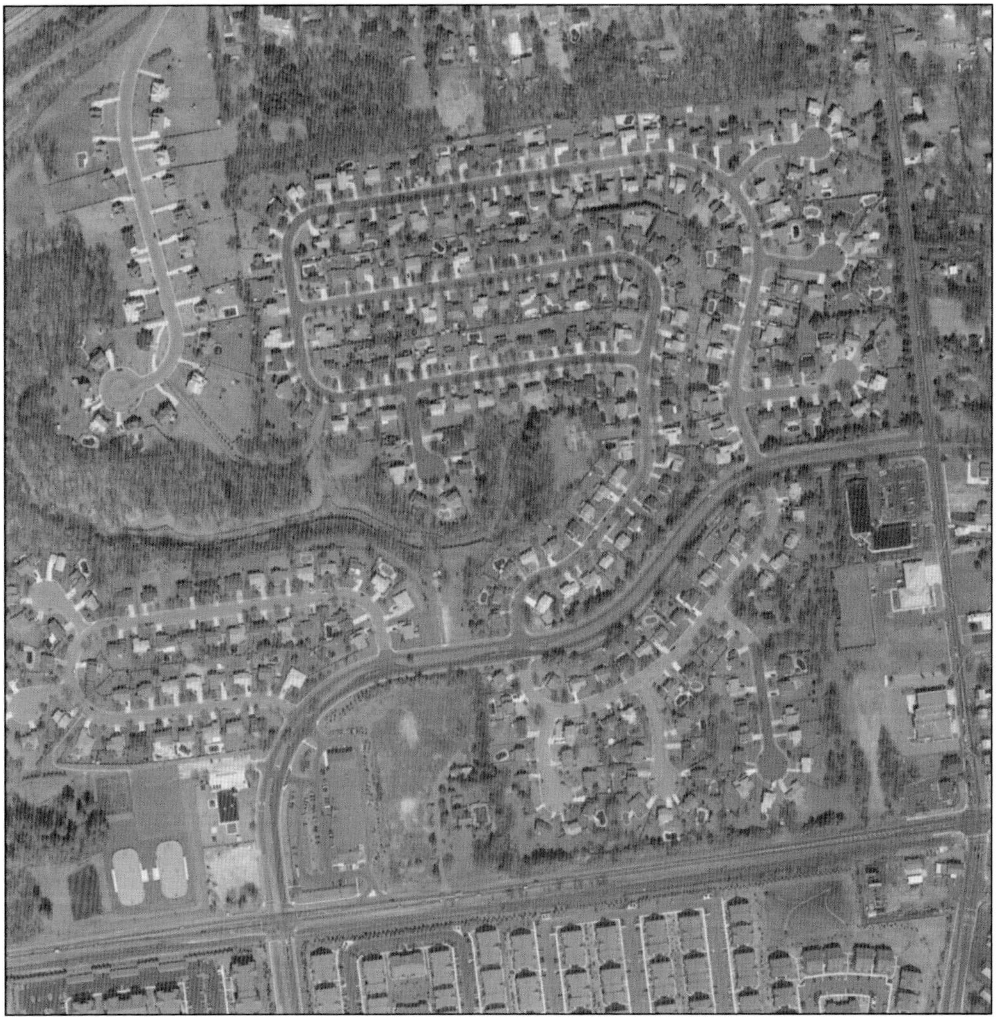

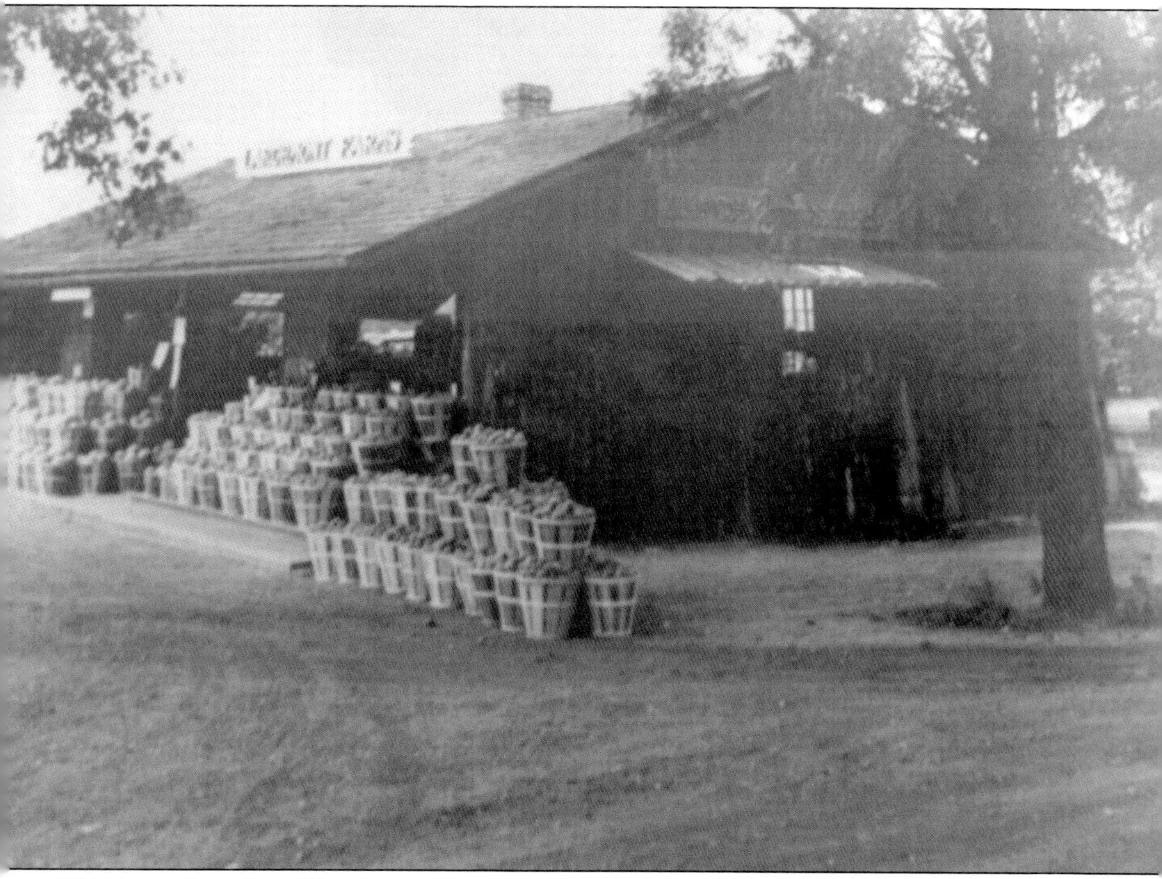

This is another view of Larchmont Farm's small roadside store, which was located next to the main farmhouse. The Haines family farmed New Jersey land since the 17th century, when the Bortons obtained the land from the Council of West Jersey Proprietors. (Courtesy of the Haines family.)

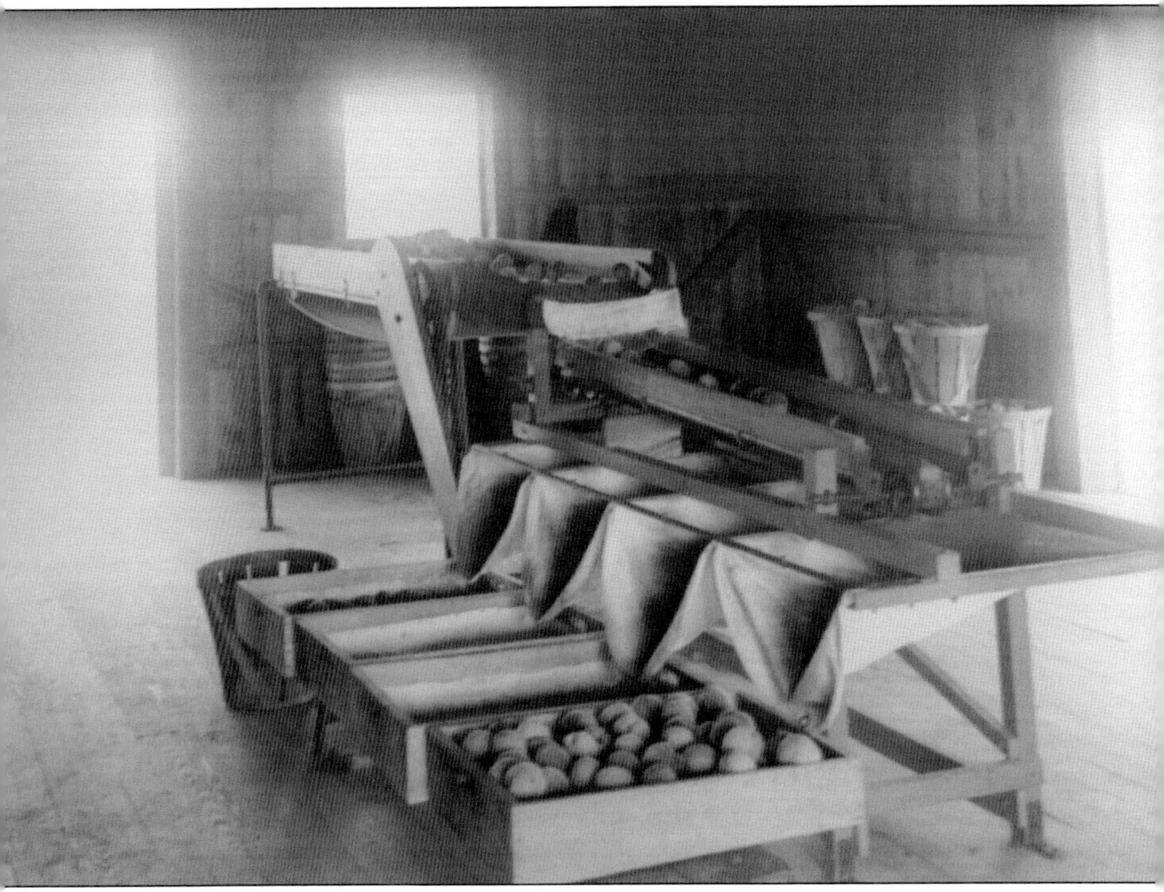

Farm equipment is set up inside Larchmont Farm. This photograph shows peaches being sorted and put into containers. These peaches were not only sold at the family's roadside store, but also at other roadside stands and in markets around the area. (Courtesy of the Haines family.)

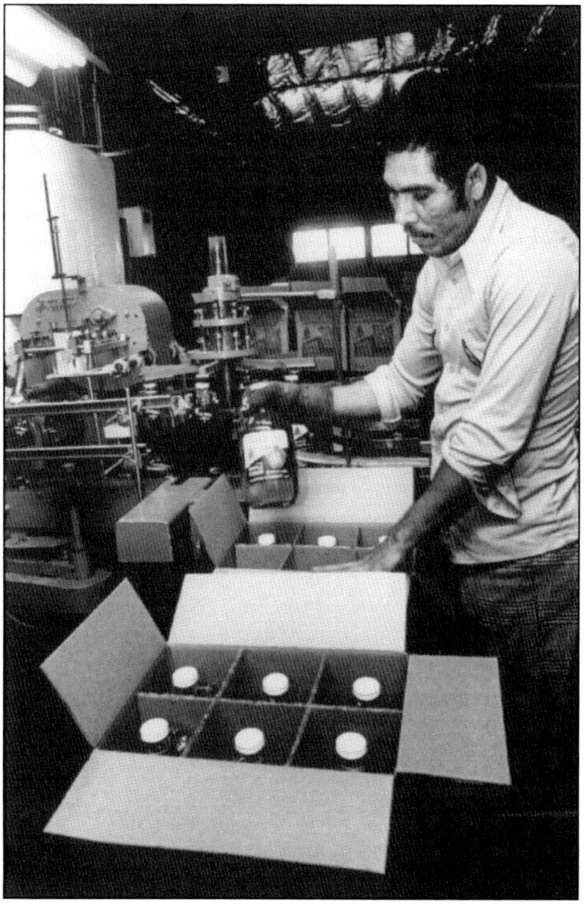

Larchmont Farm was established in 1769 in Masonville. In the late 1960s or early 1970s, the land was sold for $1.8 million and then cleared for planned developments. This area was marketed as perfectly placed between the city and the country. In the above photograph from October 1980, an unidentified worker packs apple cider for distribution. Below, apples are being packed. The farm relocated to the Elmer area of Salem County, New Jersey. (Both images courtesy of the *Burlington County Times*.)

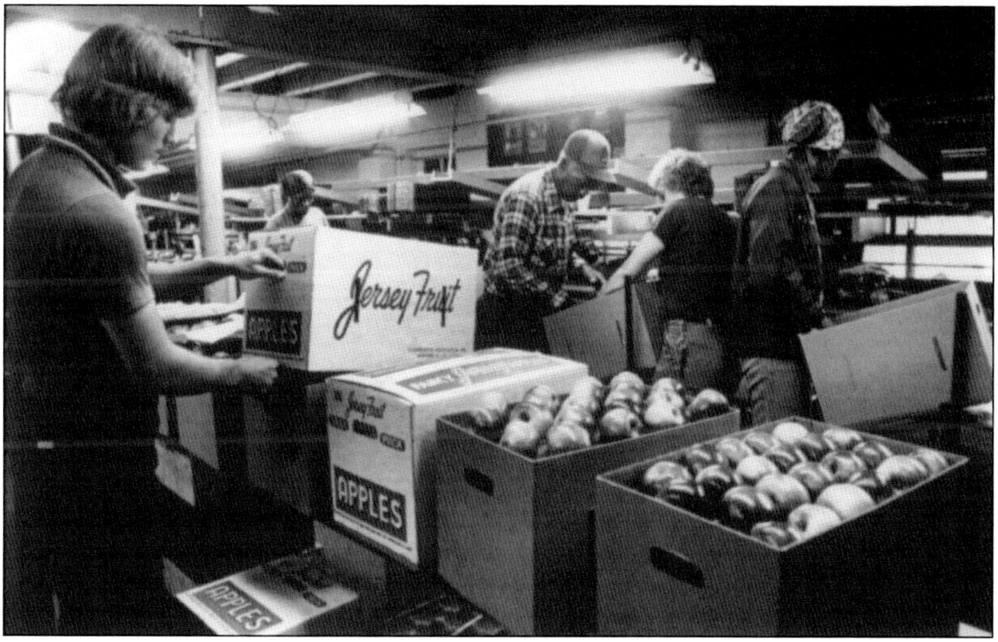

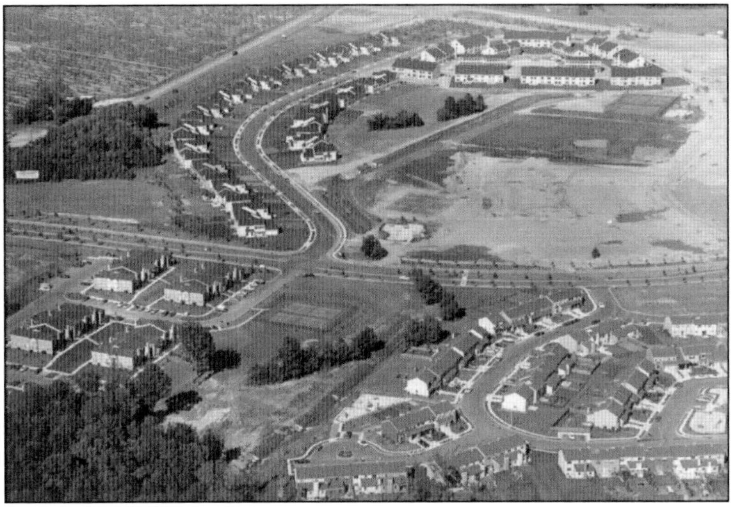

This aerial photograph shows the Larchmont apartments and condominiums, when the buildings on Willow Turn were being constructed in the late 1970s. Visible in the upper left are Route 38 and the orchards. This area is a large shopping center now. (Courtesy of the *Burlington County Times.*)

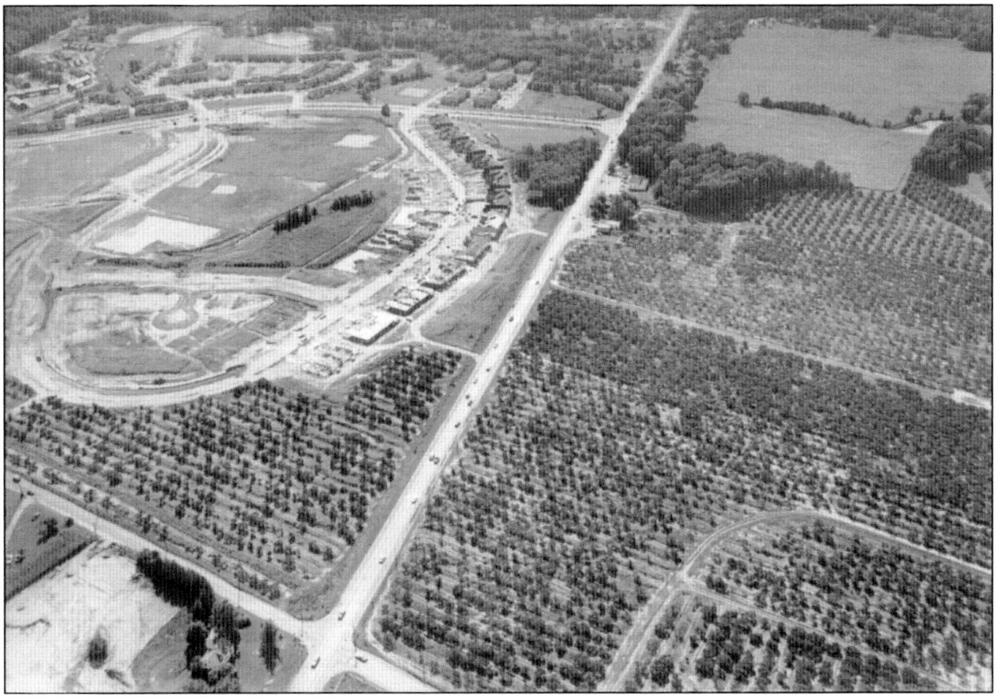

This aerial view shows the same area as above, but from a different angle. At the bottom of the photograph is the intersection of Route 38 and Ark Road. The Larchmont Farms peach and apple orchards are on the right side of the photograph, and the Willow Turn construction is in the upper left portion. (Courtesy of the *Burlington County Times.*)

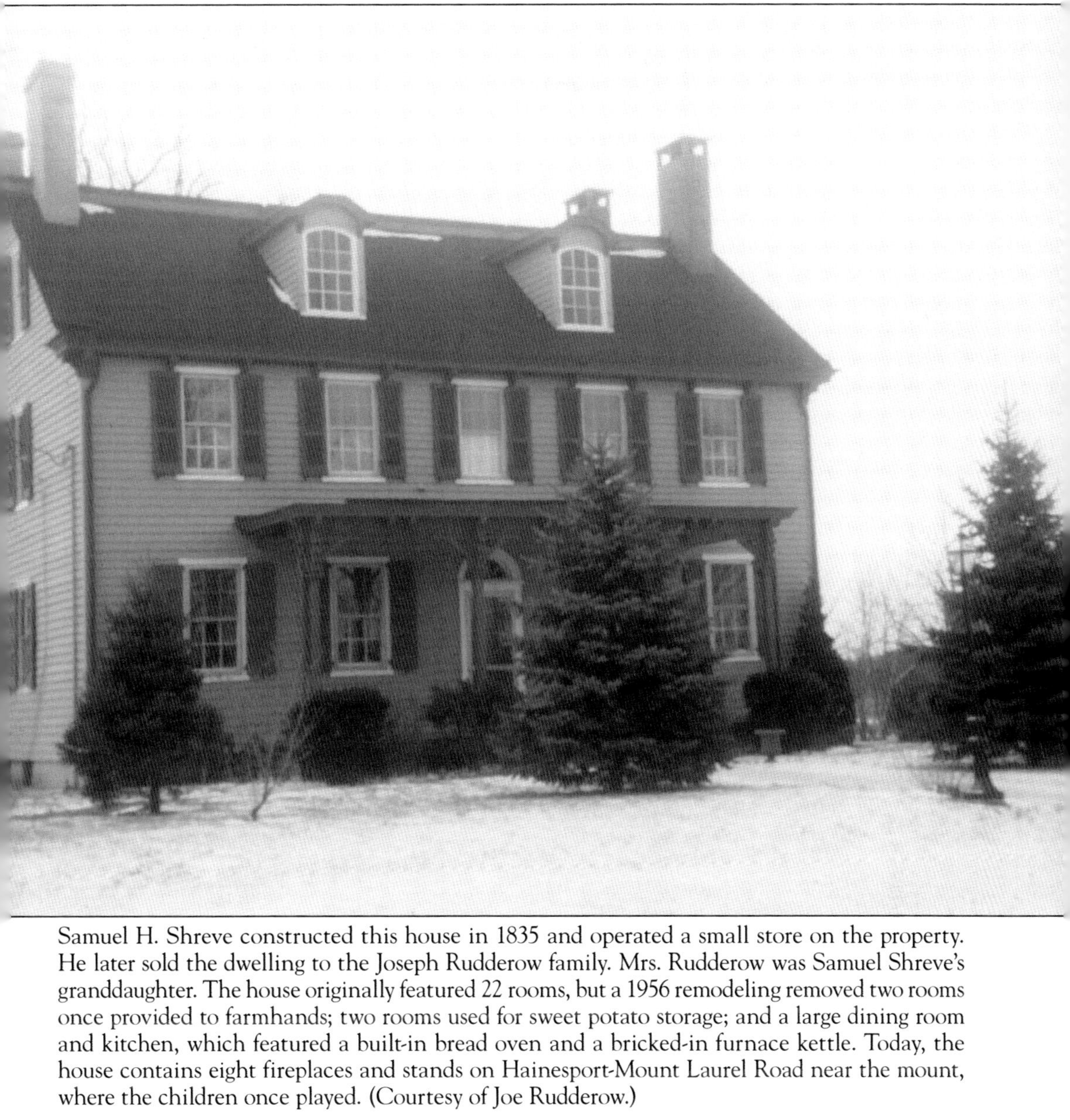

Samuel H. Shreve constructed this house in 1835 and operated a small store on the property. He later sold the dwelling to the Joseph Rudderow family. Mrs. Rudderow was Samuel Shreve's granddaughter. The house originally featured 22 rooms, but a 1956 remodeling removed two rooms once provided to farmhands; two rooms used for sweet potato storage; and a large dining room and kitchen, which featured a built-in bread oven and a bricked-in furnace kettle. Today, the house contains eight fireplaces and stands on Hainesport-Mount Laurel Road near the mount, where the children once played. (Courtesy of Joe Rudderow.)

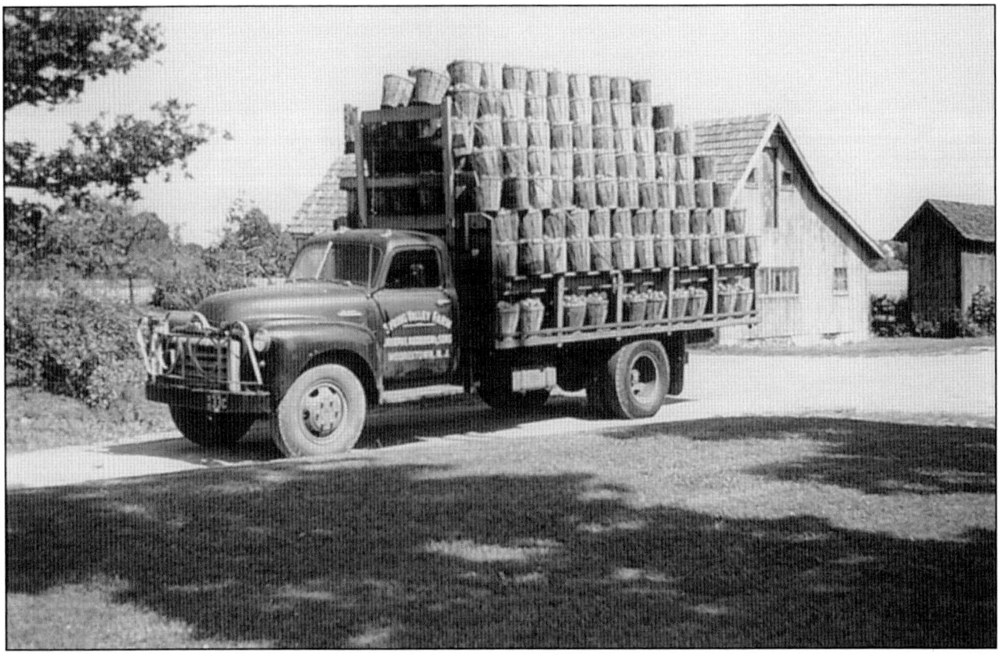

Joseph Rudderow's property, Spring Valley Farm, had over 40 acres of tomatoes that the family grew for the Campbell Soup Company. The trucks would cart them to Camden and wait in long lines for the tomatoes to be inspected and unloaded. This photograph was taken in the lower drive of the Shreve homestead. (Courtesy of Joe Rudderow.)

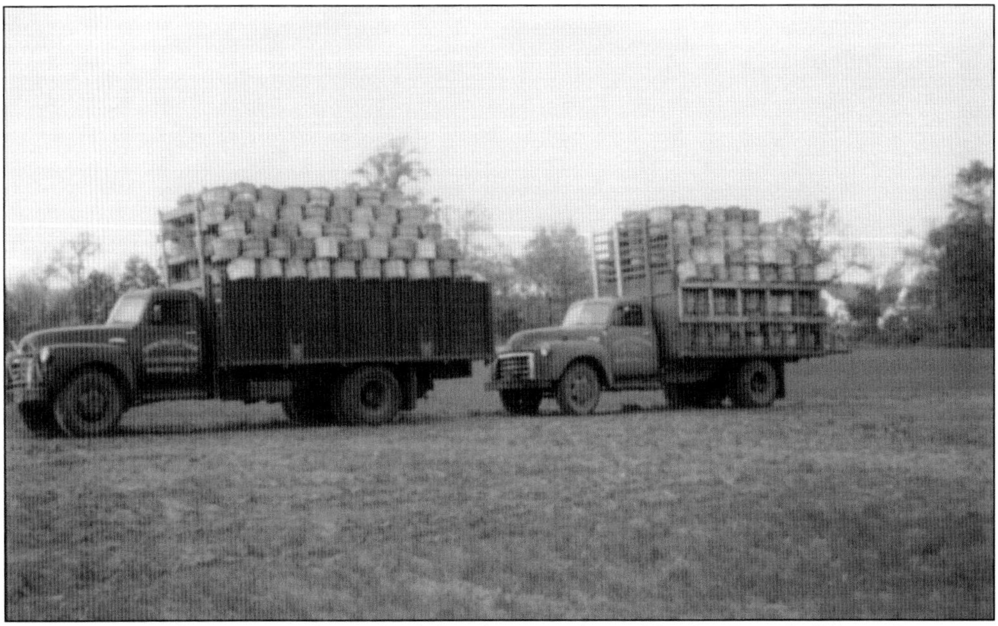

These Spring Valley Farm trucks are loaded with carrots bound for the Campbell Soup Company. Even though this farm was located in Mount Laurel, the trucks show a Moorestown address, because the Rudderows received their mail on an RFD (rural free delivery) route operated from that post office. These trucks are shown across the creek from the main farm, on land referred to as the Hurff field. (Courtesy of Joe Rudderow.)

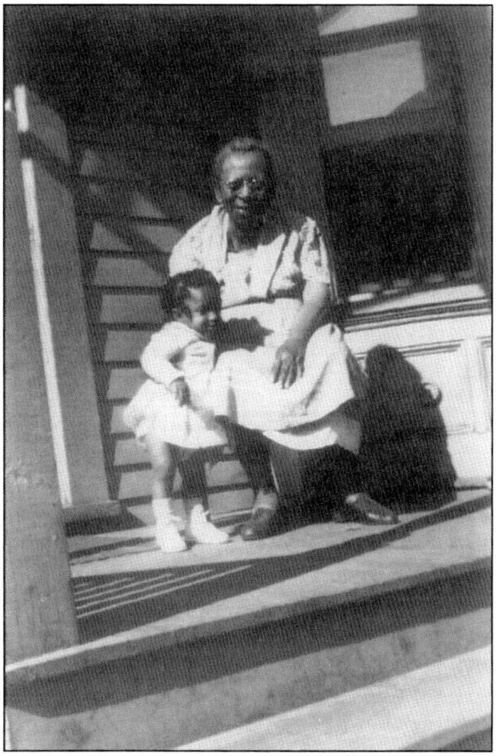

In the above photograph, Shirley Troup sits on the Moore-El family's front porch on Elbo Lane with her Grandma Sykes. Shirley was one of the family's cousins. The Moore-El family moved to Mount Laurel from Newark in the mid-1940s. Below, Grandmother Sarah Moore-El sits with two girls who are doing their hair. Aunt Patience is seated doing the hair of an unidentified girl. These photographs show daily life with the Moore-El family. (Both images courtesy of Geoffrey Hall.)

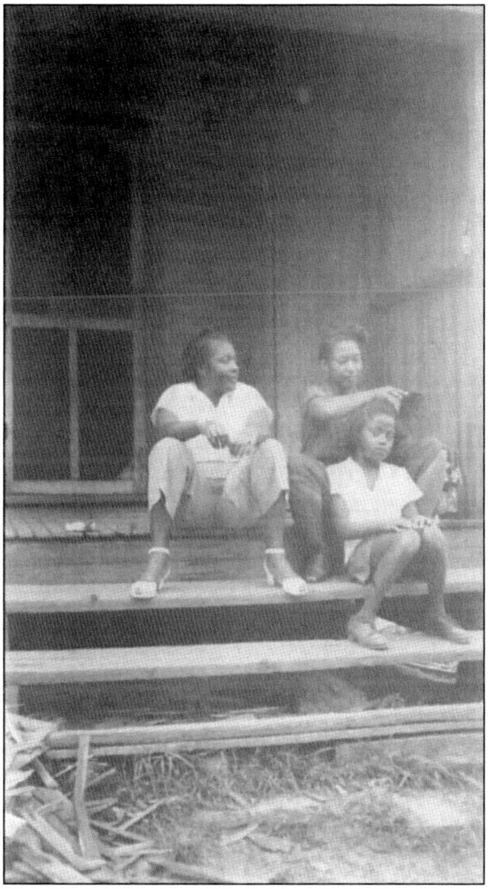

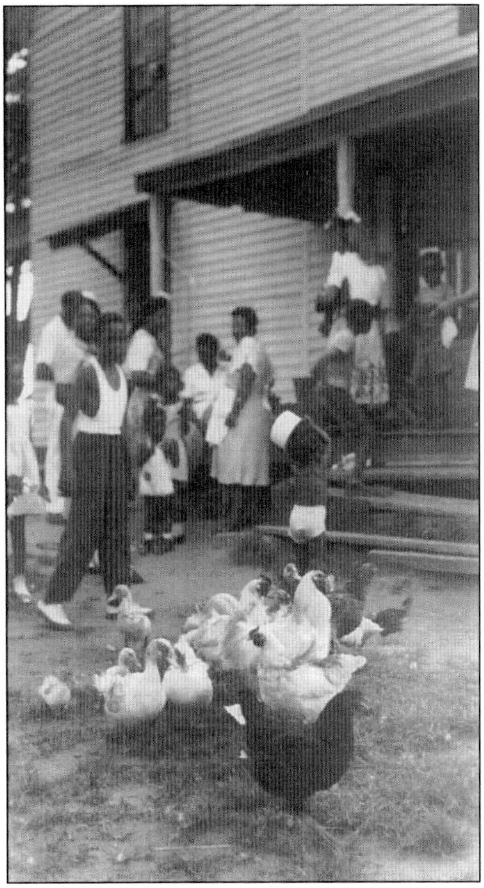

This photograph, from the early 1940s, shows the Moore-El family at their home, located next to the Rudderow farm on Elbo Lane. The family purchased the farm in the late 1930s and raised chickens to sell. They also grew various produce and had cows and horses. (Courtesy of Geoffrey Hall.)

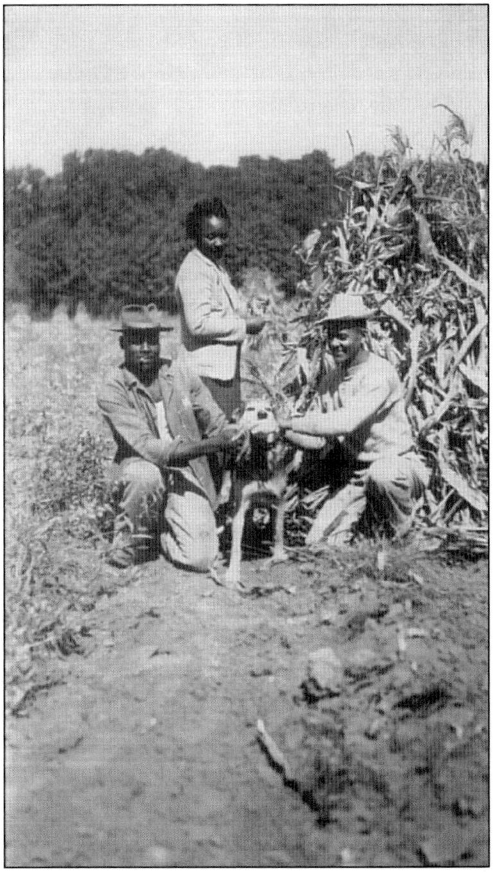

When harvest time arrived, extended family would come from Newark and help the Moore-El family on their farm. In this photograph, Sarah Moore-El poses with her brother-in-law Chester Ellis-El (right) and an unidentified person (left), and their dog, while taking a break from working with corn. (Courtesy of Geoffrey Hall.)

Emma Wiedman-Bey stands under the trellis in the yard of her family's house on Church Street. The home was located next to the Ramblewood Garden Center, across from Teal Lane. This house has since been torn down. (Courtesy of Geoffrey Hall.)

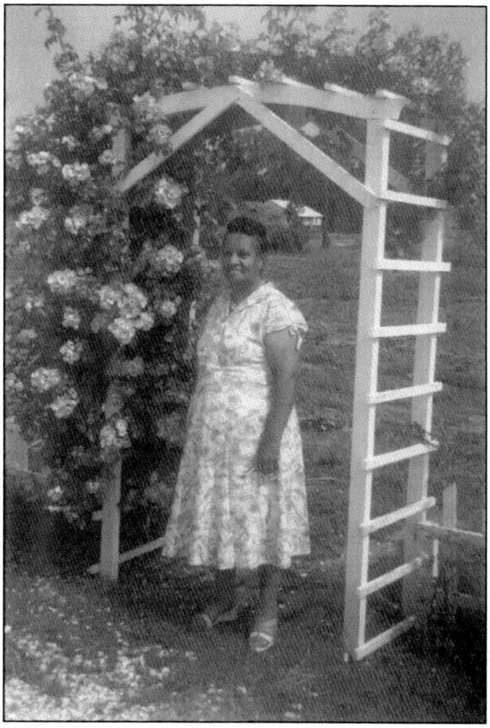

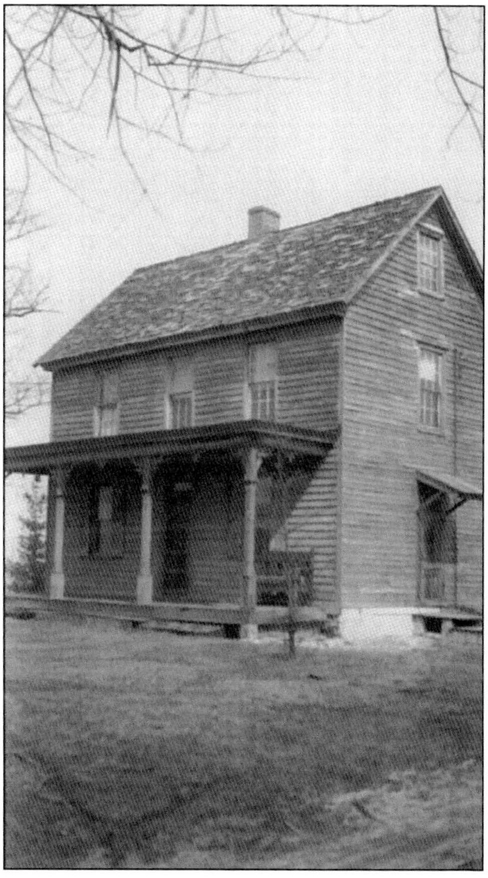

The Moore-El family lost interest in farming and sold the farm in pieces to Colonial Pipeline, who offered a lot of money to the family. A few years before most of the farm was sold, a suspicious fire occurred in the barn. Family members felt that the incident stemmed from people's resentment that an African American family owned so much property. The family kept the farmhouse, renting it out before finally selling it, just before the Stonegate development began in the mid-1980s. (Courtesy of Geoffrey Hall.)

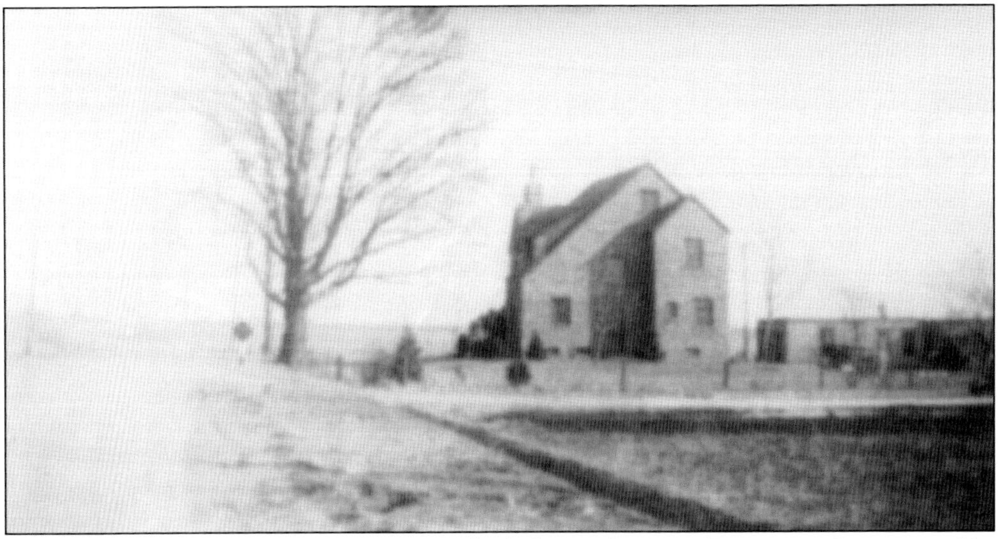

The Nardin house, pictured here in 1937, was built during the Great Depression. It was owned by William Thomas Nardin (b. 1898) and his wife, Eleanor (b. 1899). William was a farmer, mayor, and inventor who held a patent for a hot-dog cooker. He did his inventing in his machine shop. (Courtesy of Meg Ellis.)

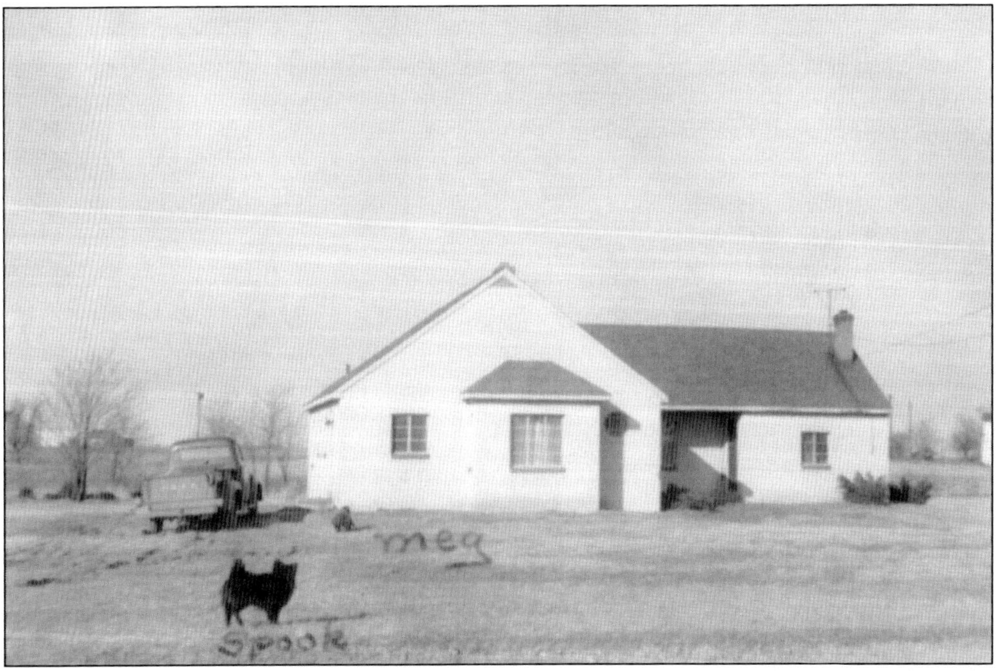

This photograph, taken in the spring of 1957, shows the William T. Nardin home across from the New Jersey Turnpike at Route 73. A hotel on Fellowship Road now stands in its place. Meg Burkhardt is shown playing in the yard with her Chow, named Spookie. (Courtesy of Meg Ellis.)

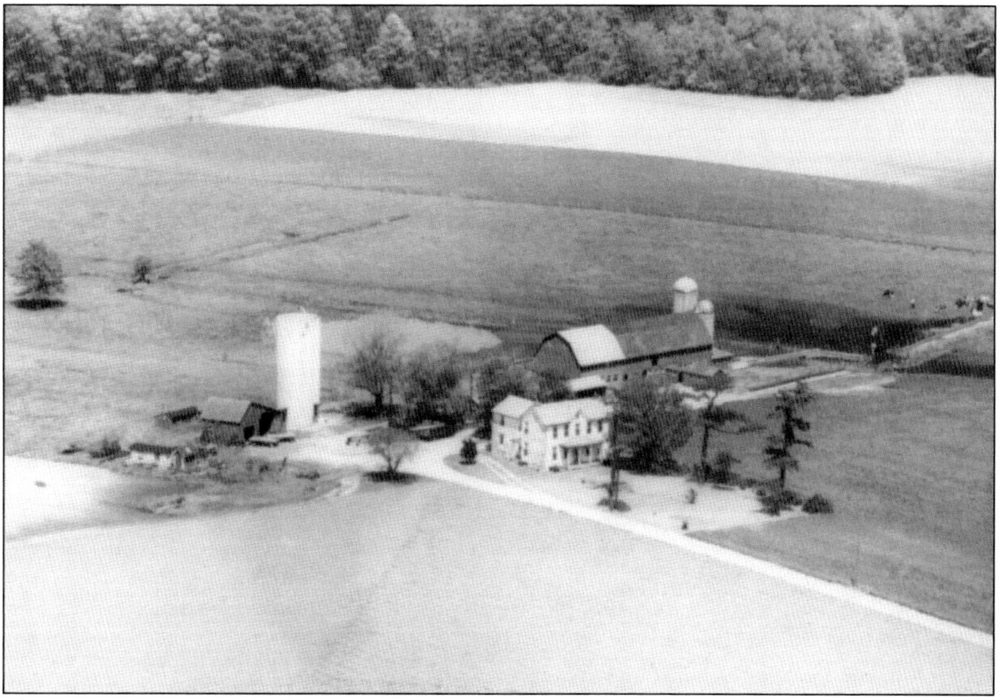

The Morris Amos Rudderow dairy farm was located on Fellowship Road. This aerial photograph, taken in 1966, shows the main house, the various barns, and some of the land. Many farmers would not only work their own land, but would lease land from other farmers in the area. (Courtesy of Buddy Rudderow.)

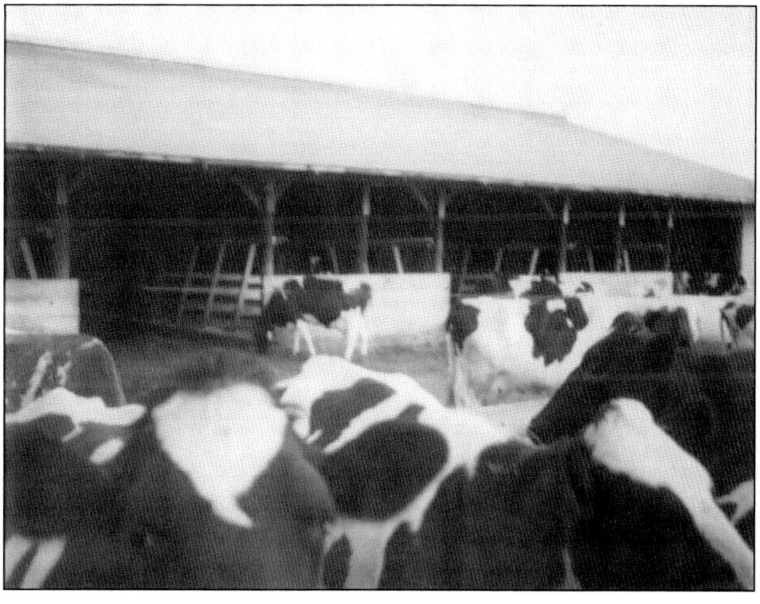

All of the cows at the Rudderow farm had to have "Mars-Haven" in their names, due to their pedigree. When the farm was active, Hank Rudderow was able to give his pet names for every cow on the family's farm. Although the Rudderow family no longer has a dairy farm, they still grow some of their own vegetables at their home. (Courtesy of Buddy Rudderow.)

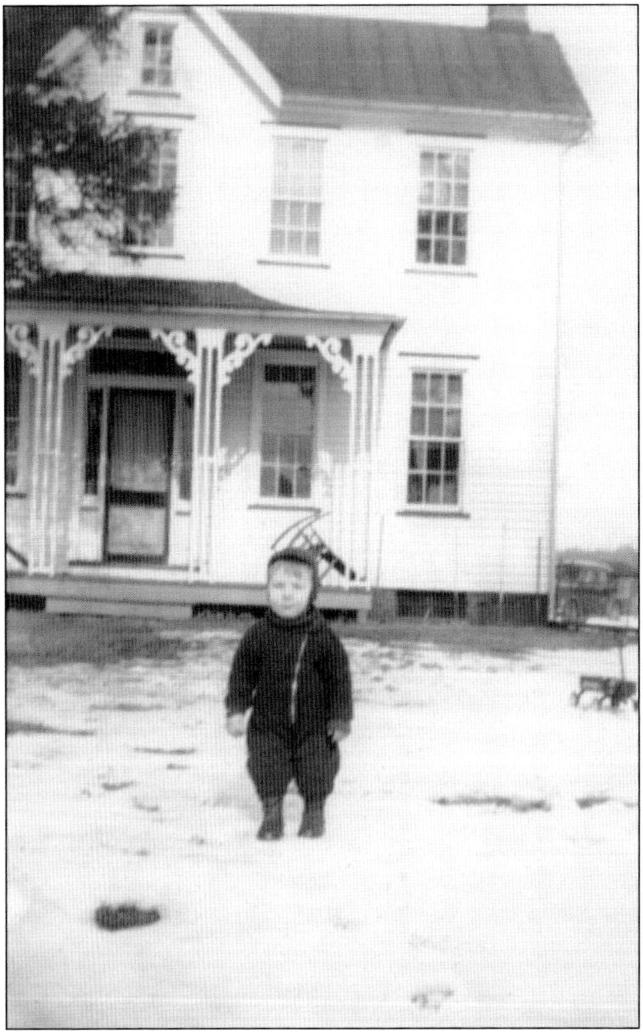

This photograph of Hank Rudderow was taken in 1942 or 1943, in front of the main house on the family's dairy farm. The Rudderow family, related to the original Evans family who settled Mount Laurel, were farmers their whole lives. (Courtesy of Buddy Rudderow.)

The Rudderow family frequently found Native American arrowheads on their farm. The Lenape Indians maintained a large presence in the Mount Laurel area before the Evans family, relatives of the Rudderows, settled on the land. There are many other places in Mount Laurel where Native American artifacts have been found. (Courtesy of the author.)

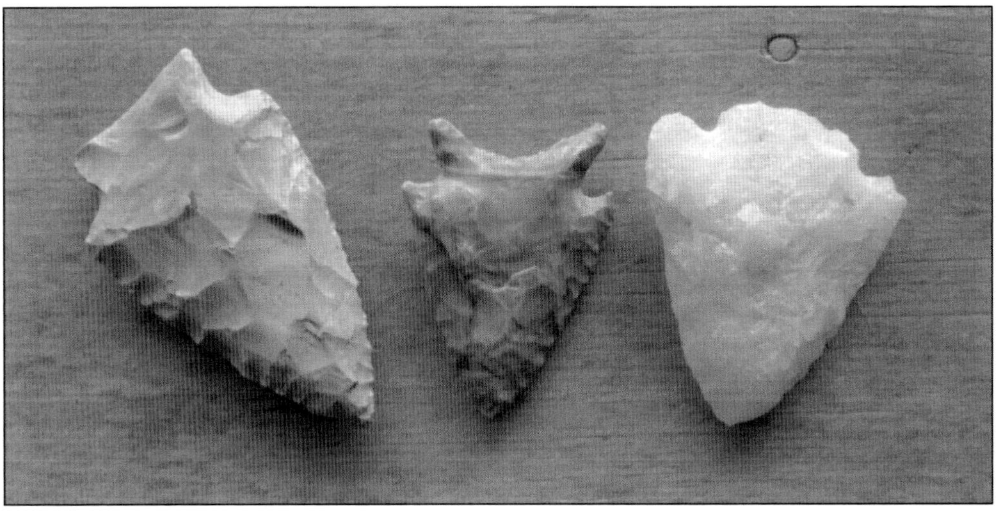

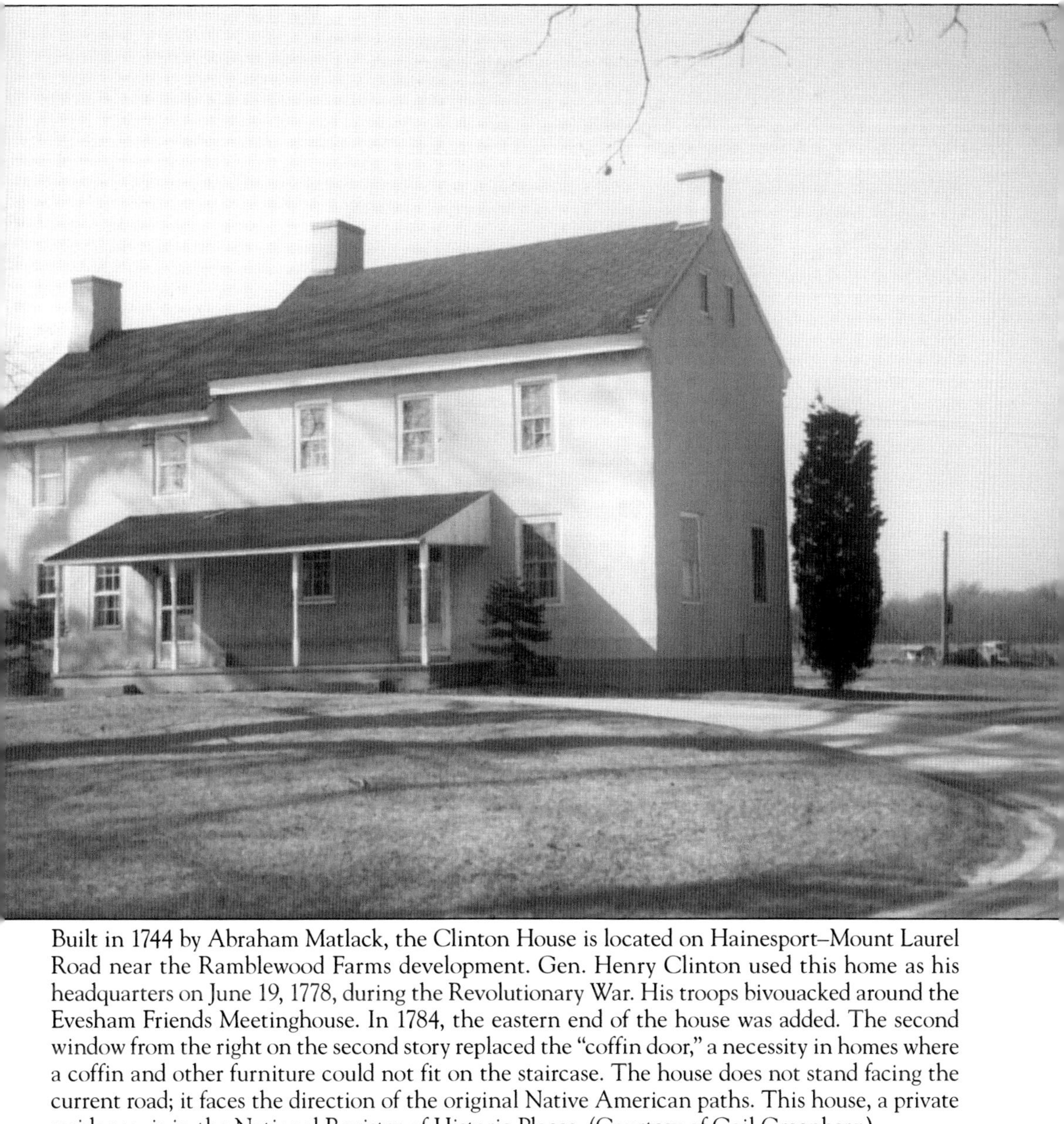

Built in 1744 by Abraham Matlack, the Clinton House is located on Hainesport–Mount Laurel Road near the Ramblewood Farms development. Gen. Henry Clinton used this home as his headquarters on June 19, 1778, during the Revolutionary War. His troops bivouacked around the Evesham Friends Meetinghouse. In 1784, the eastern end of the house was added. The second window from the right on the second story replaced the "coffin door," a necessity in homes where a coffin and other furniture could not fit on the staircase. The house does not stand facing the current road; it faces the direction of the original Native American paths. This house, a private residence, is in the National Register of Historic Places. (Courtesy of Gail Greenberg.)

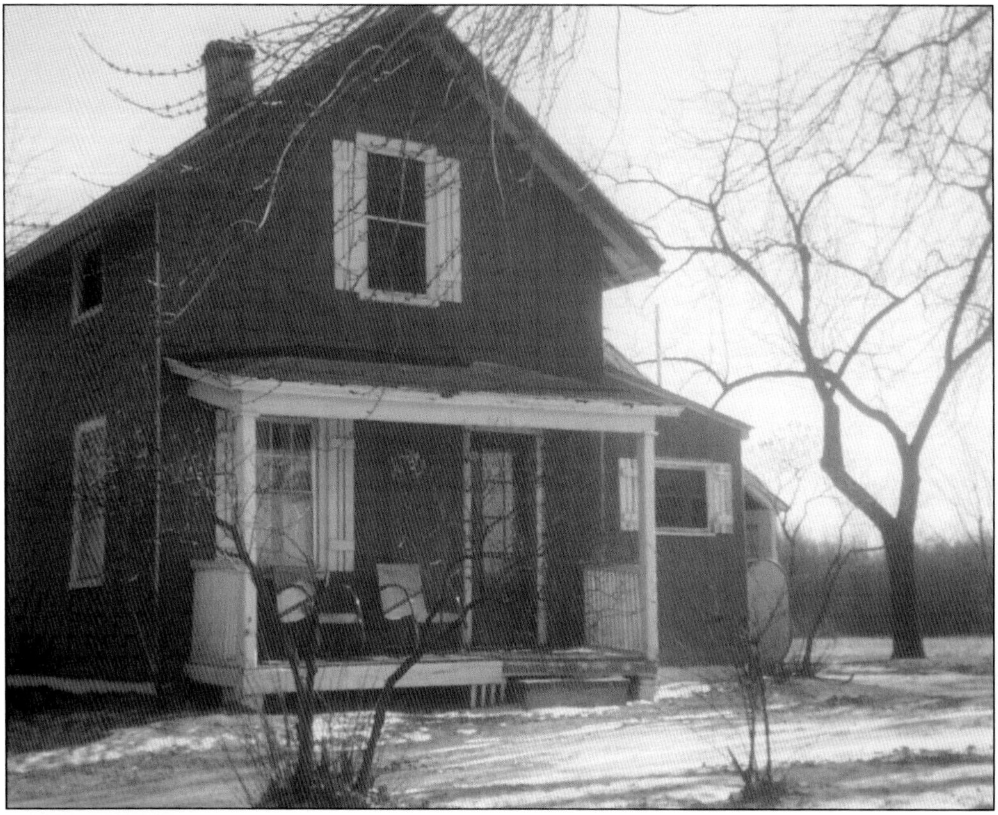

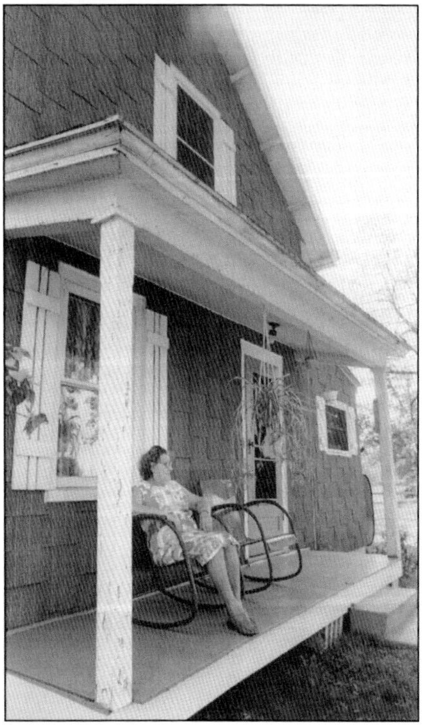

The tollhouse once had a gate in front to stop vehicles while the attendant collected the toll. In the 1800s, anyone going to church or Sunday meeting received free passage through the tollgate; others paid 10¢ and received a ticket that allowed passage all the way to Camden. Sarah Foster served as the last attendant in 1887. The tollhouse stood on the Moorestown–Mount Laurel Turnpike (present-day Moorestown–Mount Laurel Road), near the service entrance road for the current New Jersey Turnpike. With most of the roads made of crushed oyster shells, this road was the first township road to be surfaced in 1887. The tollhouse was moved in 1892 or 1912. (Above, courtesy of Gail Greenberg; below, courtesy of the *Burlington County Times*.)

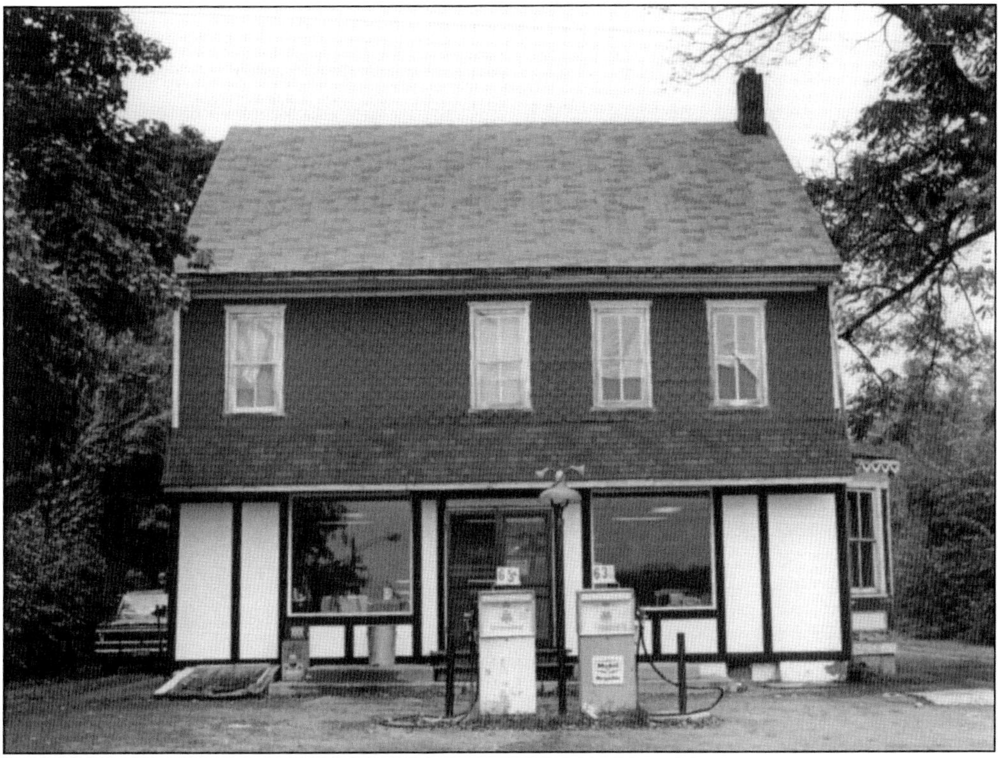

Billington's General Store (above) was located next to the Lippincott House on Hainesport–Mount Laurel Road. It sold cigarettes, lunchmeat, snacks, ice cream, and various other items. Emily Billington worked behind the counter. This store previously was a storage facility for the Mount Laurel General Store and Post Office, which were located in the Lippincott House. Billington's was converted into a restaurant called the Quiet Man (below) and was then completely renovated to become today's Cucina Carini. (Both images courtesy of the *Burlington County Times*.)

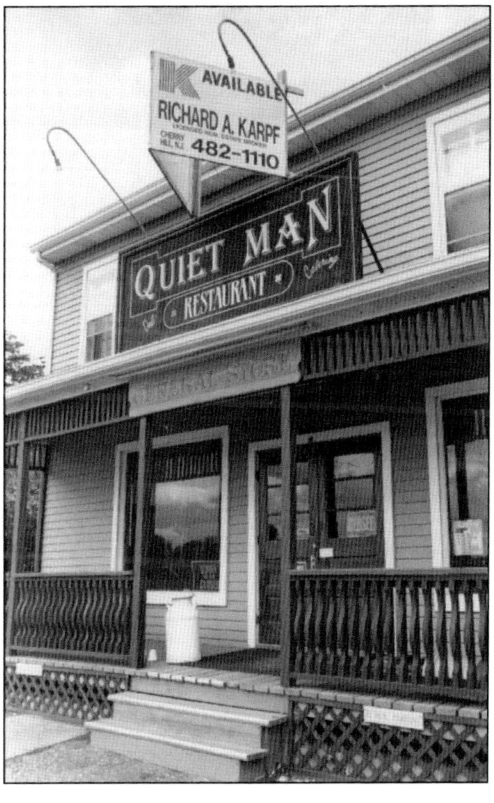

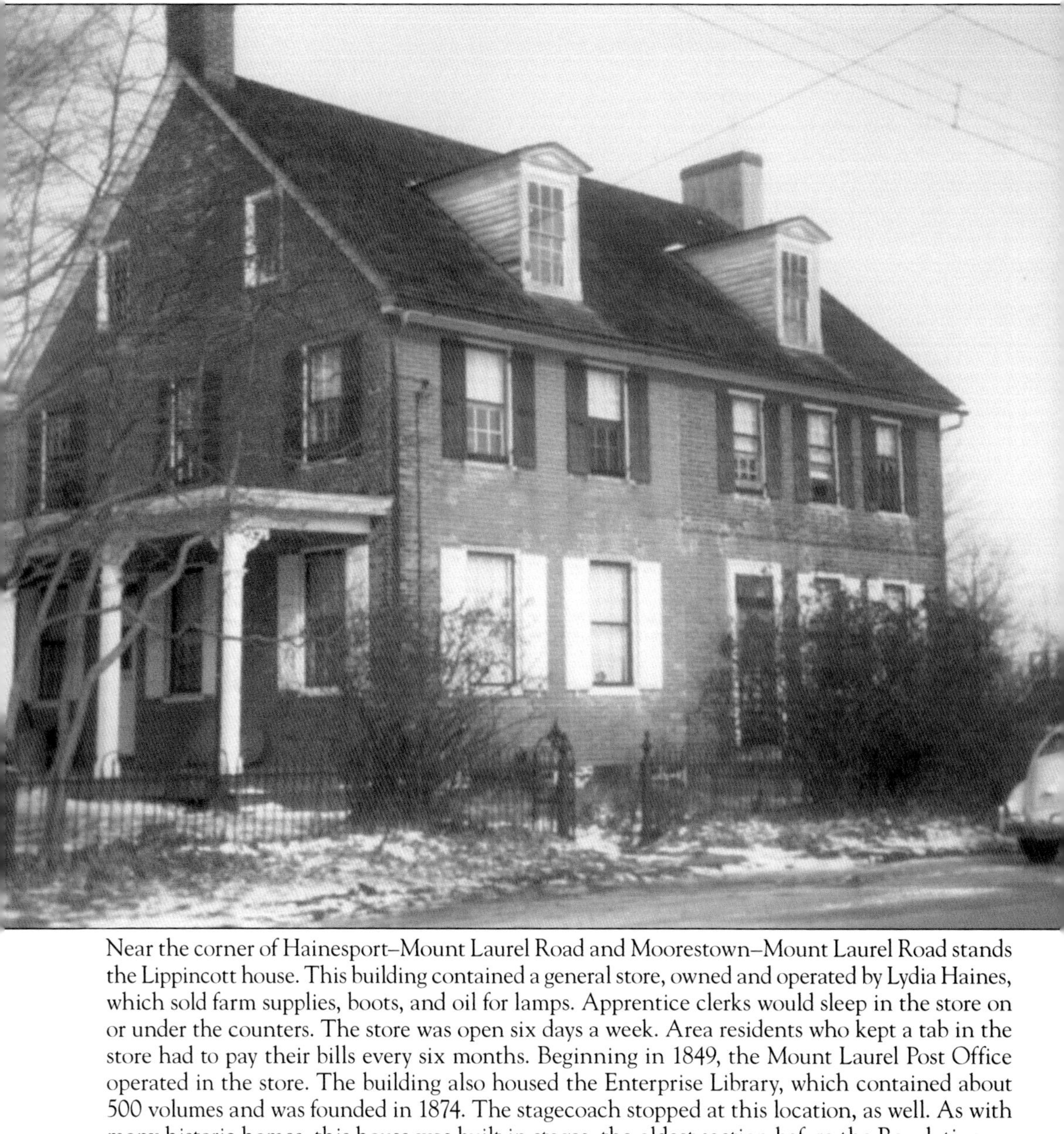

Near the corner of Hainesport–Mount Laurel Road and Moorestown–Mount Laurel Road stands the Lippincott house. This building contained a general store, owned and operated by Lydia Haines, which sold farm supplies, boots, and oil for lamps. Apprentice clerks would sleep in the store on or under the counters. The store was open six days a week. Area residents who kept a tab in the store had to pay their bills every six months. Beginning in 1849, the Mount Laurel Post Office operated in the store. The building also housed the Enterprise Library, which contained about 500 volumes and was founded in 1874. The stagecoach stopped at this location, as well. As with many historic homes, this house was built in stages, the oldest section before the Revolutionary War and the next section in 1824 with locally made bricks. (Courtesy of Gail Greenberg.)

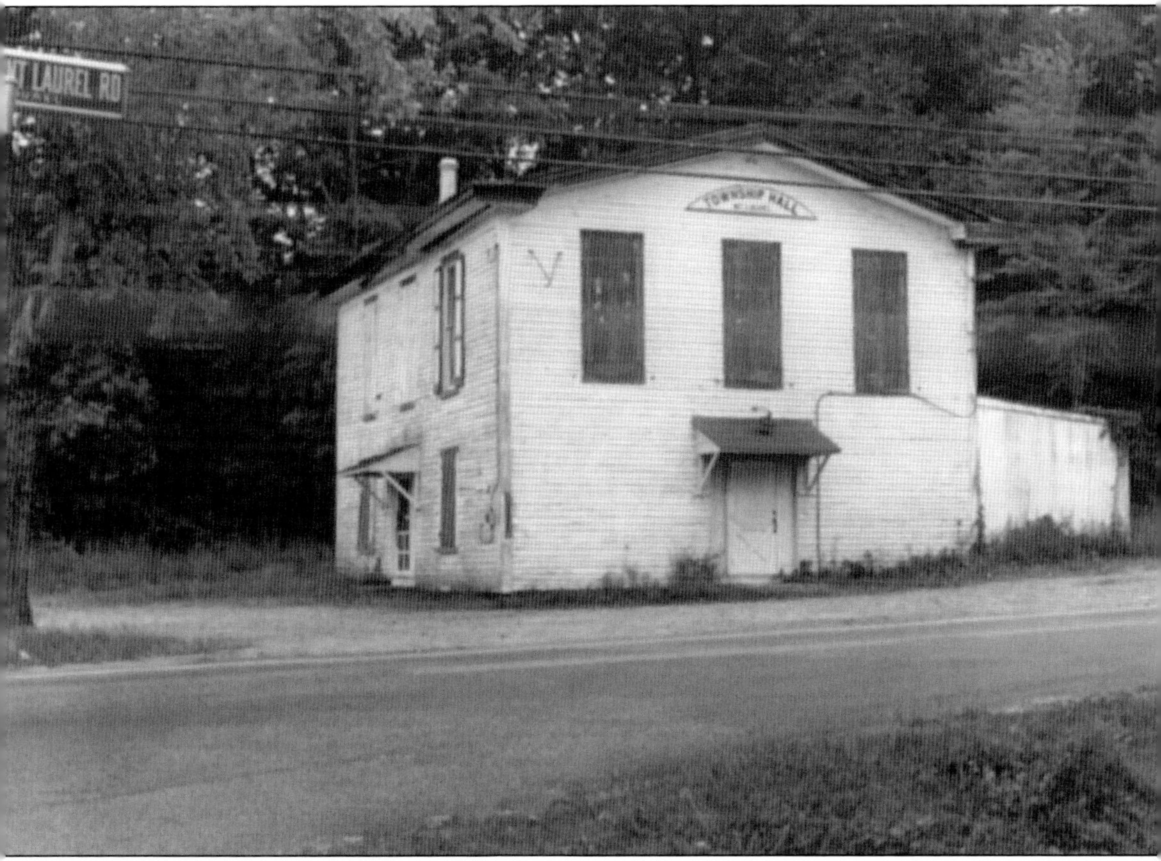

An undated photograph shows Mount Laurel's Farmer's Hall. The police department was located in Farmer's Hall, as were various other organizations. This building was renovated a few times and presently houses the Mount Laurel Historical Society. It stands at the base of the "mount," which is the smallest state park in New Jersey. William C. Bridges & Company constructed a line of signal towers on hilltops, including Mount Laurel, across the state for communication between New York City and Philadelphia. At the top of the Mount Laurel tower, above the highest trees, was a room for the operators, Edmund and Charles Darnell, who controlled complex wooden "finger" signals with ropes and pulleys. At the next station, the operator "read" the signals with powerful telescopes and relayed that information to the next station. At night, the signals employed colored lights. Owned by stockbrokers and merchants, the coded messages could not be read by the operators, but contained daily prices, tallies, shareholder reports, and other information. (Courtesy of the Mount Laurel Historical Society.)

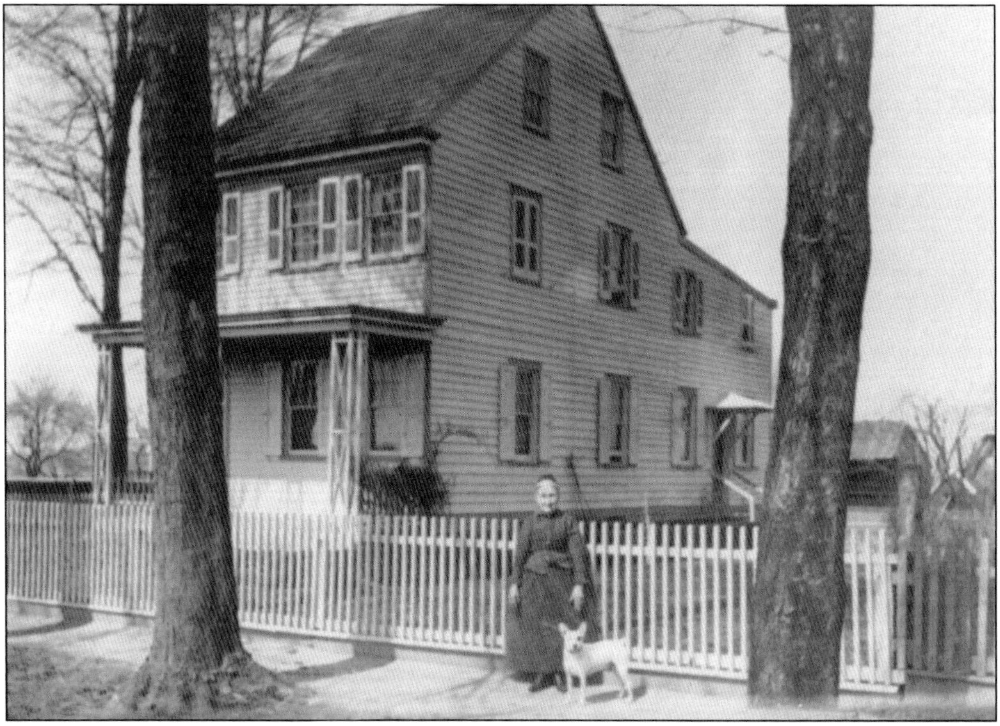

This is the home of Carlton and Sara Evans, who were relatives of the Evans family that settled Mount Laurel. The family's original farmhouse was in the middle of the planned road S-41 and was taken down in 1929 or 1930, when S-41, later Route 73, came through. (Courtesy of Marian and Jim Hartshorne.)

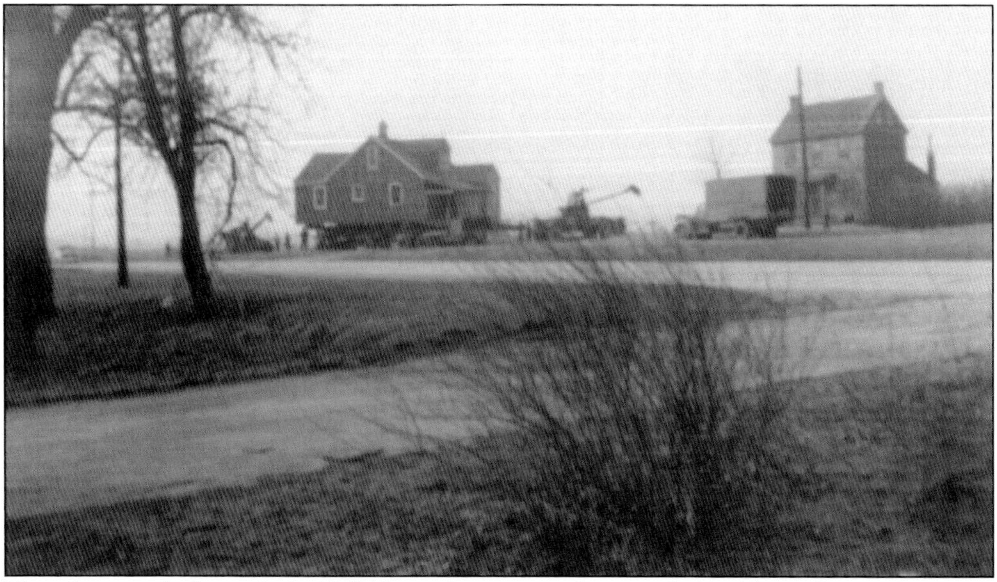

This photograph shows the Liddells' house being moved across the Rudderow farm at Route 73. Dee and Mary lived in it on the farm. The house had to be moved to Pleasant Valley Avenue between Fellowship and Church Street to get out of the way of the turnpike construction on their property. (Courtesy of Marian and Jim Hartshorne.)

In the early 1900s, Harvey E. Rudderow (left) and Alfred Rudderow pose with baskets of peaches from their farm in Fellowship near Church Road and Route 73. Their peach farm eventually became a dairy farm. (Courtesy of Marian and Jim Hartshorne.)

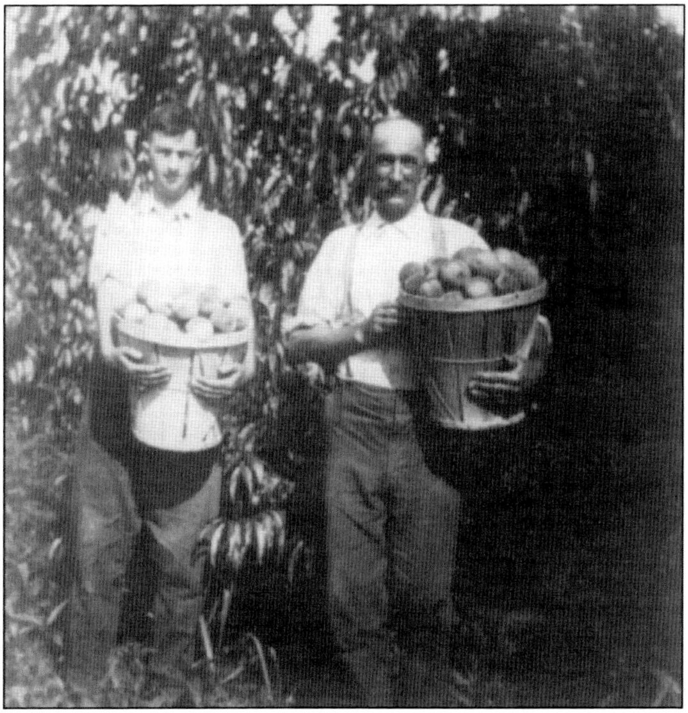

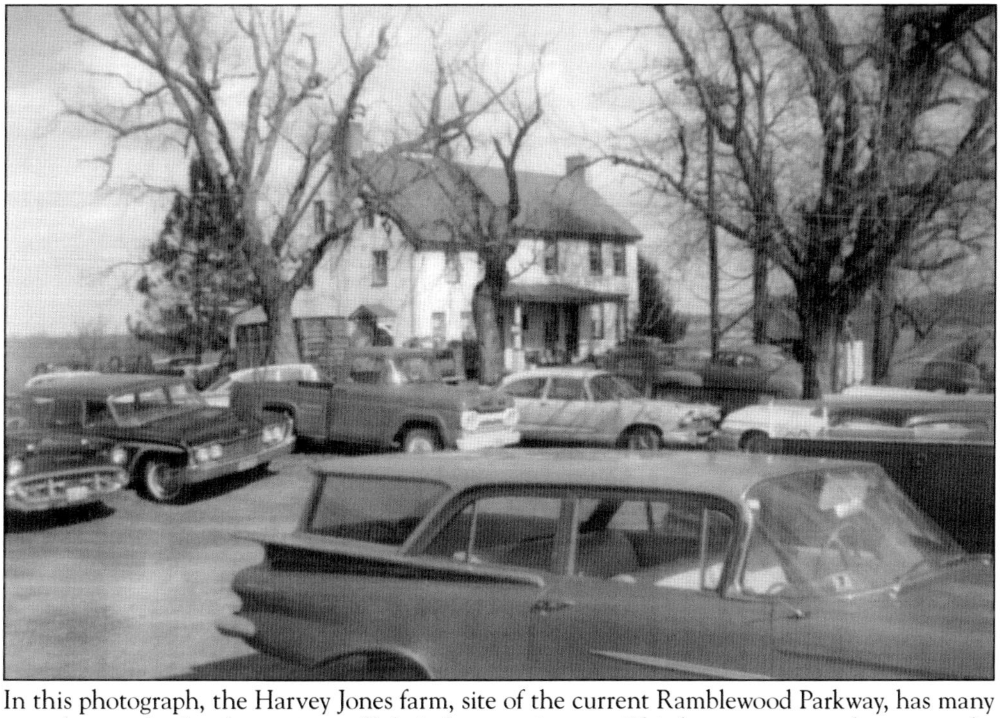

In this photograph, the Harvey Jones farm, site of the current Ramblewood Parkway, has many attendees as the family auctions off their farm equipment. This house was torn down to make way for the Ramblewood development off of Route 73. Nancy and Pete Jones had first choice of lots for their home in the new development. They nostalgically chose the spot that once was the front yard of their razed farmhouse. (Courtesy of Annetta Verner.)

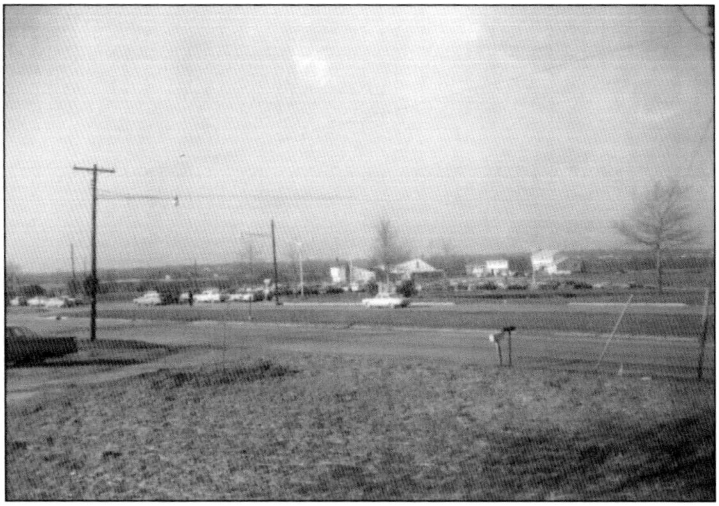

The new Ramblewood development is seen from the Havers and Verner farms across Route 73. The Havers and Verner farms were situated on the corner of Church Road and Route 73, where Copperfields Restaurant was built. Copperfields was eventually torn down. The site is now occupied by a car dealership. (Courtesy of Annetta Verner.)

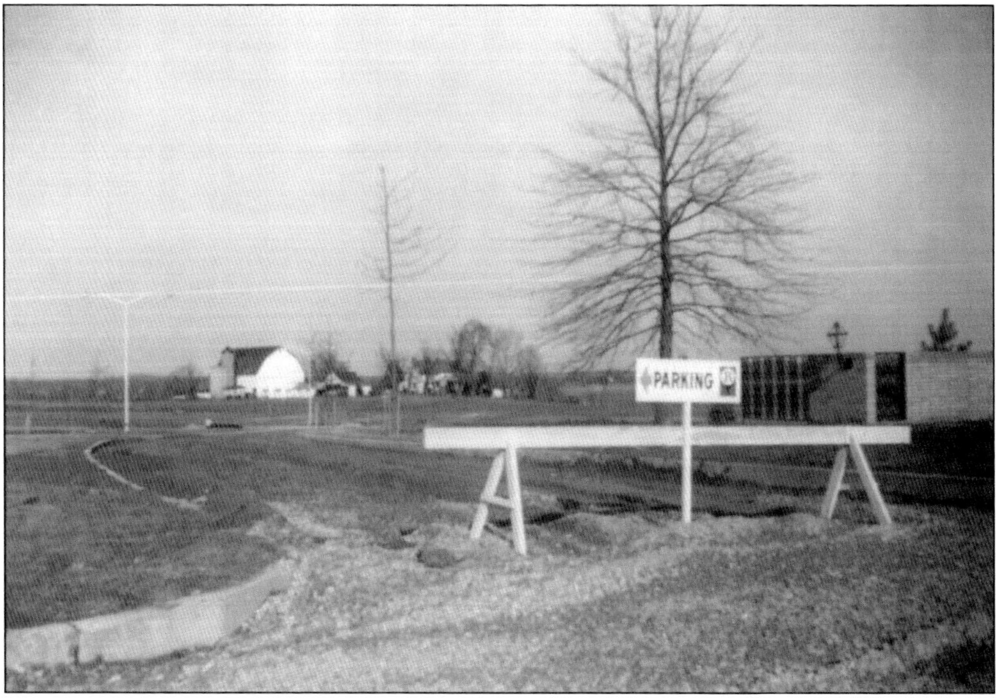

This photograph, taken around 1960, shows the entrance to the Ramblewood development at Ramblewood Parkway as seen from Route 73. The Harvey Jones farm was located there and can be seen in the background. The Jones family sold all of the land to Dick and Harry Goodwin, who created Ramblewood and then employed the Jones brothers for many years. (Courtesy of Annetta Verner.)

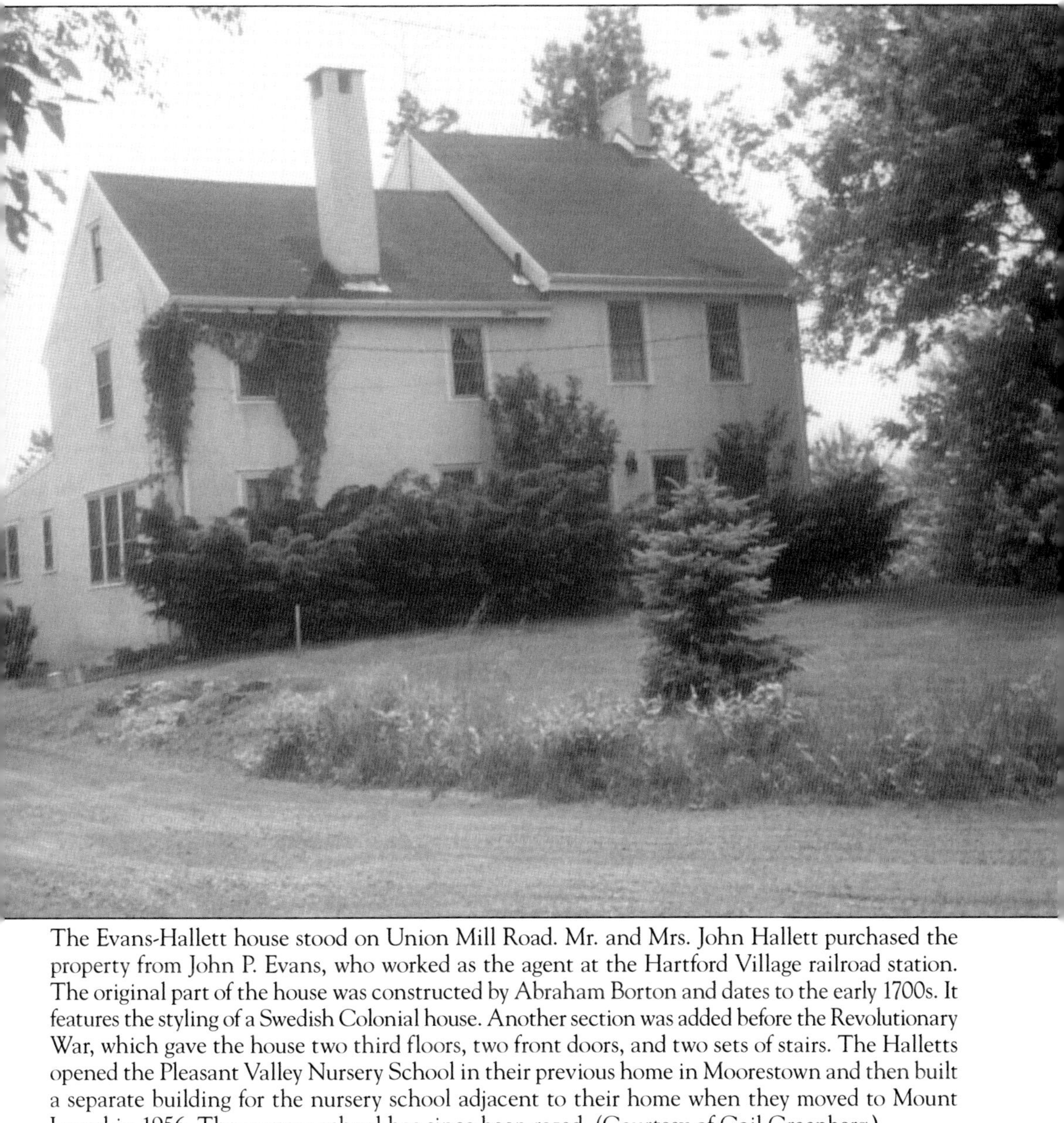

The Evans-Hallett house stood on Union Mill Road. Mr. and Mrs. John Hallett purchased the property from John P. Evans, who worked as the agent at the Hartford Village railroad station. The original part of the house was constructed by Abraham Borton and dates to the early 1700s. It features the styling of a Swedish Colonial house. Another section was added before the Revolutionary War, which gave the house two third floors, two front doors, and two sets of stairs. The Halletts opened the Pleasant Valley Nursery School in their previous home in Moorestown and then built a separate building for the nursery school adjacent to their home when they moved to Mount Laurel in 1956. The nursery school has since been razed. (Courtesy of Gail Greenberg.)

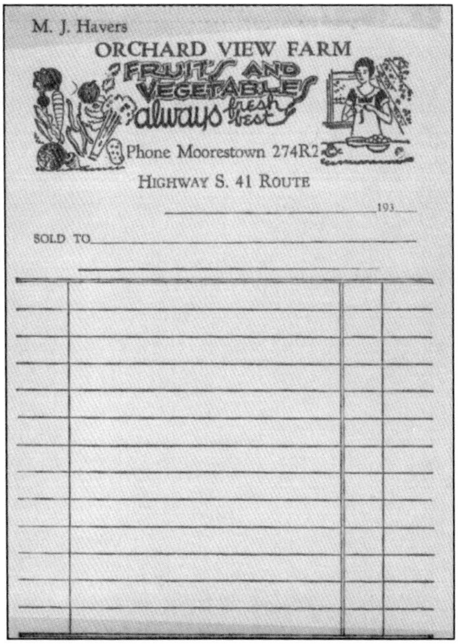
M. J. Havers
ORCHARD VIEW FARM
FRUITS AND VEGETABLES
always fresh best
Phone Moorestown 274R2
HIGHWAY S. 41 ROUTE
193
SOLD TO

This is a sales slip for the Havers' Orchard View Farm. Note the company's phone number, Moorestown 274 R2. There were no private phone lines, only party lines with, usually, eight families per line. Each house on the line had a distinctive ring. There could be anyone on the party line listening in, so whatever was said was public information. (Courtesy of Annetta Verner.)

The Havers family purchased apple cider in 50-gallon barrels from Larchmont Farm in the Masonville section of Mount Laurel. The cider would be siphoned into jugs and sold at the Havers' roadside stand with their label on it. The Havers children would fight over who got to do the siphoning. That was the only way they could sneak a drink, since all of the cider was to be sold and was not for the family to drink. (Courtesy of Annetta Verner.)

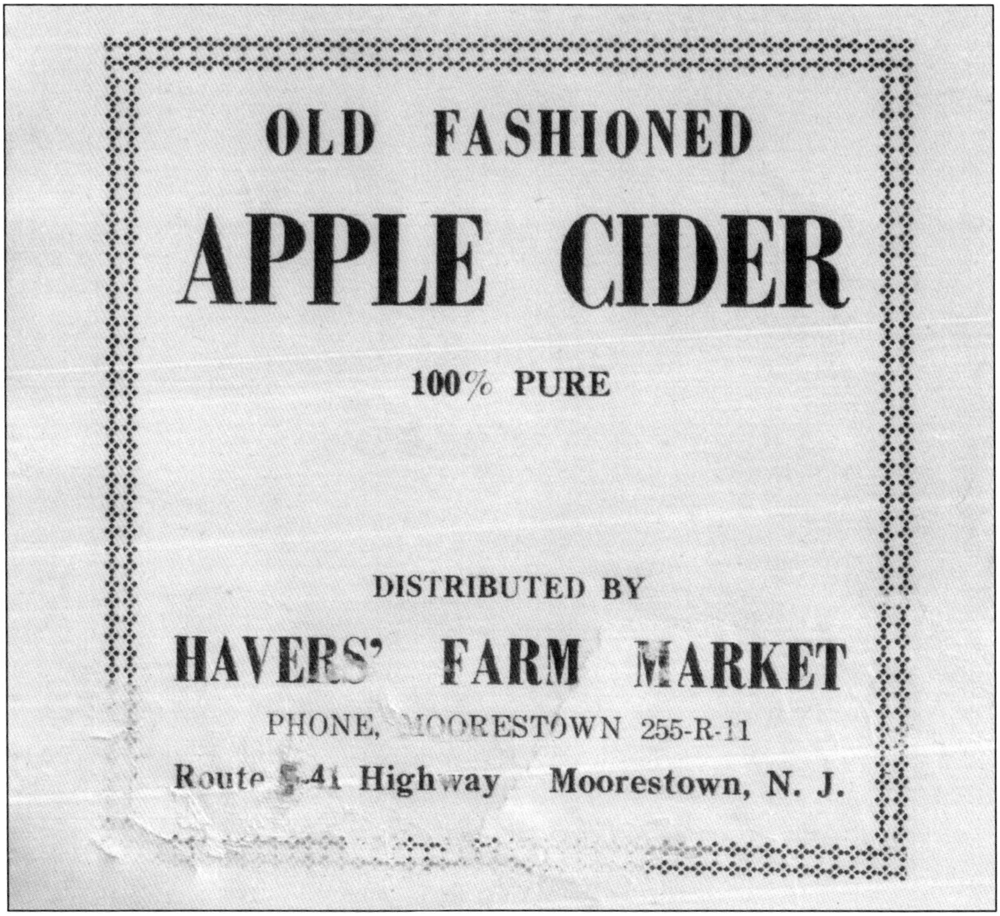
OLD FASHIONED
APPLE CIDER
100% PURE
DISTRIBUTED BY
HAVERS' FARM MARKET
PHONE, MOORESTOWN 255-R-11
Route S-41 Highway Moorestown, N. J.

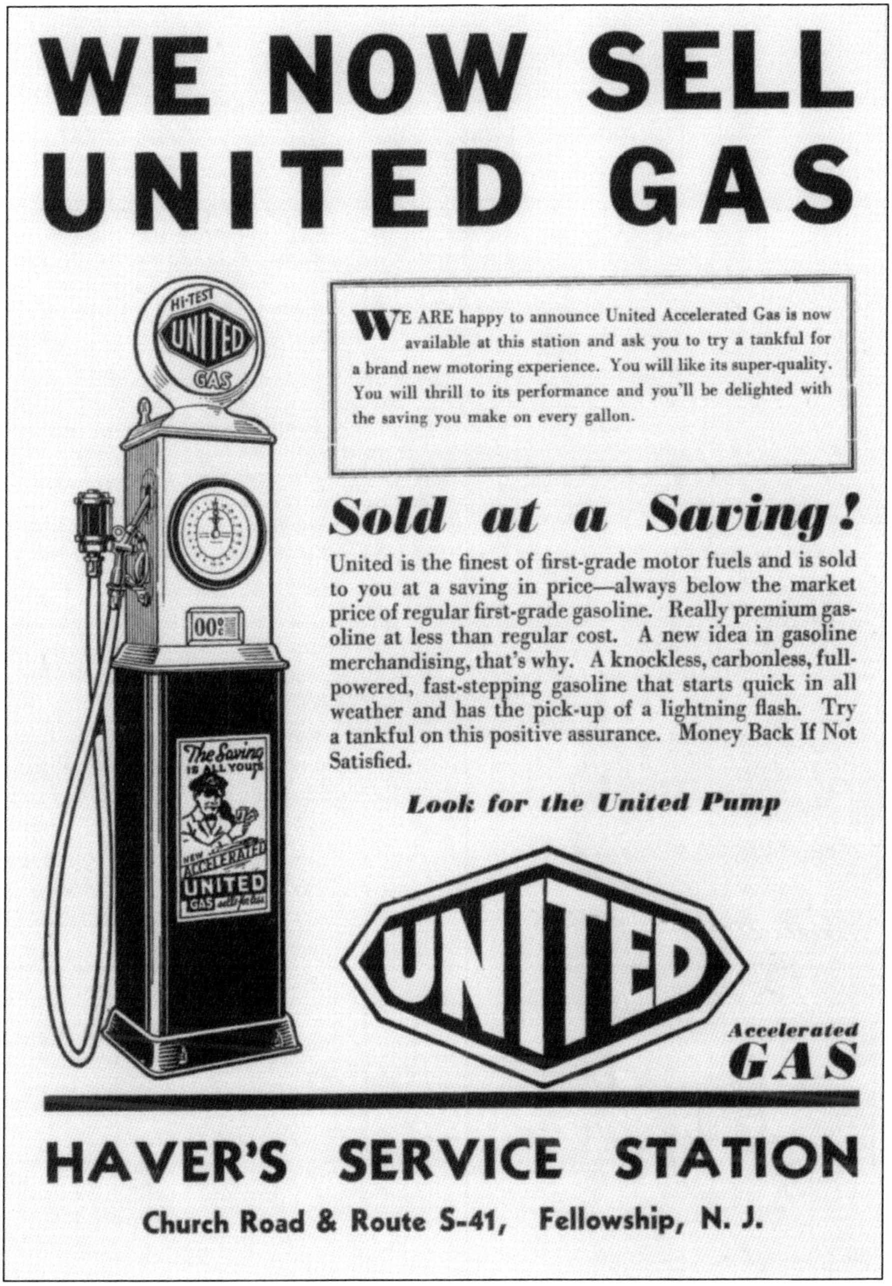

Although the Havers family's main source of income was growing tomatoes for the Campbell Soup Company, the family also owned a gas station. United Gas was an unknown brand that the Havers family sold at their station on S-41 (Route 73) for a lesser price than well-known brands. The family bought the gas through Izzy Bloom, a gas broker in Camden. In 1938, it was selling for 13.9¢ a gallon. The family never knew what brand of gas would be delivered. One time, a Shell gas truck would pull up; another time, it would be an Esso truck. Because of this, someone stopping for gas might get any brand. When someone would need gas, they would pull into the station and blow their horn, and young Annetta would run across the street to pump gas for the customer. (Courtesy of Annetta Verner.)

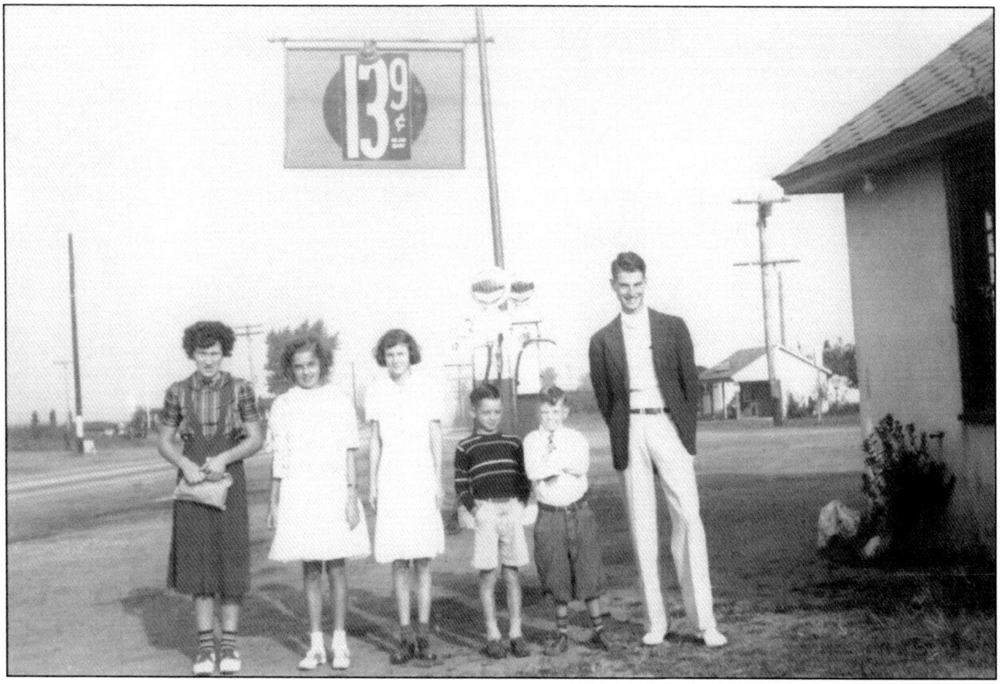

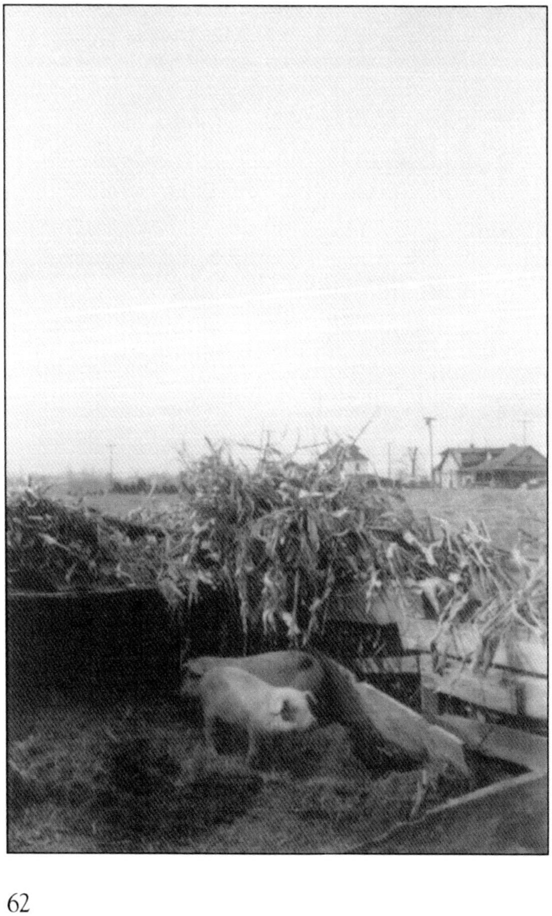

This photograph was taken in front of the Havers' United Gas station. Pictured here are, from left to right, Catherine McMullen, Anita Jones, Annetta Havers, Jarry Jones, Joseph Havers, and Pete Jones. They are getting ready to attend the first day of school in 1938. (Courtesy of Annetta Verner.)

At the Havers farm, purchased in 1915, the pigs were always getting loose on Church Road or Route 73, which was a dirt road from Fellowship to Church. A knock would come at the front door. It would be a neighbor, who would say, "Martin, your pigs are on the highway." The family would then chase the pigs down Highway S-41 and herd them back to the pen. Visible in the background of this photograph is Crawford's Log Cabin. Jim and Bertha Crawford sold beer inside and penny candy on the side porch. The Log Cabin was sold after the owners died. It became a gas station, which was torn down and became a vacant lot. (Courtesy of Annetta Verner.)

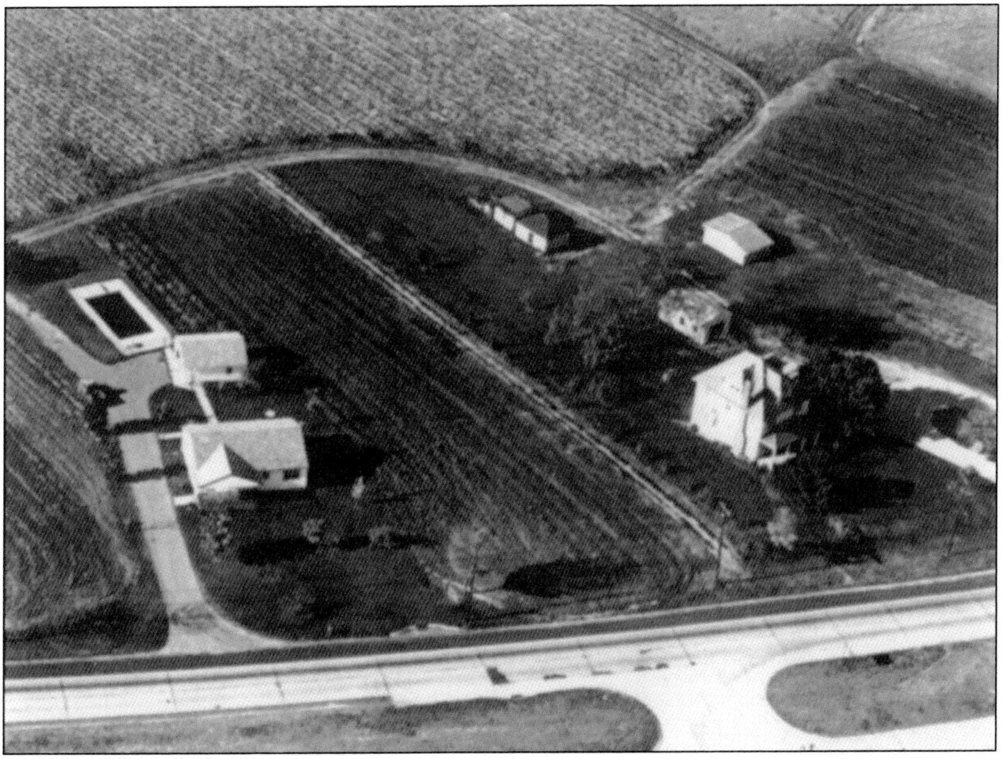

This aerial photograph of the Verner home (left) and the Havers homestead (right) was taken in 1965, across from the Jones farm. Martin Havers gave a portion of his farm to his daughter when she got married, and they maintained a path between the two houses.

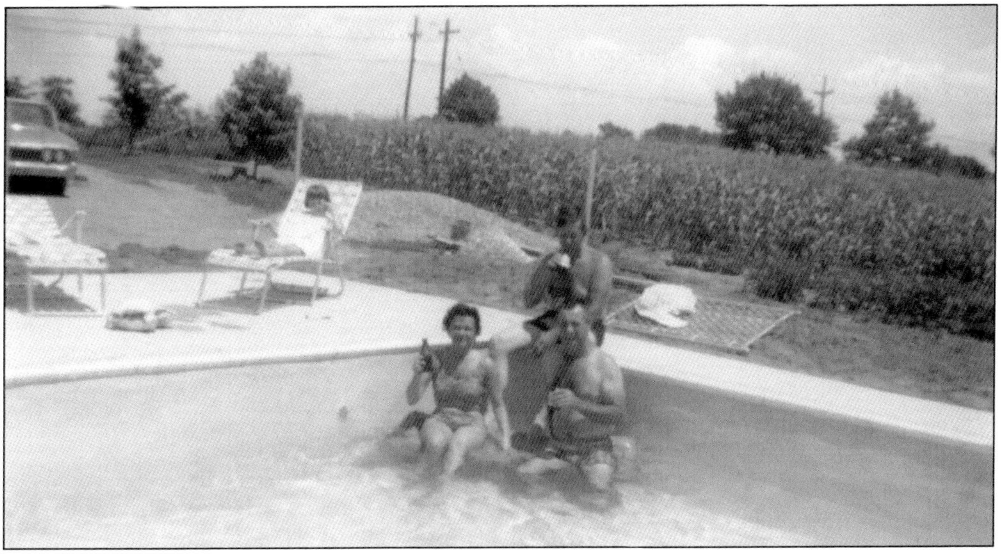

The Verners built a pool in their yard, right next to the crops. Mrs. Verner taught swim lessons to the local children. The girl pictured sitting in the chair her daughter Karen. Annetta Verner (foreground left) and Bill Verner (foreground right) are sitting in the pool. Behind them is Bud Browning, a friend who owned a farm with a roadside stand on Lenola Road in Moorestown. The farm is still in operation. (Courtesy of Annetta Verner.)

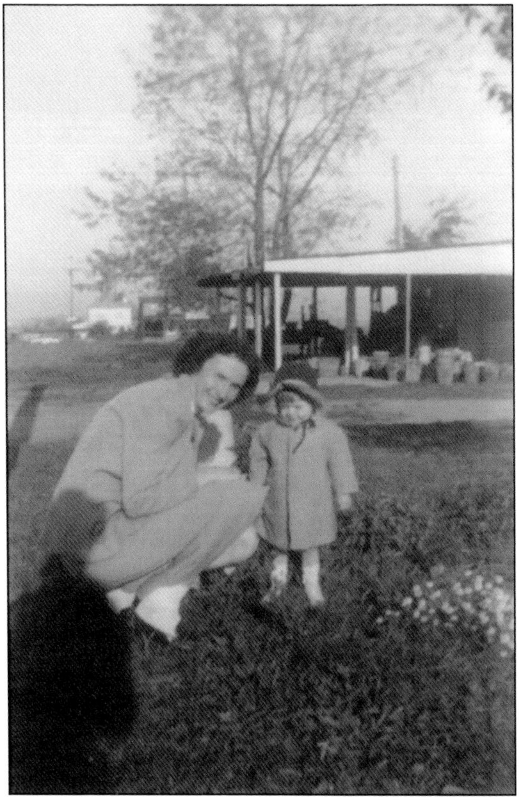

Annetta Verner poses with her daughter Kathleen in 1955. In the background is one of the Havers' roadside vegetable stands, which were located on Route 73. Martin Havers realized that he could make more money by having stands on both sides of the street. (Courtesy of Annetta Verner.)

This 1978 photograph shows the corner of Yorktown Road and South Church Street, where Mount Laurel Township purchased land for a green acres park. Now called Laurel Acres, the site contains numerous pieces of playground equipment, a pond, and a walking path. (Courtesy of the *Burlington County Times*.)

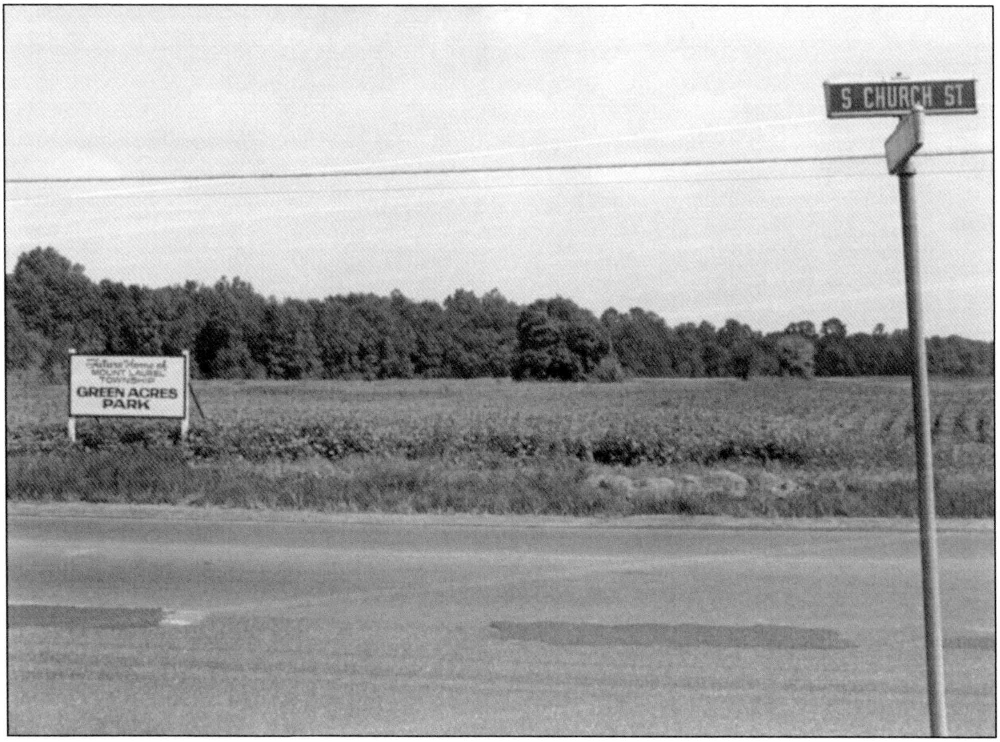

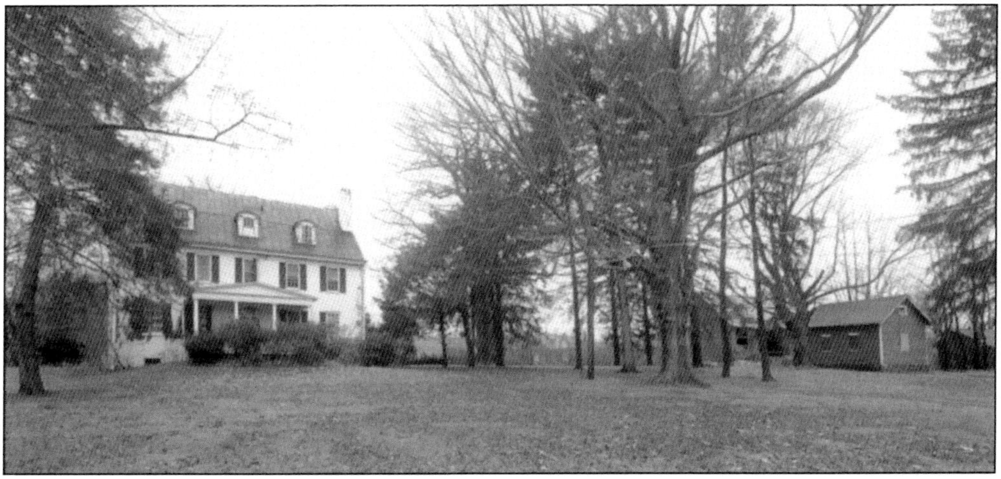

Sunnyside Farm, located on Hooten Road, was one of the most majestic Federal-style homes in the area. Arnold Neuber bought this farm from Joseph Roberts, who built the home in 1838, after over a year of construction. The bricks that were used in this house were made of clay that Samuel Stokes took from an area south of the barn. Joseph Hooten was the builder, but died soon after it was completed. This was the original Hooten homestead, and only top-quality materials were used. (Courtesy of the *Burlington County Times.*)

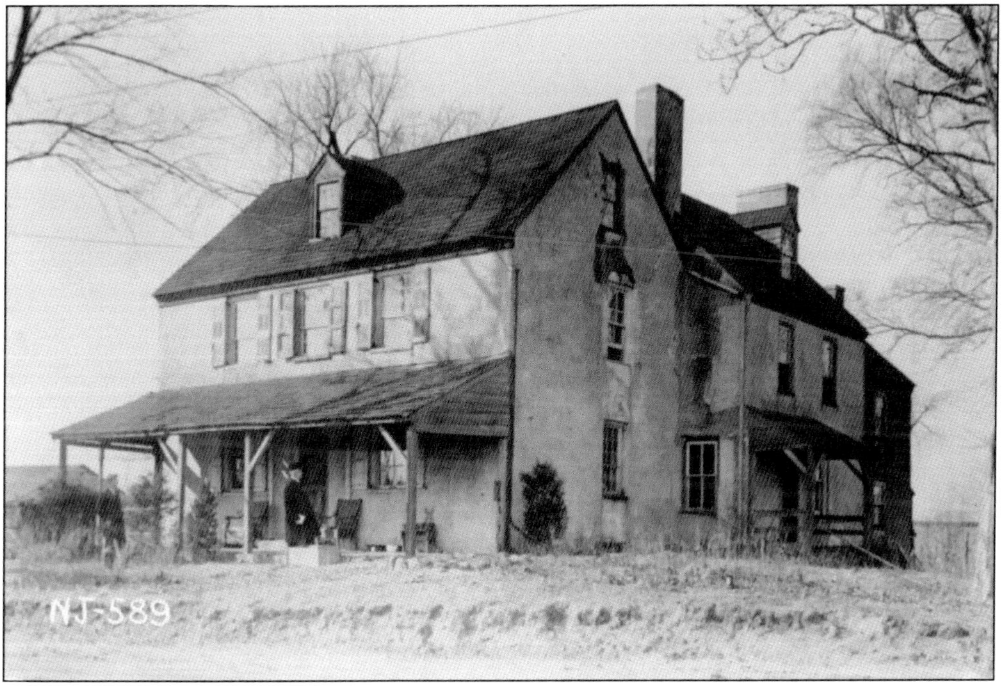

The Haines-Darnell House is located on Hainesport–Mount Laurel Road between Larchmont Boulevard and Hartford Road. The house is on the property of the PAWS Farm, a wildlife preservation society established in 1980, and is used for educational presentations and learning opportunities. The Darnell family cemetery is located on one of the nature trails. This house, constructed in 1736, is one of the few remaining homestead farms from that century. The Darnell family also owned most of the land around the mount before settling in this location, two miles away. (Courtesy of the Library of Congress.)

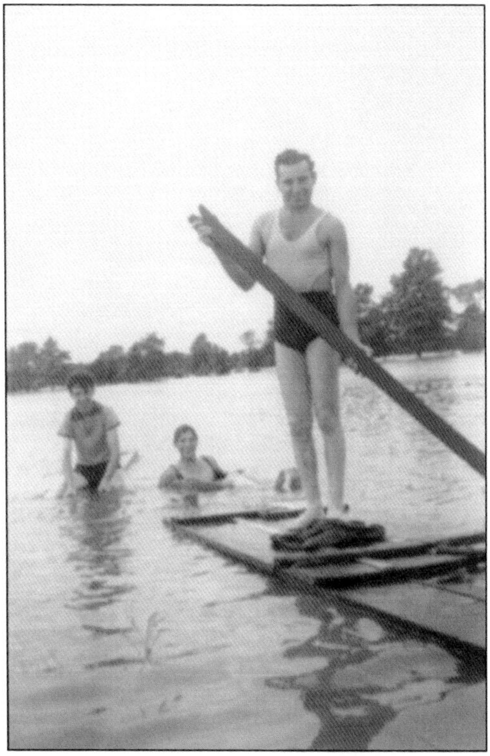

This photograph, taken in 1938 or 1940, shows the backfields and meadows flooded in six feet of water on the Monte farm on Hartford Road. Alex Monte stands on the boards while Mike Monte (left) and Johnny Carfagno get wet. (Courtesy of Judith Monte.)

Posing at a Brownie meeting in 1956 are, clockwise from bottom left, Dolores Starliper, Linda Mason, Linda Stevenson, Judy Monte, Diann Monte, Jeannie Lee, two unidentified leaders, Sherry Wagner, Nancy Clark, Margaret Janssen, Shirley Elbertson, Alice Bain, and Madeline Simpers. (Courtesy of Judith Monte.)

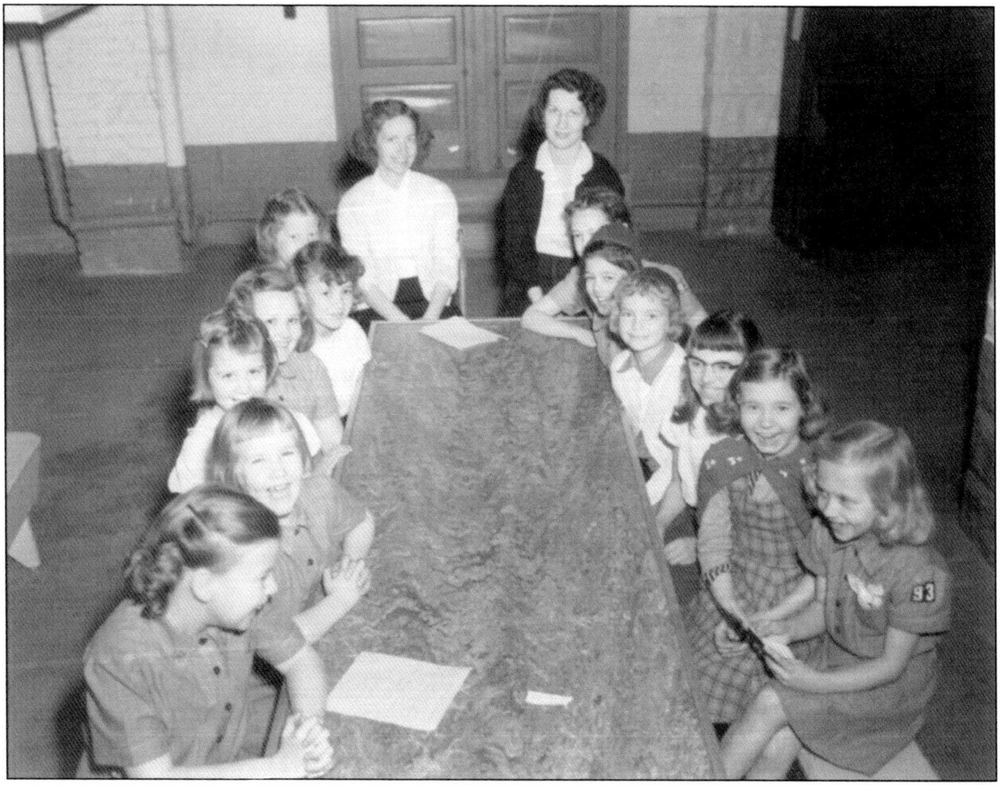

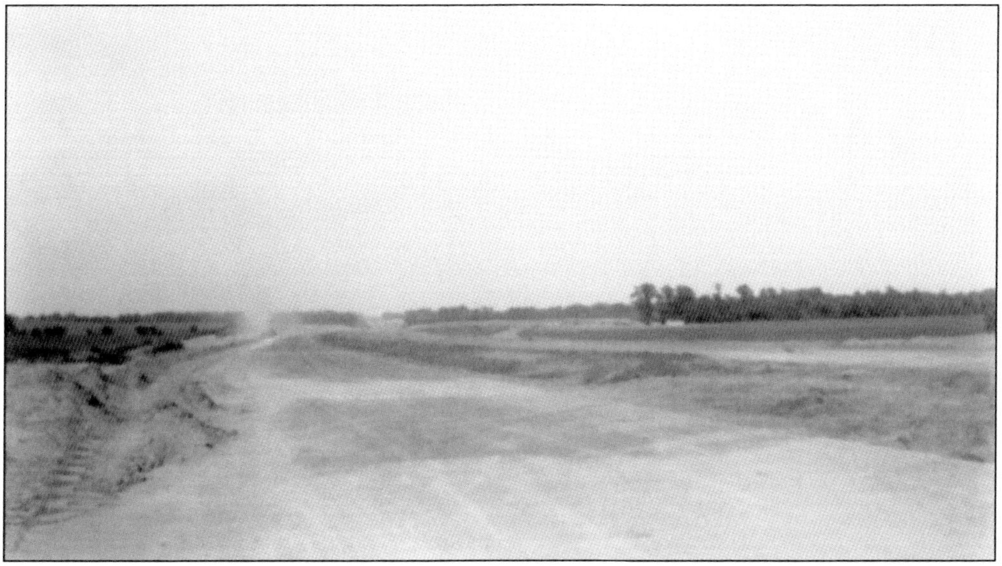

Seen here under construction in 1951, the New Jersey Turnpike passed through part of the Monte family's farm and through portions of various other farms. On the other side of town, near Fellowship, excavations for the turnpike near the Rudderow farm at Church Road turned up a rare fossil of a giant sloth and fossilized oyster shells, found by 14-year-old Jimmy Ruhle. It was determined that the shells were over 50 million years old and the ground sloth, *Megalonyx jeffersonii*, was 100,000 years old. (Courtesy of Judith Monte.)

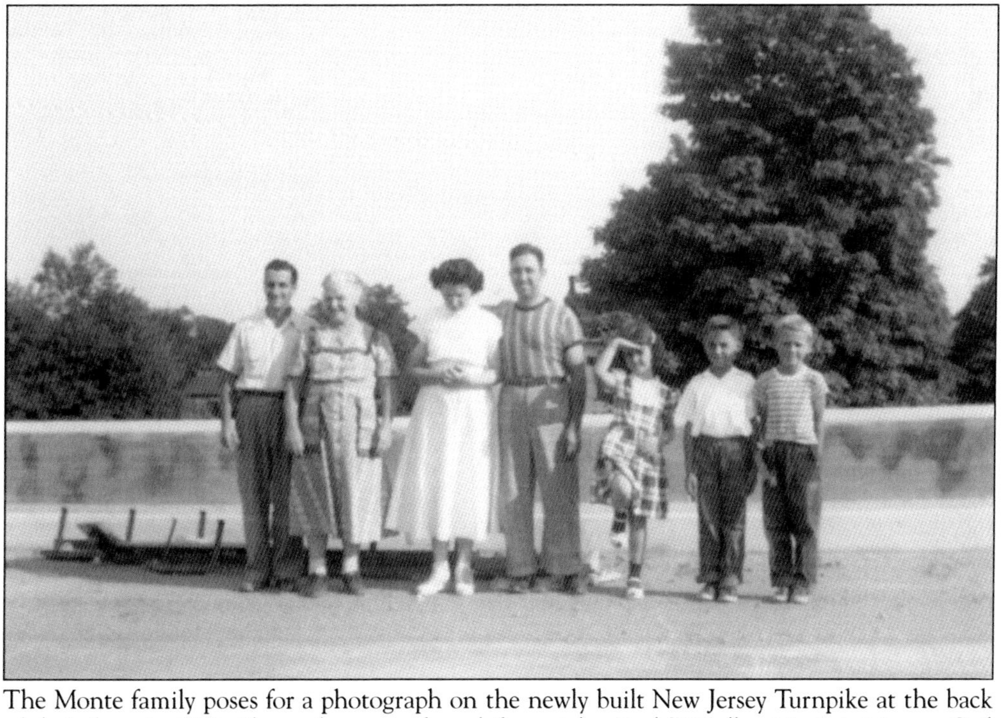

The Monte family poses for a photograph on the newly built New Jersey Turnpike at the back of their farm in 1951. Shown here are, from left to right, Paul DiGalbo, Virginia Monte, Ceil Calabrese, Don Calabrese, Rosalie Calabrese, Frankie Calabrese, and Frankie's friend Stevie Radcliff. (Courtesy of Judith Monte.)

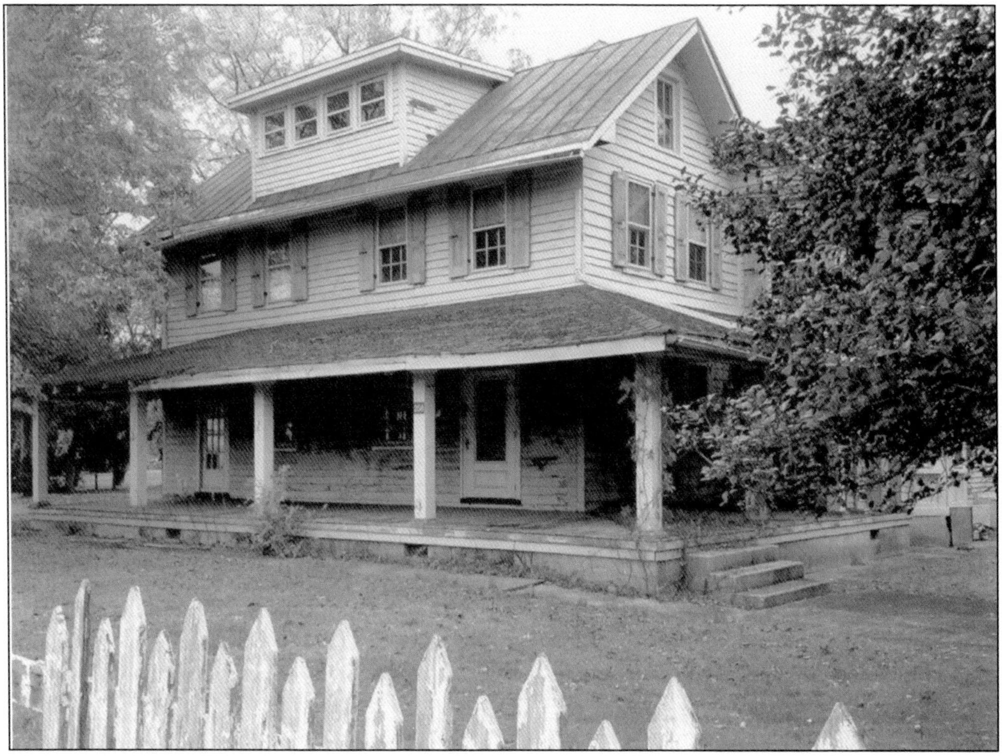

The Middleton-Nelson house, built in 1765 by a Mr. Evans, stood along Moorestown–Mount Laurel Road. This house was built for two spinster sisters who did not speak to each other. The house had separate entrances, and each floor featured partitions so that the sisters did not have to interact. The Middleton family purchased the house with six acres in 1914. This photograph was taken just before the house underwent demolition. (Courtesy of Dr. O. Kirk Spurr.)

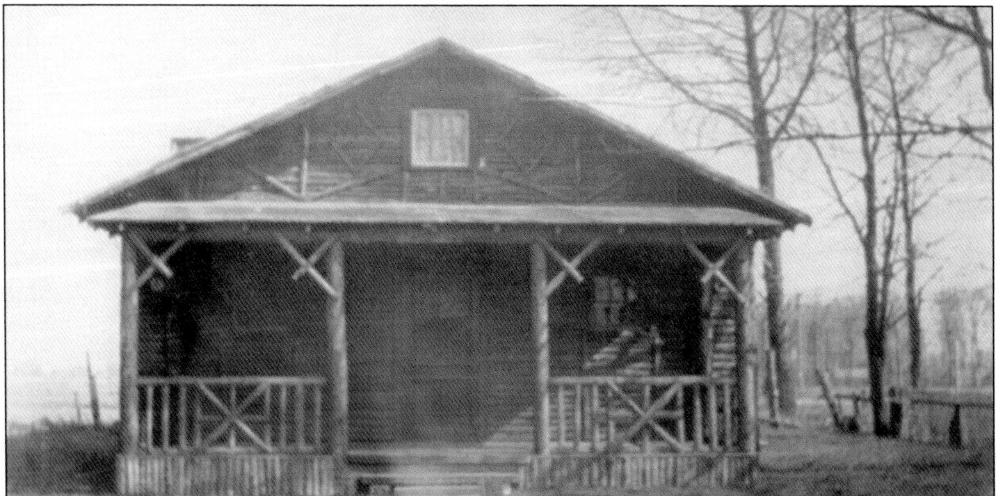

In 1925, Dorothy Middleton built her "Ranch House Museum" east of the main house, very close to the road, and filled it with Native American artifacts from her growing collection. A white picket fence, visible in the previous photograph, separated the museum from the road. This photograph dates to 1926. (Courtesy of Dr. O. Kirk Spurr.)

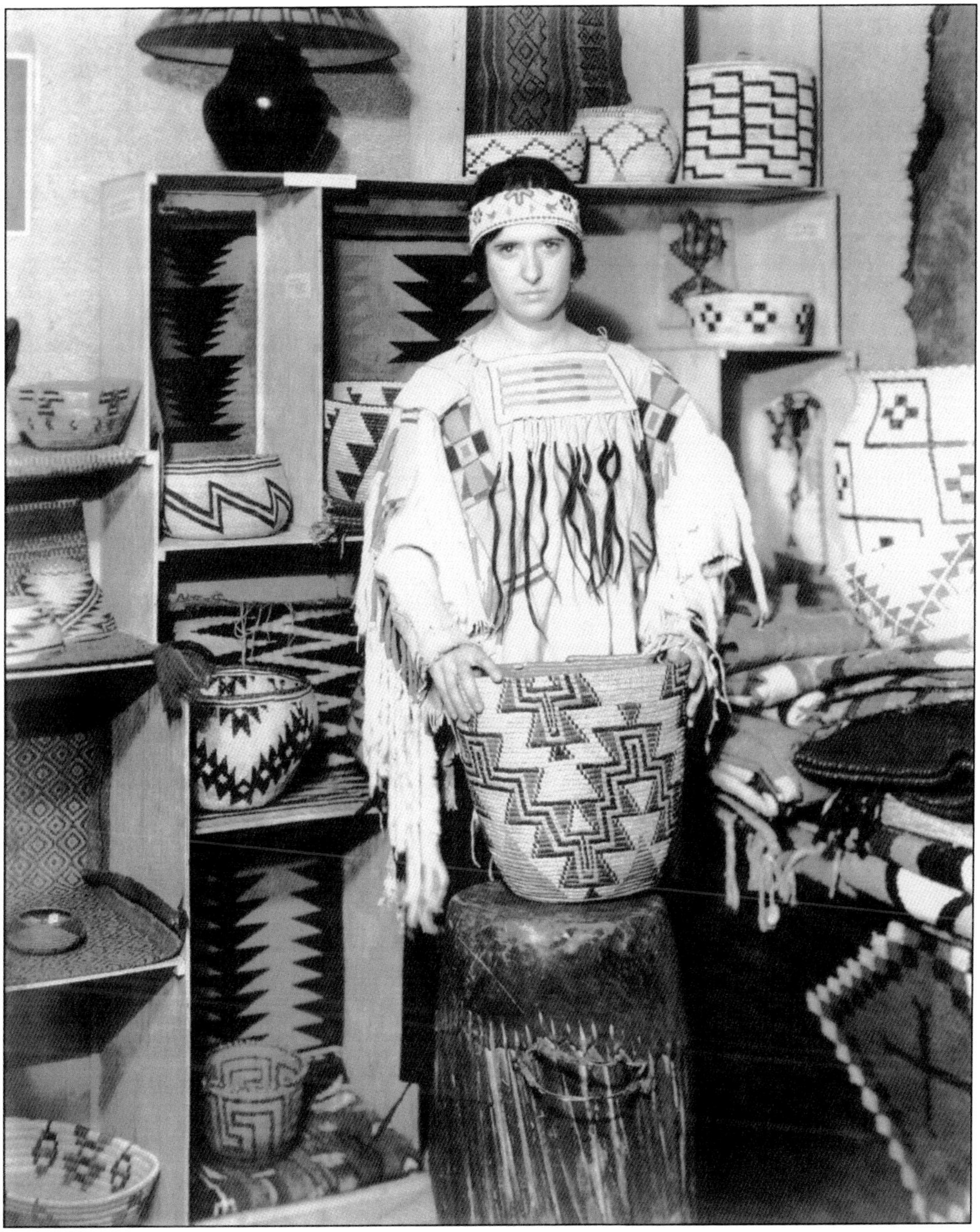

An addition was built to Dorothy Middleton's museum in the late 1920s or early 1930s. She called it her gallery and, because of the narrow nature of the walkways, restricted its viewing to adults only. Dorothy loved to dress in the artifacts she collected. This photograph of Dorothy Middleton, taken on December 20, 1931, shows her at an exhibit called The Arts & Crafts Exhibit of the American Indian in the New Jersey State Museum in Trenton, New Jersey. She enjoyed showing off her best artifacts and wearing authentic Native American clothing, like this ceremonial Blackfoot chief's coat, made of doeskin and trimmed with beads and human hair. At this event, she saw a replica of an outdoor Pueblo baking oven, which she acquired and installed in her museum. It is shown on the next page. (Courtesy of Dr. O. Kirk Spurr.)

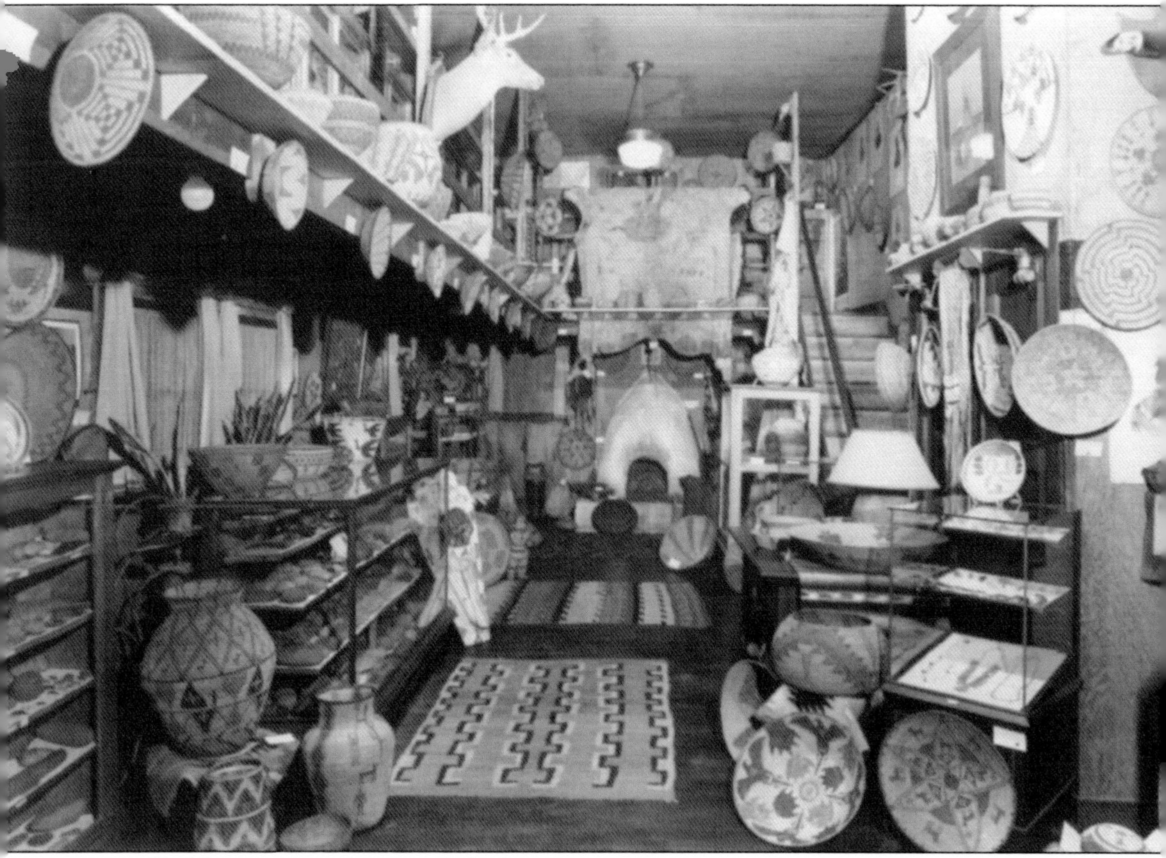

Half of the interior in the Thunderbird Museum, as it was now called, is shown in this photograph, taken in December 1947. A stairwell in the right rear led to another floor of Native American artifacts. Hanging above the baking oven is a buffalo hide rug, and the display cases contain numerous artifacts, such as arrowheads, baskets, totem poles, and tools from various tribes. Unfortunately, the Thunderbird Museum had a sad ending. After Dorothy Middleton-Nelson moved her rare, valuable collection to the "Turtle," the Native American Center for the Living Arts located in Niagara Falls, New York, the struggling museum had to sell off the collection piecemeal, without each item's documented history. The museum has since closed and all of Dorothy's well-catalogued artifacts ended up at an auction, selling for a fraction of their value. (Courtesy of Dr. O. Kirk Spurr.)

Three

Jacob's Chapel, Colemantown, and the Underground Railroad

Because the Underground Railroad comprised clandestine operations, it is hard to identify conductors, locations, and specific buildings used as stations. The Colemantown Meeting House, built as a schoolhouse around 1820 and moved to Colemantown in 1840, was a recognized stop. Of three known routes for fugitive slaves, two had a stop near what was then called Evesham Mount, which most likely referred to the Colemantown Meeting House, located very near the mount. The Quaker values of the area influenced local farms and industry to hire free African Americans rather than to own slaves. This situation allowed working black families to pursue their own business opportunities and farms because they had a source of income. Escaped slaves who took temporary shelter among the residents of Colemantown probably worshiped at the Colemantown Meeting House, Burlington County's oldest African Methodist Episcopal Church. The Colemantown Colored Cemetery contains the graves of numerous black Civil War soldiers, both identified and unknown. There are 110 headstones, but many graves are unmarked. Additionally, members of the prominent Still family are buried in the cemetery, which shares a common property line with the Quaker cemetery.

For many years, members thought Jacob's Chapel was built on land donated by a Quaker named Albert Jacobs. New research, however, has found that the chapel derives its name from Jacob Mitchell, the pastor who oversaw completion of the building in September 1867. Both the Colemantown Meeting House and Jacob's Chapel are listed in the New Jersey Register of Historic Places. Jacob's Chapel is also important because it served as a meeting place for Ethel Lawrence and other township African Americans as they organized their efforts to bring affordable housing into Mount Laurel. In 1970, Mayor William Haines told a group of 60 African Americans that Mount Laurel was denying their request for affordable housing. This started the long road of litigation. The New Jersey Supreme Court ruled that the law was exclusionary, and this paved the way for changing the face of communities throughout New Jersey. The Mount Laurel decisions of 1975 and 1983 required all municipalities to provide a fair share of affordable housing for low- and moderate-income households.

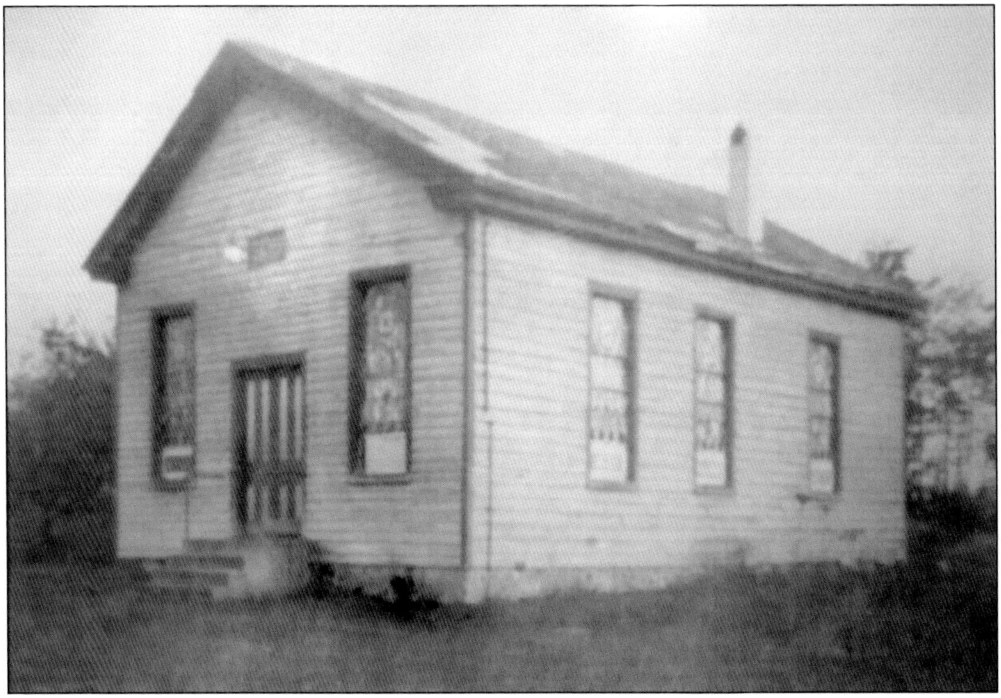

The above photograph, taken in the 1920s or 1930s, shows Jacob's Chapel, a building dedicated in September 1867 and still in use today. This building is listed in the New Jersey Register of Historic Places and will soon be nationally listed. The stained-glass windows were installed in the 1920s. The below photograph shows Jacob's Chapel as it looks today. (Courtesy of the *Burlington County Times*.)

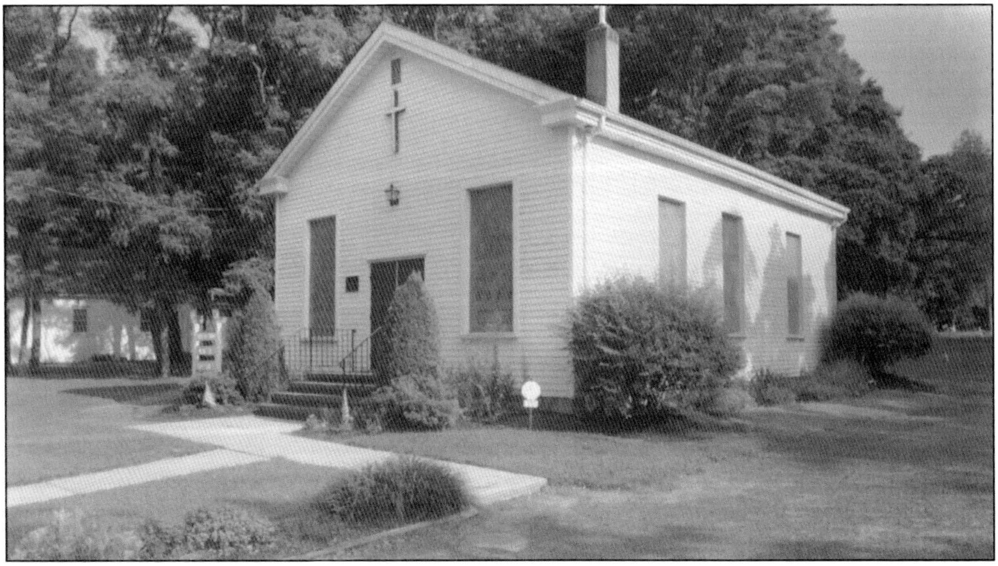

Jacob's Chapel, a small, one-story building, has three stained-glass windows on each side of the building, as well as two in the front. These windows have been preserved through the years and have been recently restored. (Courtesy of the author.)

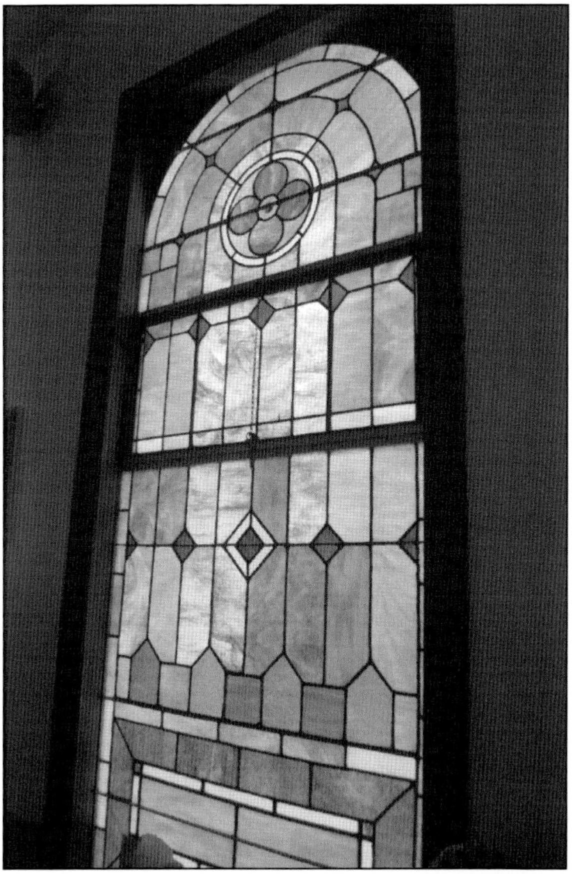

The Colemantown Meeting House, built around 1820 as a school building, was moved to Colemantown in 1840, where it continued to serve as a school as well as a church. It is the oldest black church in Burlington County and served as a stop on one of the three lines used for fugitive slaves moving north. Until the mid-1960s, the building stood on the other side of the road. (Courtesy of the *Burlington County Times*.)

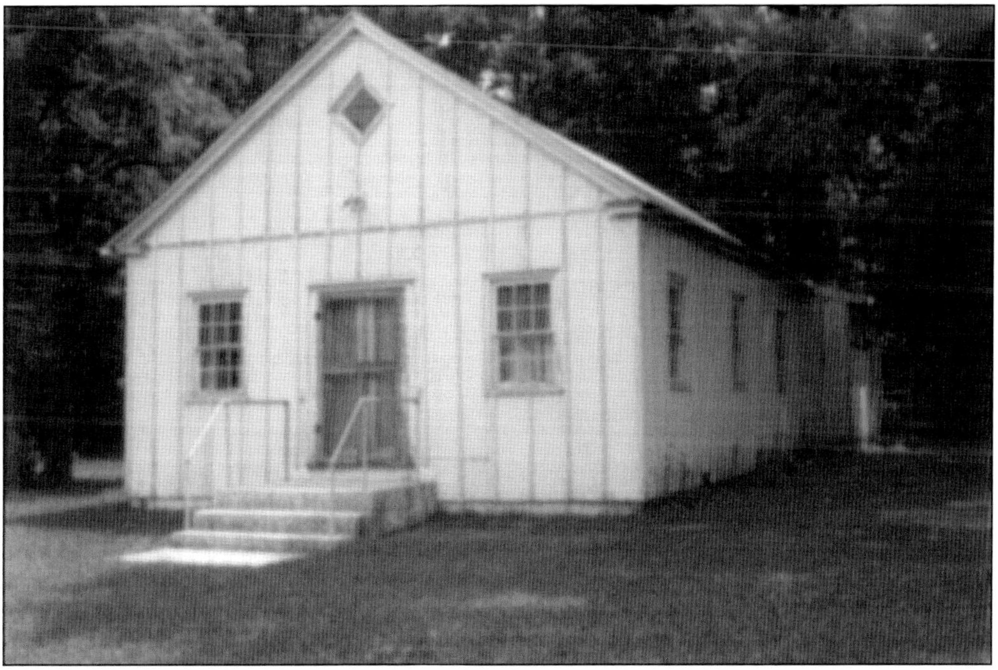

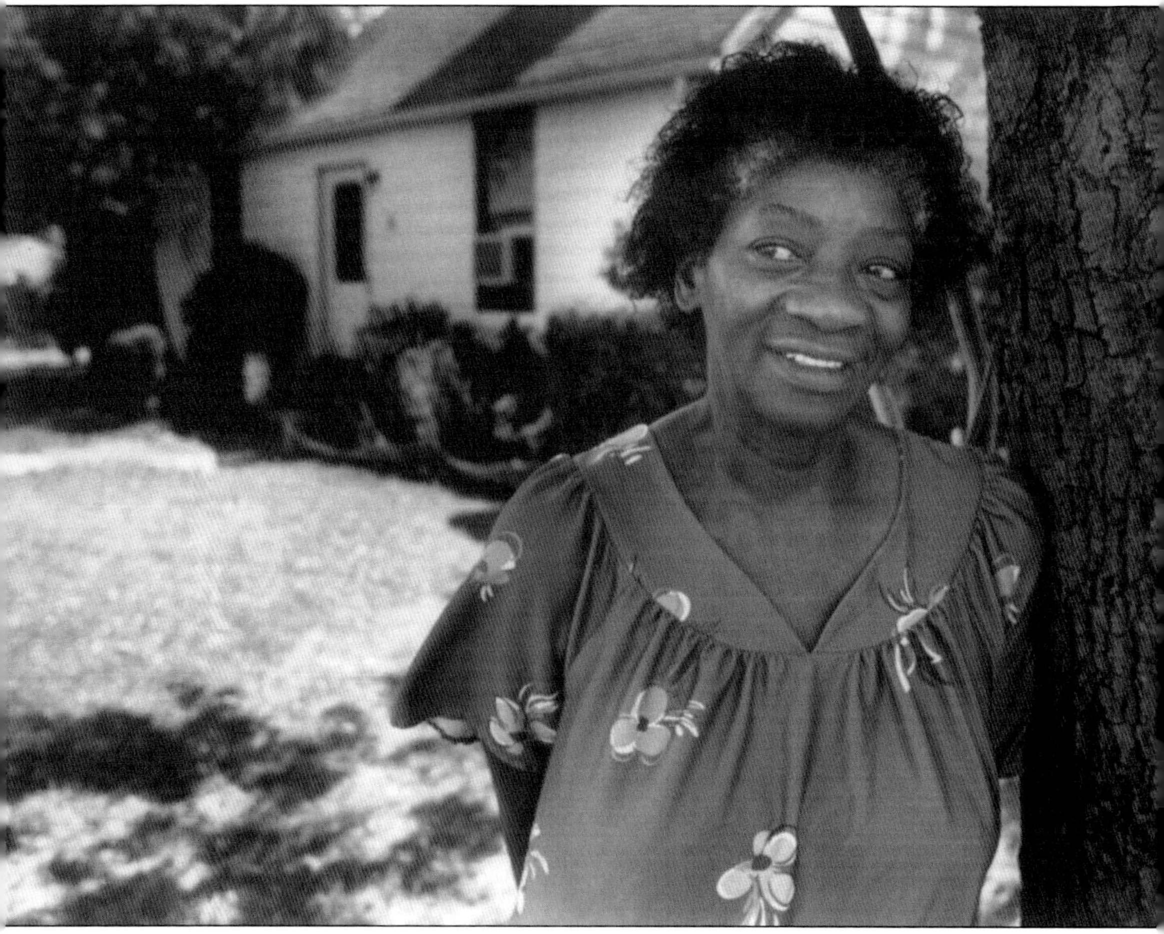

In 1968, Ethel Lawrence (above) was a key organizer of a multiracial group of Mount Laurel residents who formed a nonprofit corporation, the Springville Community Action Committee. Its purpose was to develop low- and moderate-income housing. The group designed a plan for a 36-unit apartment complex; however, in 1969, the Township Zoning Board denied the variance that was necessary for the housing to be built. This began a court battle that lasted over 25 years to open Mount Laurel and similar communities to low- and moderate-income residents. The courts eventually ruled that the poor may not be excluded from New Jersey's municipalities by local zoning ordinances that make housing too expensive for them to rent or own. According to the courts, in the Mount Laurel I (1975) and Mount Laurel II (1983) decisions, all municipalities have a constitutional obligation to adopt zoning that accommodates the community's "fair share" of the regional need for low- and moderate-income housing. (Courtesy of the *Burlington County Times*.)

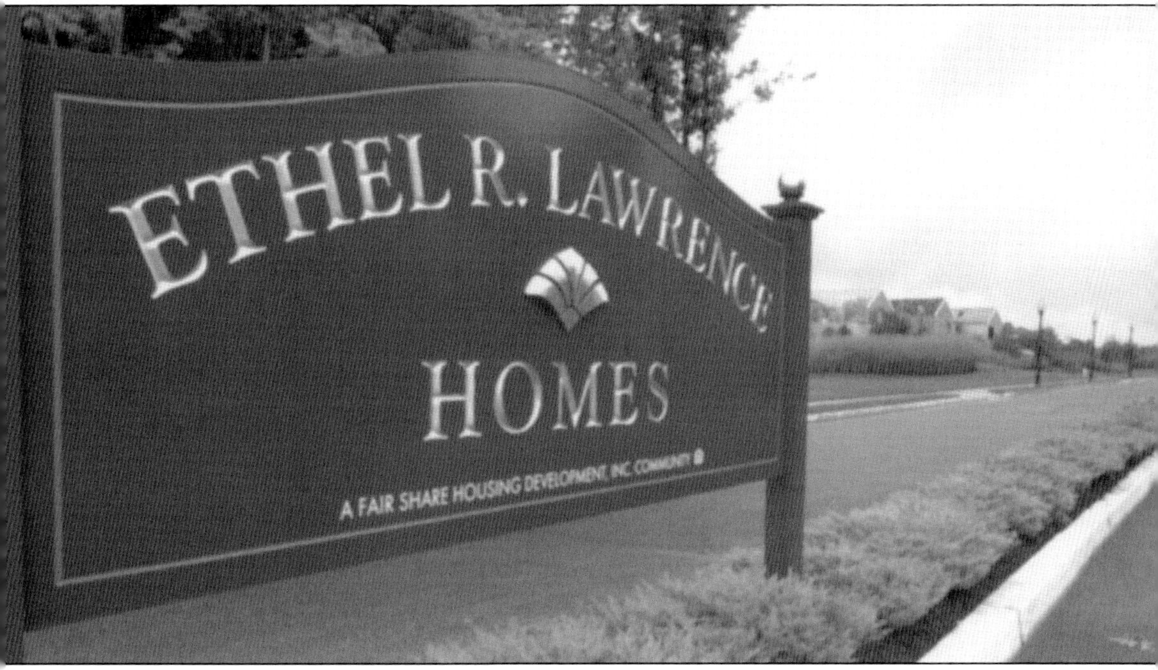

The Mount Laurel decisions guarantee the right of the underprivileged to live in places where economic opportunities for advancement are highest. Ethel Lawrence, called the Rosa Parks of the housing movement, fought for all New Jersey residents to have affordable housing. Although Ethel Lawrence died before seeing her dream come to fruition, she probably would have been amazed that 868 families showed up the first weekend to apply for housing in the development named for her. (Courtesy of the *Burlington County Times*.)

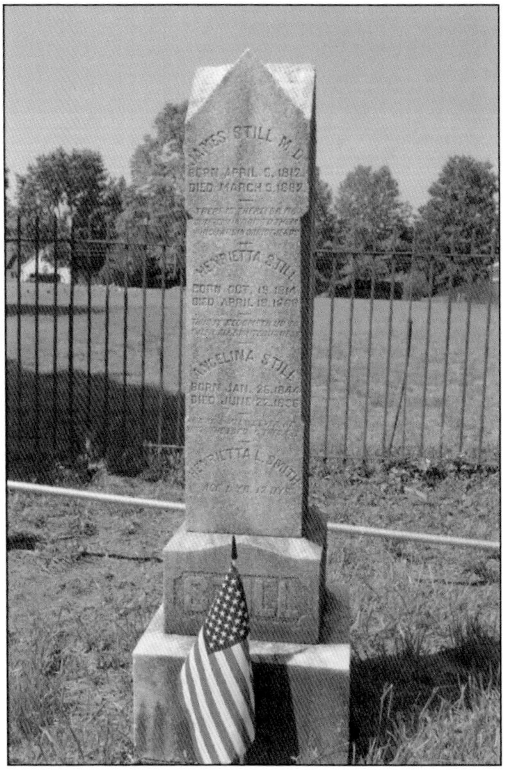

Colemantown is a small antebellum African American hamlet in Mount Laurel on Elbo Lane named for its founder, Charles Coleman. The African Methodist Episcopal edifice, now known as Jacob's Chapel, sits in front of a cemetery that contains the graves, both marked and unmarked, of many Civil War soldiers, as well as the grave of Dr. James Still and his family members. Recognized as the "black doctor of the pines," Dr. Still gained a well-deserved reputation for treating patients with local herbs that he distilled. He had only three months of education and read books on anatomy and physiology. Dr. Still, whose parents were slaves, died in 1882 as one of South Jersey's wealthiest landowners. (Both images courtesy of the author.)

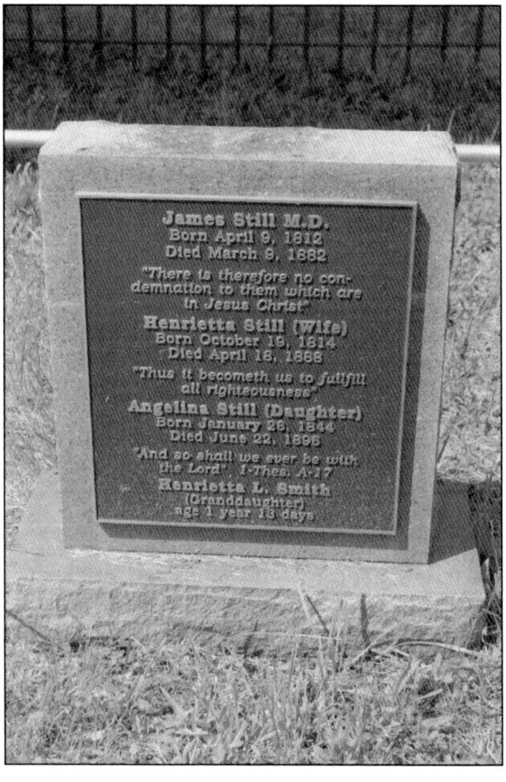

Four

Religious Life in Mount Laurel

In 1698, William Evans Jr. gave one acre of land to the Society of Friends, which constructed a meetinghouse in 1717 of Jersey sandstone quarried from the mount. It is the oldest meetinghouse in the county and is still in use today.

Masonville became home to a Methodist Episcopal Church. Village women who attended Sunday school in Hartford persuaded Edward Idell in 1869 to start a Sunday school in their village. These meetings began in the kitchen of a private residence and soon outgrew the space. The Sunday school leaders asked Joseph Brooks to sell a piece of his meadow, and residents of Masonville donated their time and labor to help ready the lot and build the edifice. Dedication of the Masonville Methodist Episcopal Church occurred on February 19, 1872, and it soon became part of the Rancocas Circuit after local preachers had served the church.

In Springville along Hartford Road, Russian Jews, looking for a summer getaway from Philadelphia, formed Congregation Agudas Achim in 1927. Approximately 25 Orthodox families built homes within walking distance of the synagogue and received their mail addressed to them in "Jewtown." The Springville area included a kosher butcher, the Sandler Farm, Springville Day Camp, Mitten's Day Camp, Betchen's Overnight Camp, Rosen's Chicken Farm, Akerman's Tailor Shop, Kitchman's Farm, a dress factory, and a general store called Litwans, which later became Marmons. Martin Sclaroff owned a tavern, Martin's Inn, and obtained a liquor license the day after Prohibition ended. There was also a community center where parties, roast beef dinners, and shows were hosted on its stage. Eventually, the summer homes were winterized and the Jewish families moved away. In 1971, when the congregation disbanded, Temple Sinai received most of the relics from Agudas Achim, while a few went to Adath Emanu-El.

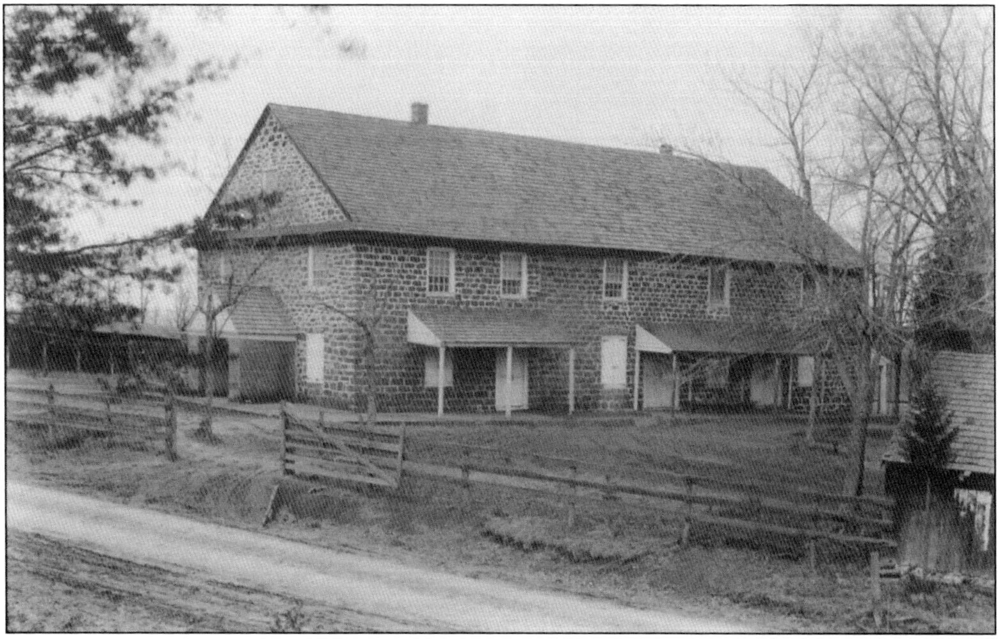

William Evans deeded the land for a meetinghouse to the Society of Friends in 1717. Local Quakers had held meetings in homes since 1694. William Evans's wife, Elizabeth, served as a Quaker minister. In 1759, the Haddonfield Monthly Meeting authorized Evesham Meeting to establish a monthly meeting, which the members did the following year. The meeting's eastern end dates to 1760, when the members appended it to the 1717 meetinghouse to accommodate the monthly meeting. The members added the western end to the meetinghouse in 1798, after demolishing the 1717 meeting and reusing the materials. The meetinghouse is constructed from iron or sandstone quarried from the mount across the road. Today, the meetinghouse is the oldest one still in use. (Above, courtesy of Jarry Jones; below, courtesy of the author.)

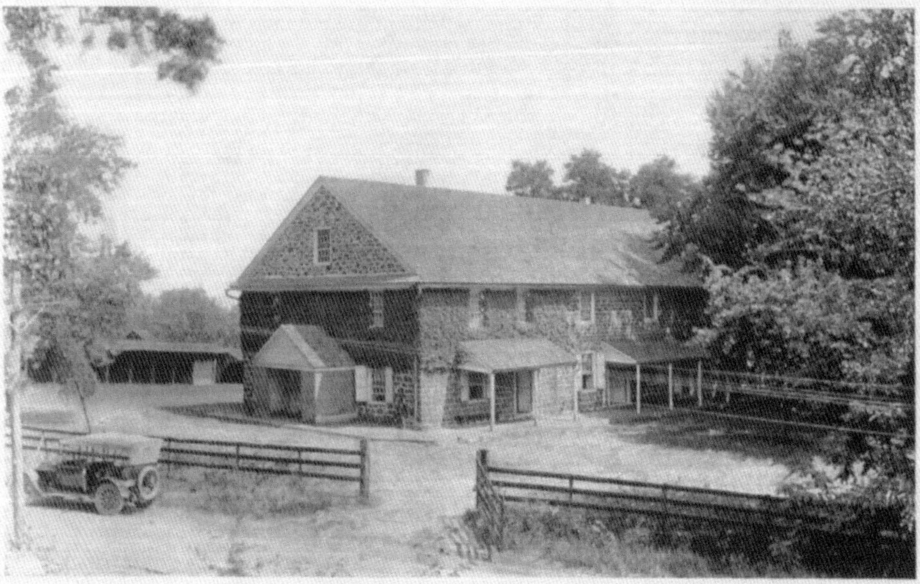

FRIENDS' MEETING HOUSE, Mount Laurel, N. J. Built 1798

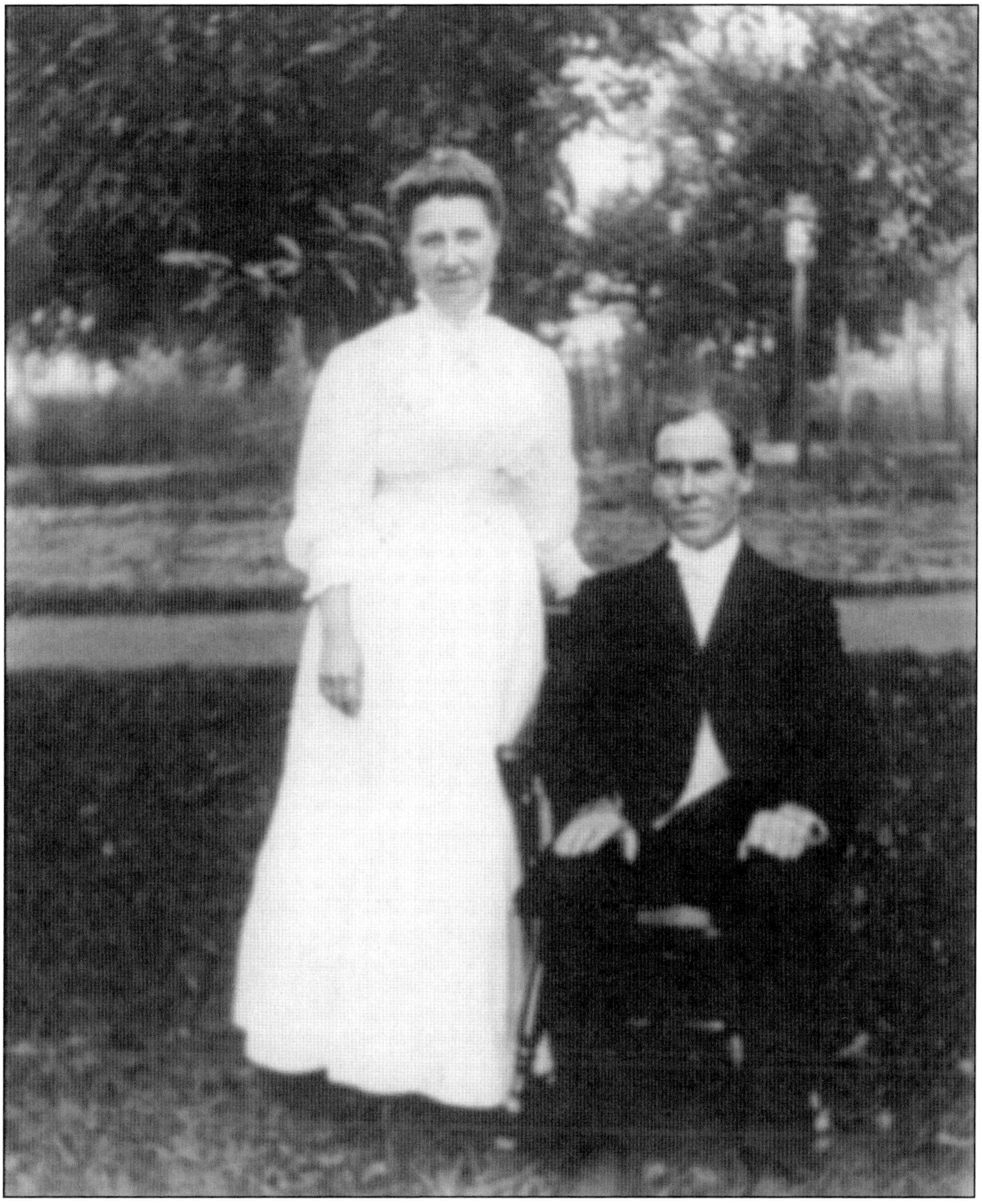

The Reverend S.H. Evaul was pastor of the Masonville United Methodist Church from 1909 to 1911. This photograph of the reverend and his wife was taken at the circuit's parsonage in Rancocas Village. The church was started in someone's kitchen in 1869 after several ladies had been going to Hartford for Sunday school. The group soon grew too large for a kitchen space, so the church was officially founded in 1872, the same year as Mount Laurel Township. When completed, after having been built by local residents, preachers of various denominations from Mount Holly would serve the church. Soon after, the church became a part of the Methodist Conference and joined a three-church circuit that included the Methodist churches in the Village of Rancocas and Charleston (Willingboro). This meant that the churches shared the same minister. The first pastor was David Stewart, who served from 1872 to 1874. (Courtesy of the Masonville-Rancocas United Methodist Church.)

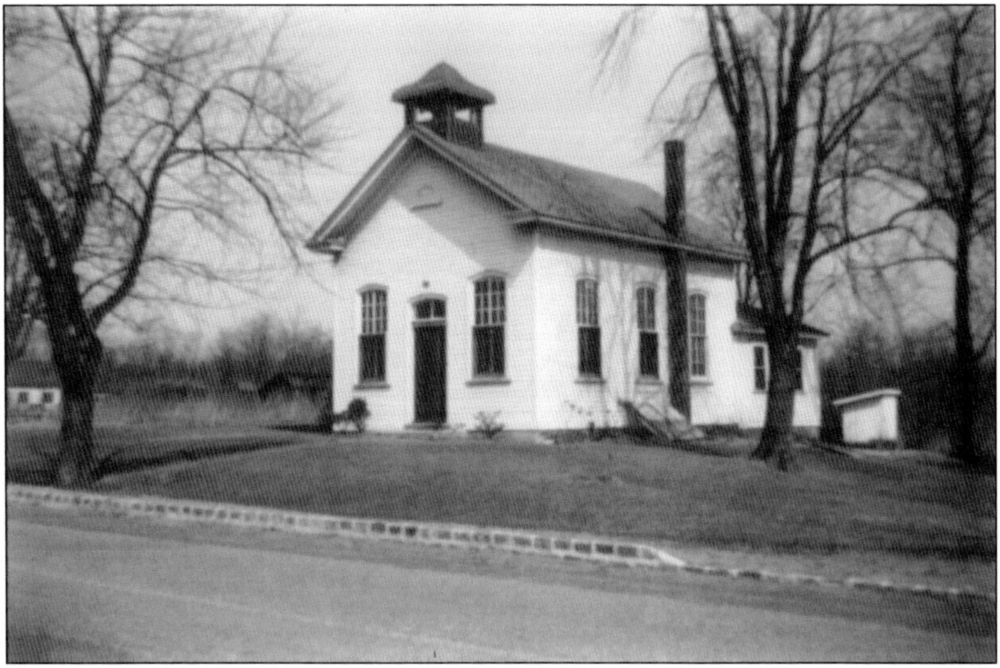

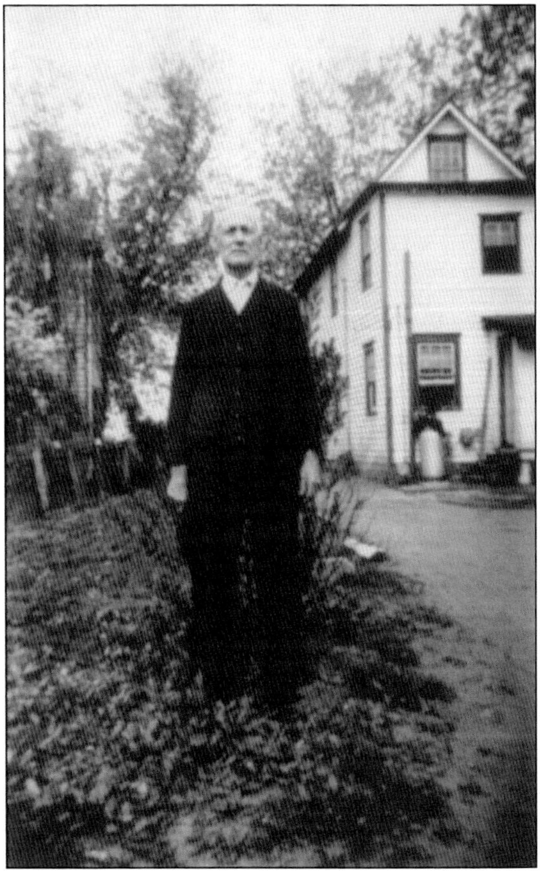

In this photograph, the Proud family house is on the far left, and the church is shown with the addition of the Sunday school room, built during the late 1930s. An outhouse stands to the rear of the church in this photograph. (Courtesy of the Masonville-Rancocas United Methodist Church.)

Edward Proud poses for a photograph. The Proud family home was located next to the Methodist Church, across from the Larchmont Farm's orchards on Masonville Road. The home was demolished in 1983. Edward Proud worked for the Mount Laurel Schools. (Courtesy of the Masonville-Rancocas United Methodist Church.)

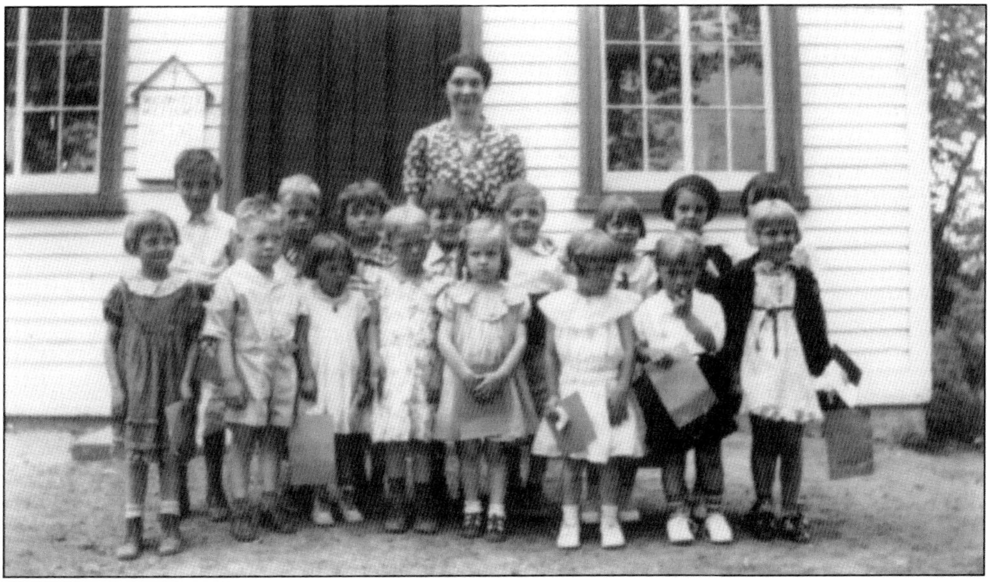

In 1938, Mrs. Burkman, the pastor's wife at that time, poses in front of the Methodist Church with a group of Sunday school boys and girls. The Reverend E.T. Idell organized the Sunday school in 1869. The original church structure dates to 1872. Prior to that, the congregation met in a Masonville home for two to three years. The congregants purchased a lot for the church for $135. (Courtesy of the Masonville-Rancocas United Methodist Church.)

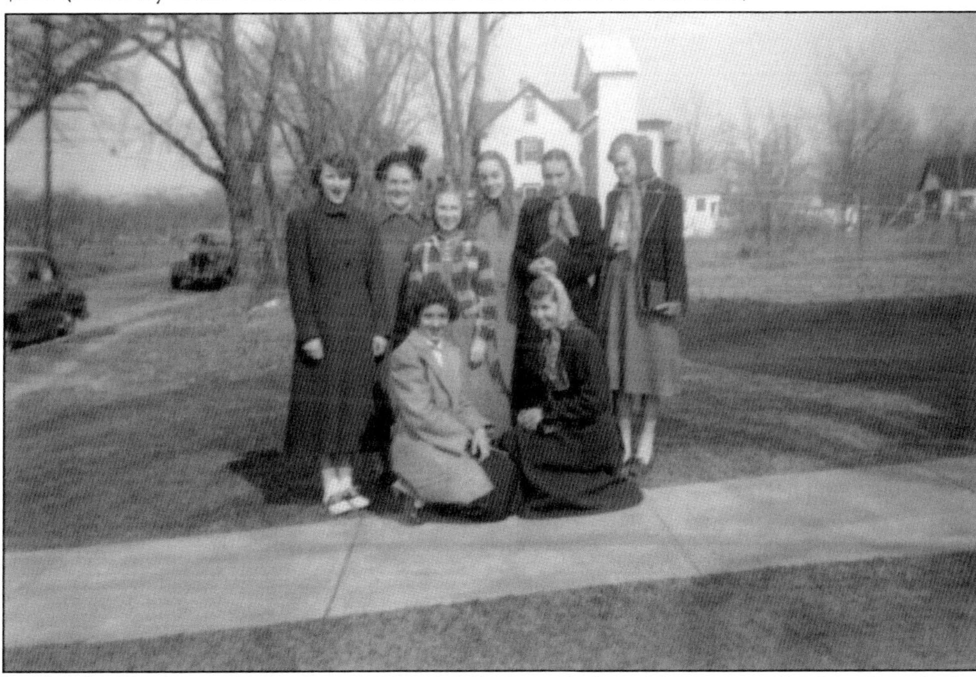

This photograph, taken in 1946, shows some of the young ladies of the Masonville United Methodist Church before an outing. Among those shown here are Rebecca Clevenger (standing, second from left), MaryEllen Harrison (standing, far right), Evelyn Stevens (kneeling, left), and Ginger Johnson (kneeling, right). Cars are parked on the street across from the orchards. (Courtesy of the Masonville-Rancocas United Methodist Church.)

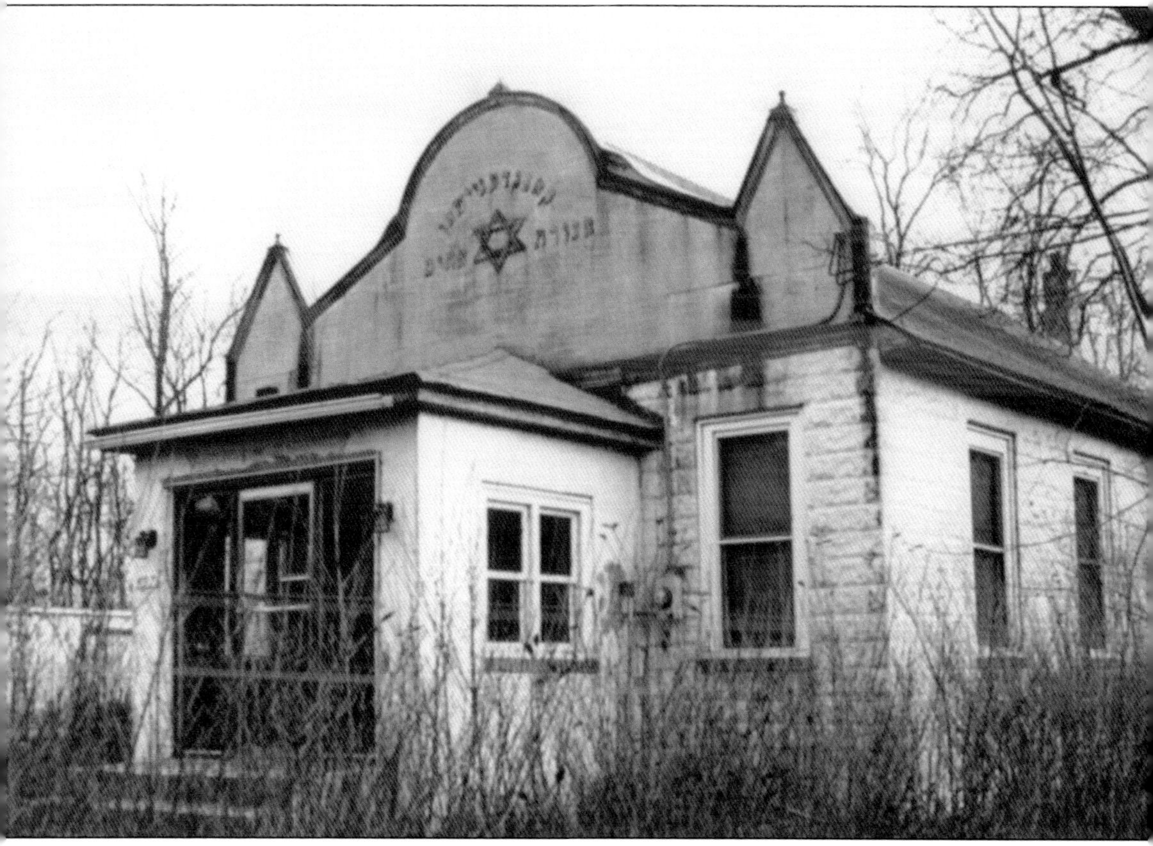

The Baron De Hirsch Fund helped Jews find new lives in many parts of the world, including a settlement in Philadelphia. Some of those who came were not happy in the city, so they formed two separate realty corporations and bought land in the Springville section of Mount Laurel. They called the area Springville, but their neighbors called it "Jewtown." From approximately 1924 until the early 1940s, it was a popular place to spend the summer. They formed Congregation Agudas Achim and organized a community center. The Jewish families who lived there, primarily merchants from Philadelphia, would walk to the synagogue shown here on Saturdays and worship together. There was also Mitten's Day Camp and an overnight camp for the Jewish children. A number of year-round businesses operated in this group of cottages, including Litwan's grocery store, Brook's candy store, Ackerman's tailor shop, and Becker's chicken farm. Some of the families who lived in this community still reside in the area. (Courtesy of the *Burlington County Times* and Ruth Bogutz.)

Shown here is the ground-breaking ceremony for the Evangelical Presbyterian Church, located on Union Mill Road at Walton Avenue. This congregation had previously been in Camden, but it found a new home in Mount Laurel across from silos and farmland. (Courtesy of the Evangelical Presbyterian Church.)

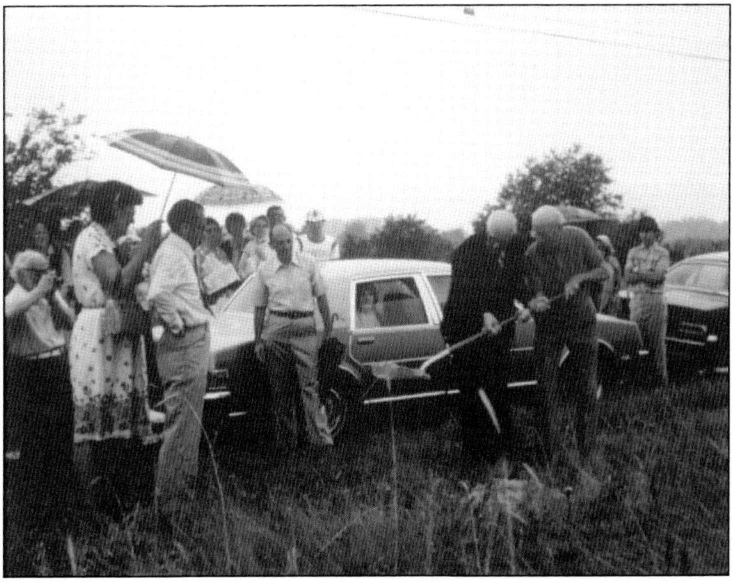

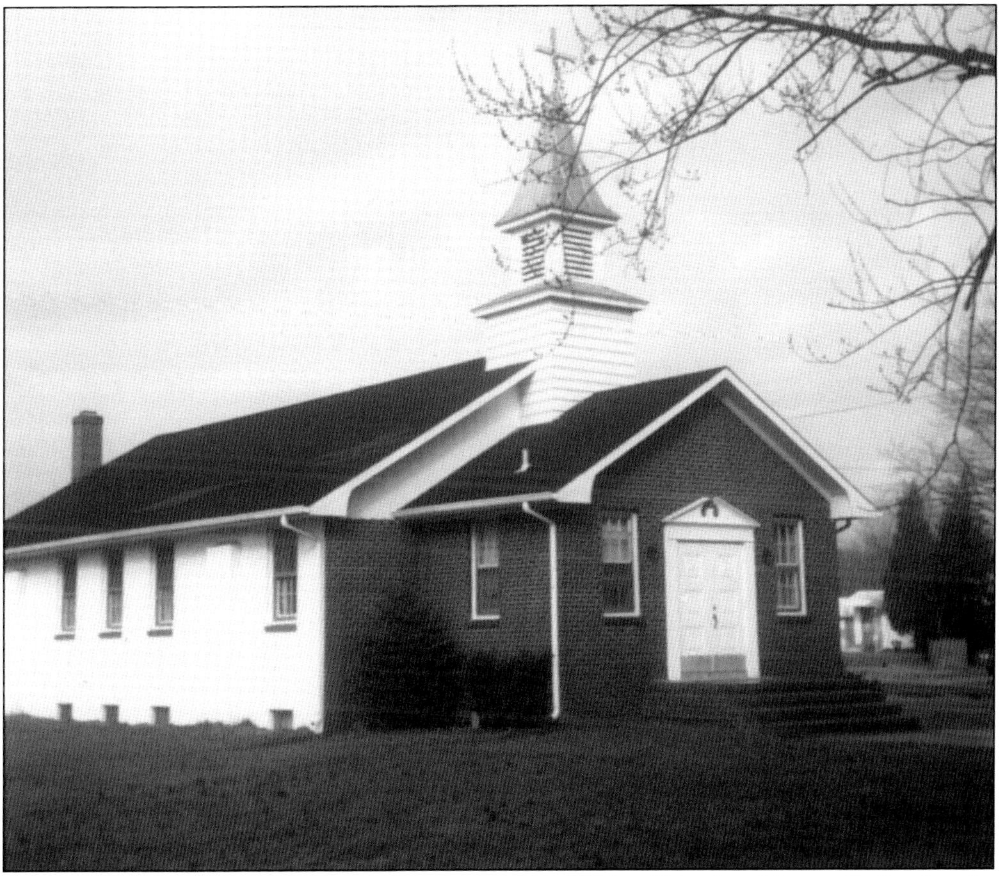

Calvary Bible Church, located across from Mount Laurel School No. 2 on Masonville Road at the corner of Memorial Lane, has been in Mount Laurel for over 50 years. This photograph of the brick-front church was taken in the early 1970s. (Courtesy of the Mount Laurel Historical Society.)

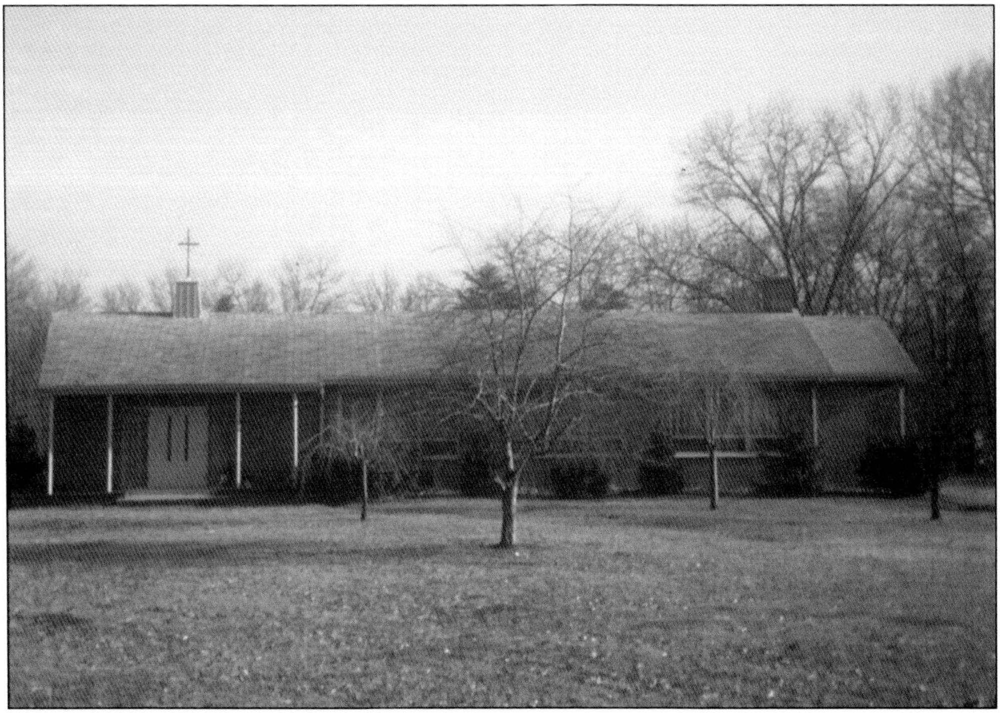

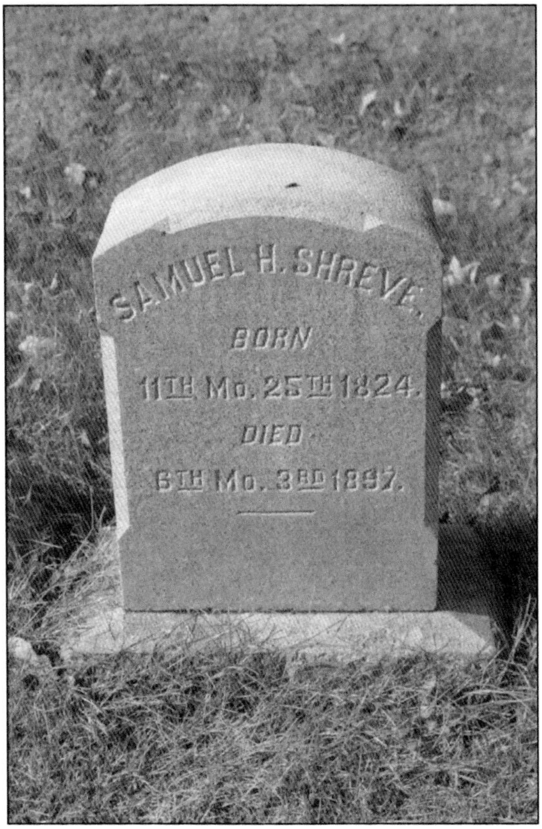

The New Covenant Presbyterian Church is a small church located in a wooded area off of Creek Road, between the Timbercrest development and Rancocas Woods. This photograph was taken in the early 1970s. (Courtesy of the Mount Laurel Historical Society.)

There are numerous cemeteries in Mount Laurel. A pauper's field is located on Union Mill Road, near where it intersects with Church Road and Church Street. There are no grave markers. The Mount Laurel Cemetery and the Eldridge Cemetery are located on Cemetery Road. They look like one large cemetery, but they are really two separate private cemeteries. This photograph of Samuel Shreve's gravestone was taken in the Mount Laurel section. (Courtesy of the author.)

Five

Mount Laurel Schools

Schools in Mount Laurel have been educating residents since the 1760s. In 1783, the Religious Society of Friends constructed a schoolhouse across Moorestown–Mount Laurel Road from the Friends' meetinghouse. In 1850, they built a school across from the Farmer's Hall that operated as a Friends' school until 1869. It then became a public school and was used until 1882. Because of the overcrowding in this school, it reverted back to being a Friends' school, and the township constructed a new two-room public school. Unfortunately, this building burned down in January 1917, less than a year after improvements were made on it.

Mount Laurel's African American population attended the Black Shutter School, located near the corner of Hainesport–Mount Laurel Road and Oliphant's Mill Road, now Hartford Road. The Green Grove School stood on Union Mill Road in 1868; in 1870, the township moved the building across the street and improved it. Once the township schools underwent consolidation, officials moved this school again to Mount Laurel Road, and it became the "colored" school, Mount Laurel School No. 3. Decisions concerning desegregating Mount Laurel schools began in the 1940s.

Around 1880, each hamlet contained one- or two-room schoolhouses. The Masonville School, which also served Centerton residents, was moved in 1898 to its present site on Masonville Road. In 1918, the township closed the Hartford School and transported those children to the Masonville School, which was enlarged to four rooms. Hartford parents were involved with their children's education through the Hartford Parent-Teacher group, which joined with the Masonville Home and School. They helped keep parents informed, ran the lunchroom, provided playground equipment, and worked with the community.

The Fellowship School closed in 1920 under the township school consolidation plan, so the children began taking a bus to the Mount Laurel School. Each school received new indoor bathroom facilities, along with adequate space for playgrounds. Until Lenape High School opened in 1958, all Mount Laurel students attended the Moorestown Junior and Senior High School.

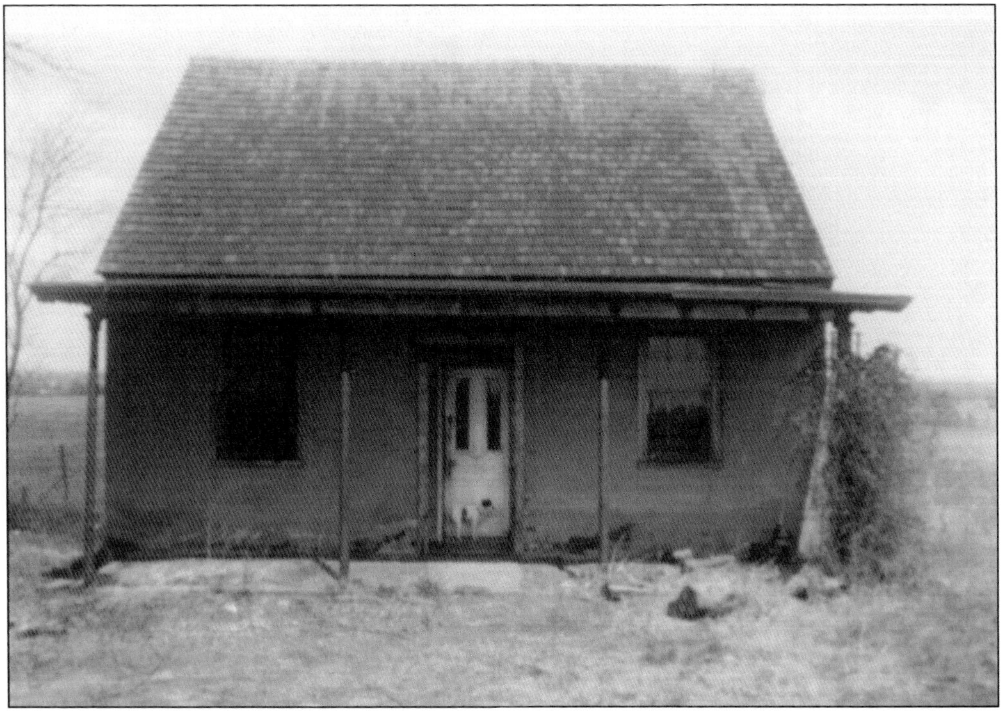

The Fellowship section of Mount Laurel had a one-room schoolhouse, built in 1819 and used until about 1920. This school stood along S-41 (Route 73). After the Fellowship school closed, the township bused the children to the Mount Laurel School No. 1. The Fellowship School was torn down in 1962. (Courtesy of Marian and Jim Hartshorne.)

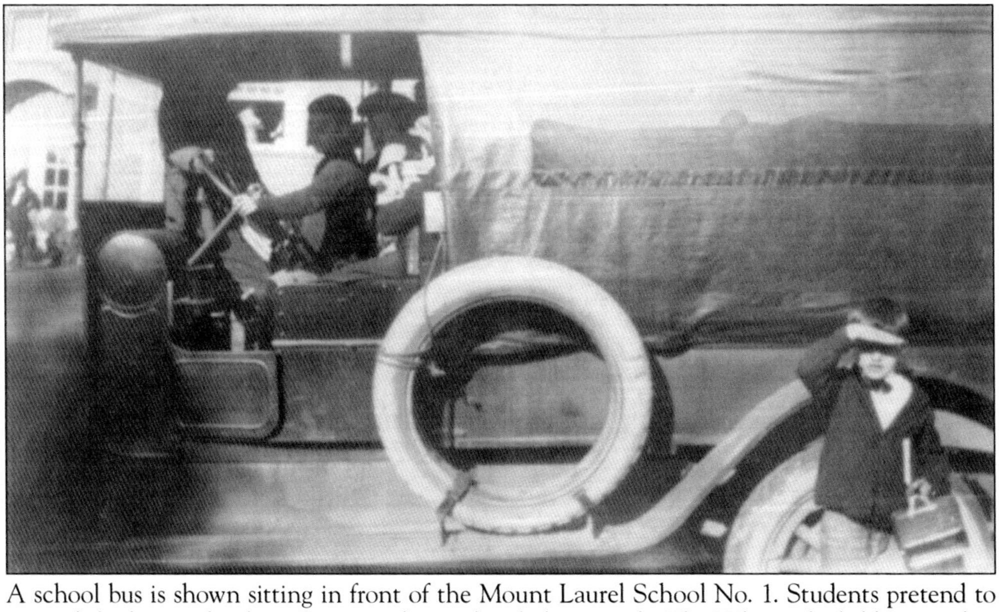

A school bus is shown sitting in front of the Mount Laurel School No. 1. Students pretend to control the bus in the driver's seat in this undated photograph. The Whitcraft children used to take this bus to school in the late 1920s or early 1930s. (Courtesy of Meg Ellis.)

Hazel Wells taught sixth grade at the Mount Laurel School No. 1, now called the Hattie Britt Administration Building. She attended New Jersey State Normal School in Trenton for her teacher education, catching the train in Moorestown every day to commute there. Wells was born in 1894 and married Robert Godfrey in 1920. This photograph was taken before they were married. (Courtesy of Meg Ellis.)

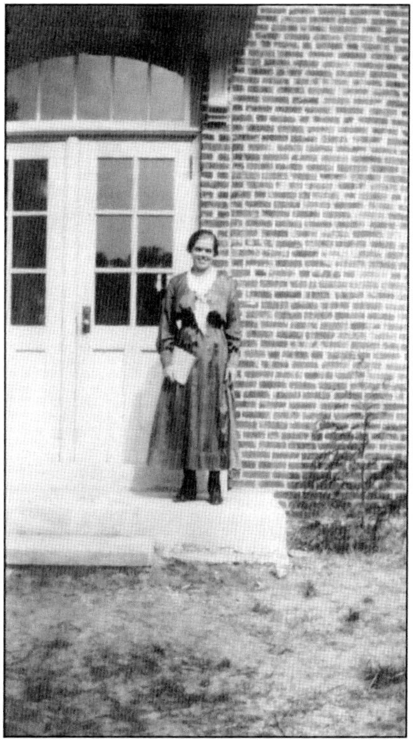

This is Mount Laurel School No. 1's first-grade class in 1960–1961. Throughout the years, students had to attend different schools because of space issues. During one year, classes were held at the Beeler School in nearby Marlton, where Meg Burkhardt's mother coincidentally worked. A different group of students attended classes in Farmer's Hall another year. (Courtesy of Meg Ellis.)

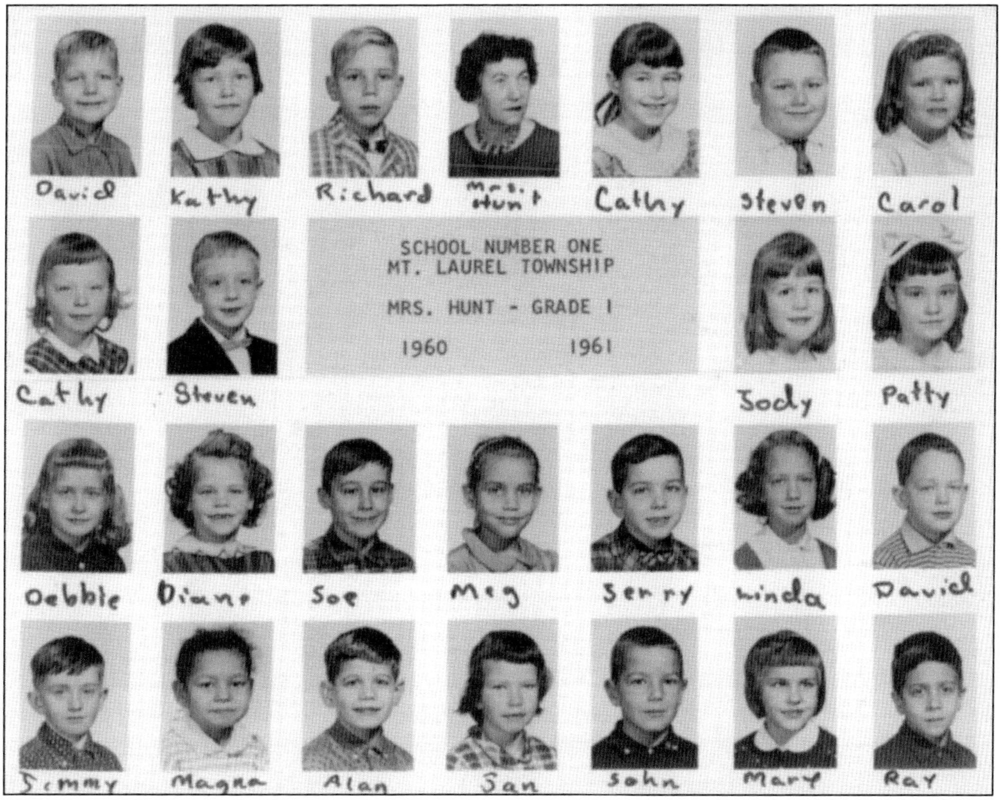

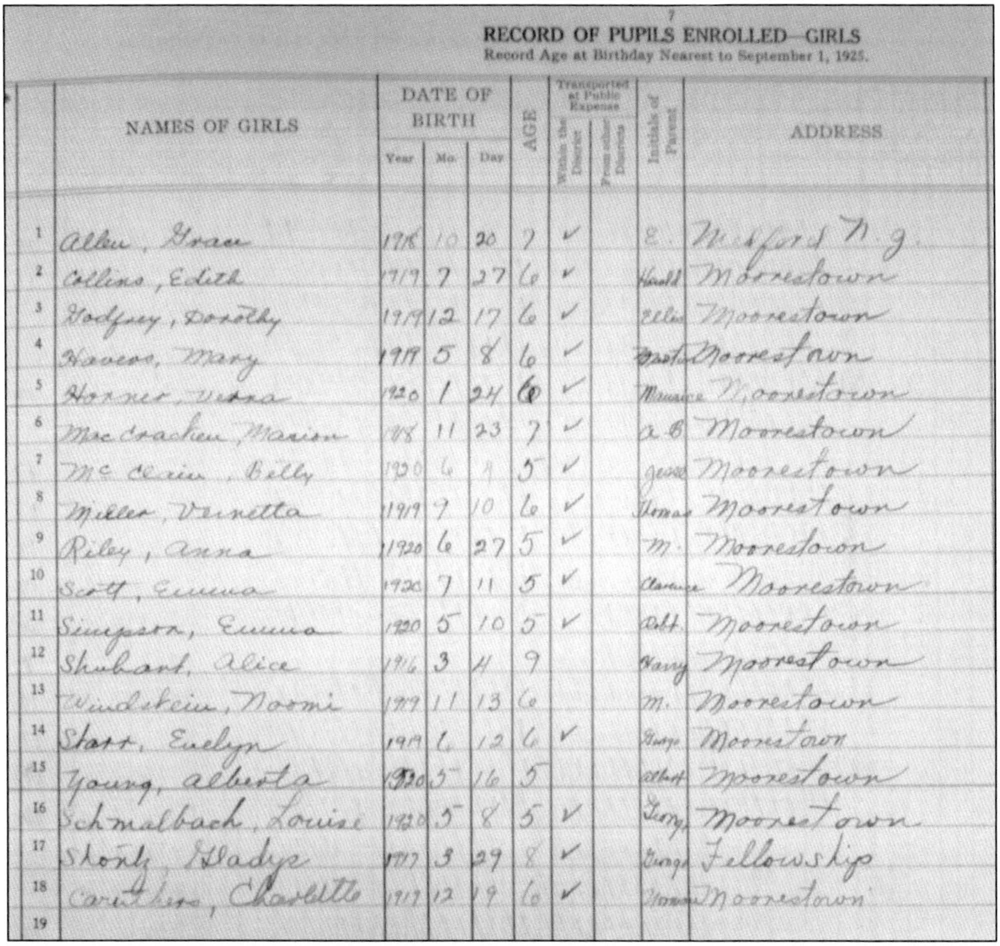

RECORD OF PUPILS ENROLLED—GIRLS
Record Age at Birthday Nearest to September 1, 1925.

	NAMES OF GIRLS	Year	Mo.	Day	AGE	Transported at Public Expense: Within the District	From other Districts	Initials of Parent	ADDRESS
1	Allen, Grace	1918	10	20	7	✓		E.	Medford N.J.
2	Collins, Edith	1919	7	27	6	✓		Harold	Moorestown
3	Godfrey, Dorothy	1919	12	17	6	✓		Ellis	Moorestown
4	Haveos, Mary	1919	5	8	6	✓		[illegible]	Moorestown
5	Horner, Verna	1920	1	24	6	✓		Maurice	Moorestown
6	MacCracken, Marion	1918	11	23	7	✓		A.B.	Moorestown
7	McClain, Betty	1920	6	4	5	✓		Jesse	Moorestown
8	Miller, Vernetta	1919	9	10	6	✓		Thomas	Moorestown
9	Riley, Anna	1920	6	27	5	✓		M.	Moorestown
10	Scott, Emma	1920	7	11	5	✓		Clarence	Moorestown
11	Simpson, Emma	1920	5	10	5	✓		Albt.	Moorestown
12	Shubart, Alice	1916	3	4	9			Harry	Moorestown
13	Windstein, Naomi	1919	11	13	6			M.	Moorestown
14	Starr, Evelyn	1919	6	12	6	✓		George	Moorestown
15	Young, Alberta	1920	5	16	5			Albert	Moorestown
16	Schmalbach, Louise	1920	5	8	5	✓		George	Moorestown
17	Shontz, Gladys	1917	3	29	8	✓		George	Fellowship
18	Caruthers, Charlotte	1919	12	19	6	✓		Norman	Moorestown
19									

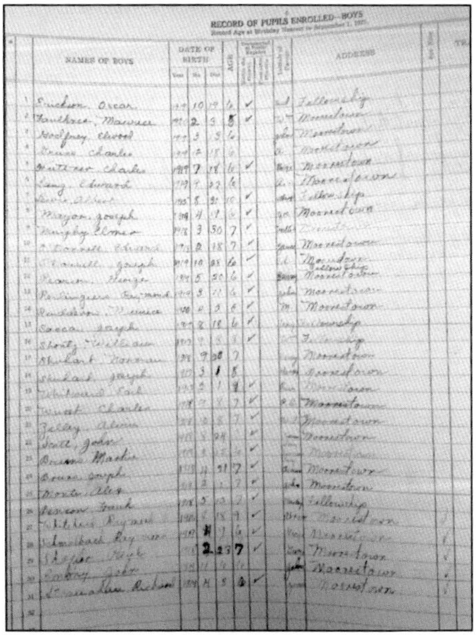

RECORD OF PUPILS ENROLLED—BOYS

The Mount Laurel Post Office operated from 1849 until 1908. The Masonville Post Office operated from 1868 to the late 1970s or early 1980s, when it moved and became the new Mount Laurel Post Office, retaining Masonville's zip code, on Whitman Drive. Prior to this consolidation, many citizens of Mount Laurel Township received their mail though Moorestown via a RFD route, which operated out of select post offices, like Moorestown. The Hartford Post Office operated from 1868 to 1954. As seen in the above photograph, the students in the record of pupils enrolled were listed as having an address in Moorestown, with a few in Fellowship. The above photograph shows the boys list, and the below photograph shows the girls list for 1925. (Both images courtesy of Mount Laurel Schools.)

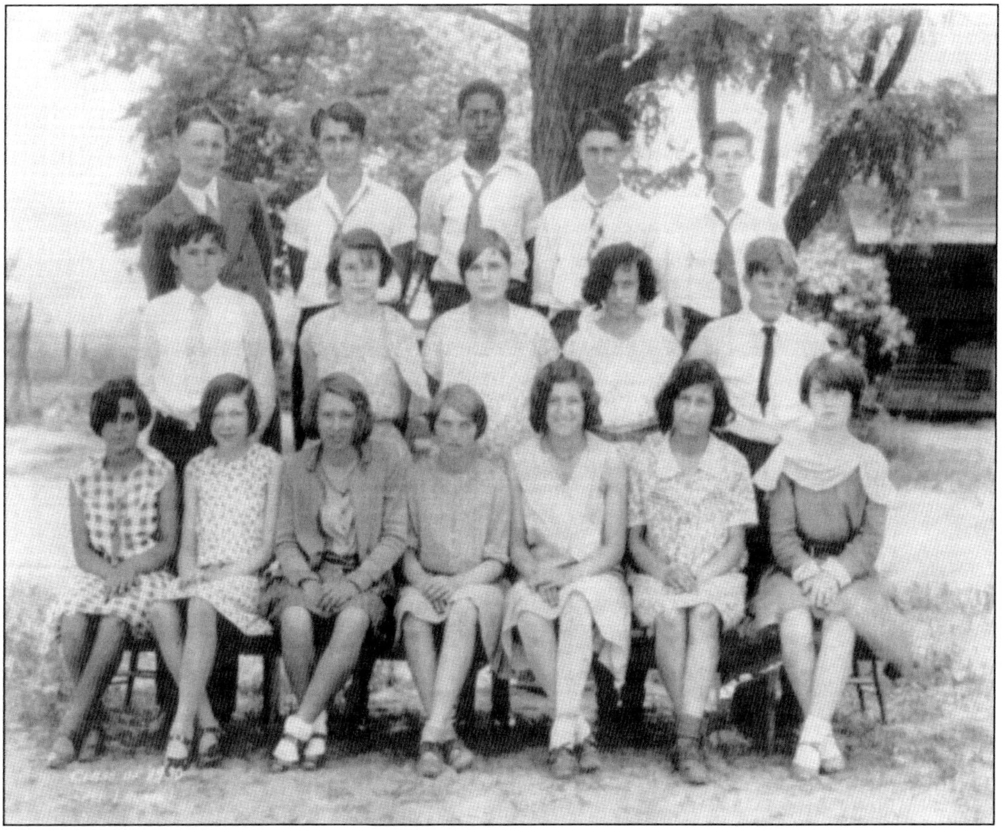

The Mount Laurel School No. 1 class of 1930 poses for an eighth-grade graduation photograph. Shown here are, from left to right, the following: (first row) Lillian Ackerman, Elenor Hurff, I. Huttner, Marion Murphy, Grace Monte, Rita DiLossi, and Veronica O'Donnell; (second row) Willis Gruno, Marie O'Donnell, Grace Slimm, Evelyn Pelengiero, and Walter Pearson; (third row) Irving Dorfman, Fred Lewis, Warner Hunters, Tony Carino, and Leon Schaffer. (Courtesy of Judith Monte.)

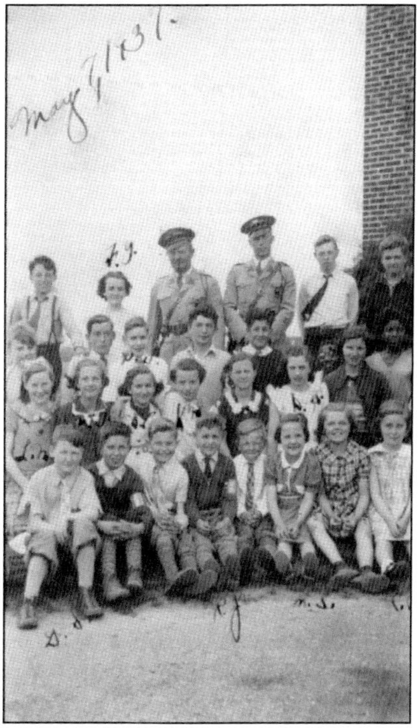

Students pose with New Jersey State Troopers in this photograph from May 1937. Among those identified by their initials are the following; (first row) G. Strannahan, Warren W., R. Jones, M. Slimm, Gen. Godfrey, and Ruth Carey; (second row) B. Litwen, K. McKraken, Louise M., M. Godfrey, Gruno, M. Strannahan, and D. Hoffman; (third row) William Godfrey, N. Jones, Kitch, and Jack Louis; (fourth row) Florence Grota and Trooper Stetson. (Courtesy of Annetta Verner.)

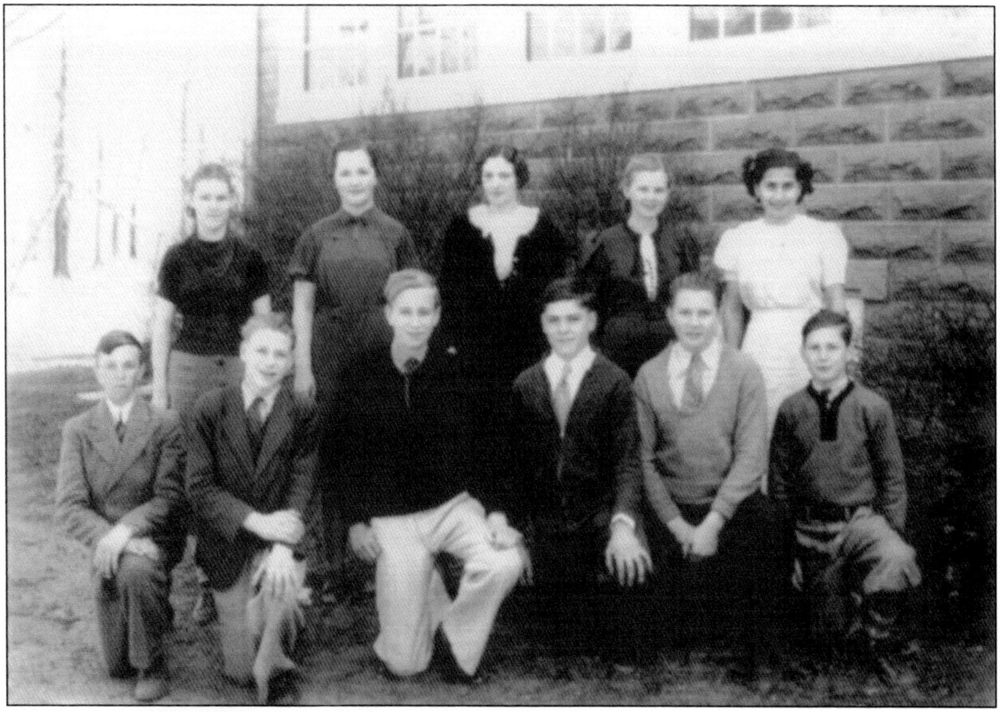

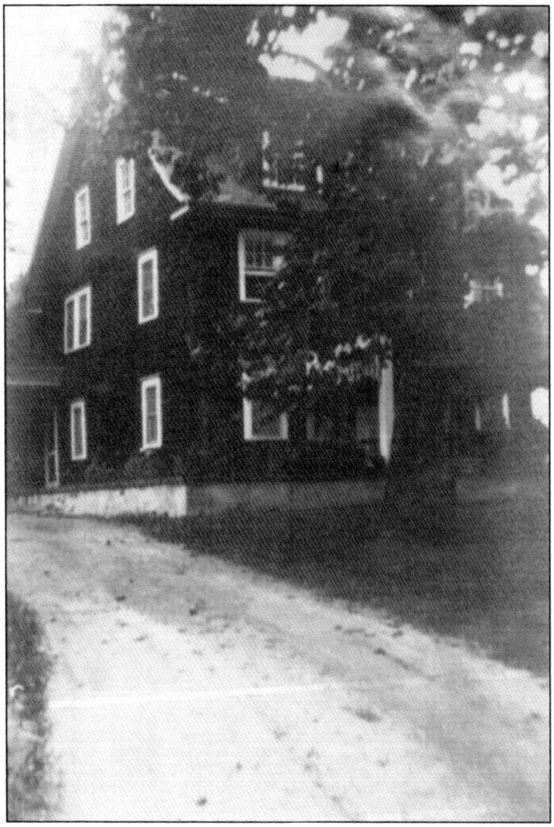

Students of the graduating class of 1937–1938 pose at the Masonville School No. 2. In this photograph, the only identified person is Nancy Comfort (second row, far left). (Courtesy of the Mount Laurel Schools.)

The Comfort farm, located near Masonville, is shown in the 1930s. Dr. Rubin Sharp and his wife, Mary, purchased the farm when the Comfort family could no longer afford to live there. The house had a very large, casual kitchen table. (Courtesy of Nancy Jones.)

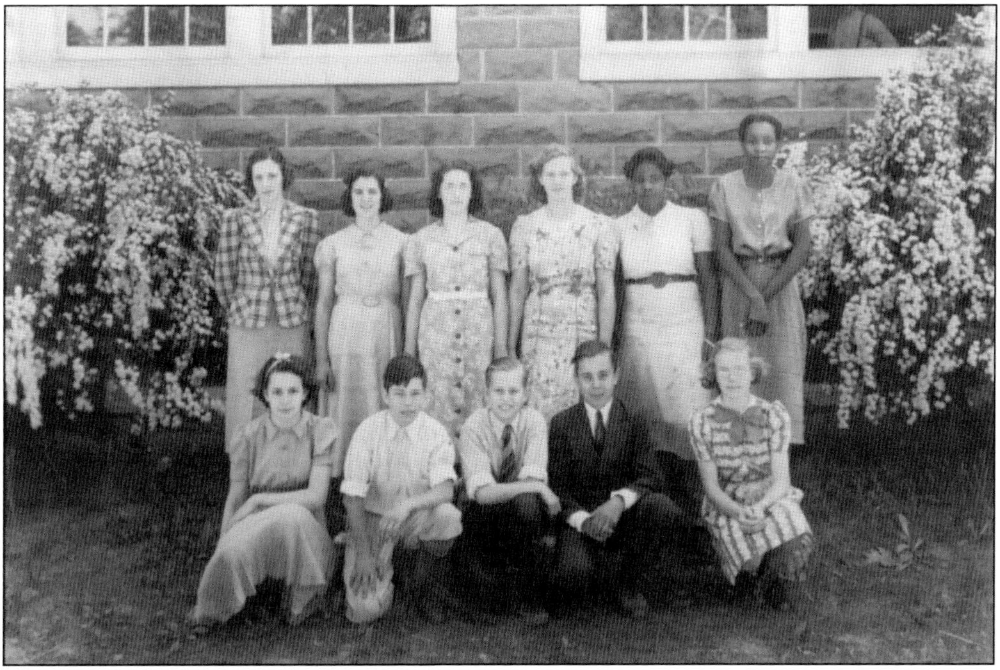

Mary G. Allsip, a teacher at the Masonville School, poses with her students in 1938. Shown here are, from left to right, (first row) Marion Sandelle, John Cann, Harry Bungees, Lester Van Sciver, and Gladyn Laveman; (second row) Allsip, Anna DiGalbo, Norma Schemly, Mary Davison, Fenton Garnett, and Mary Hunter. Mary Davison eventually married Mike Monte and developed, with her in-laws, the Monte farm on Marne Highway near Hartford Road. (Courtesy of Judith Monte.)

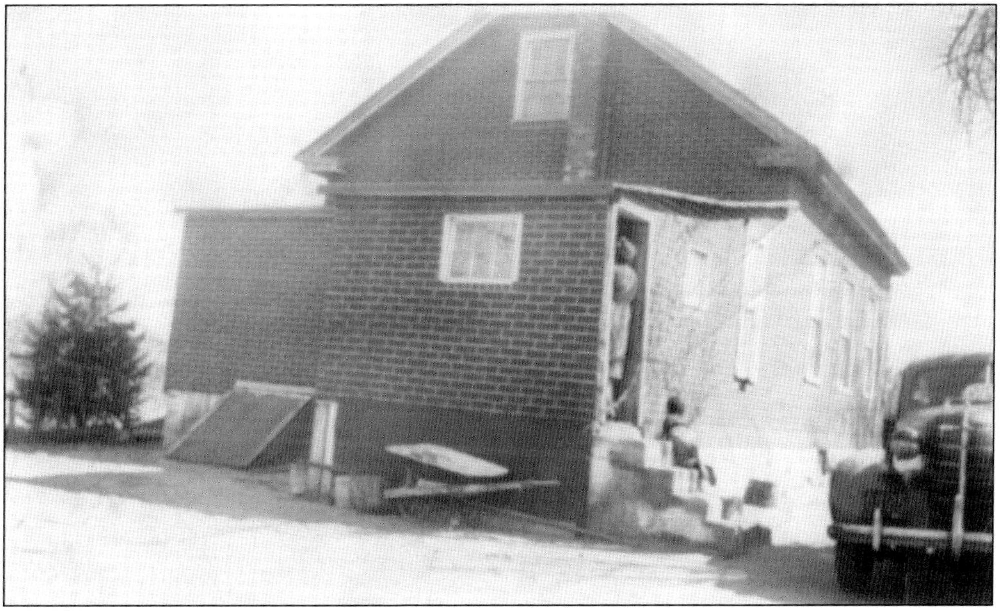

A 1936 Pontiac or Buick automobile is shown next to the old Masonville schoolhouse. The DeBolt family purchased this house from the school district when the new Masonville School No. 2 was built. This house is still located behind the Masonville School. (Courtesy of Robert E. DeBolt.)

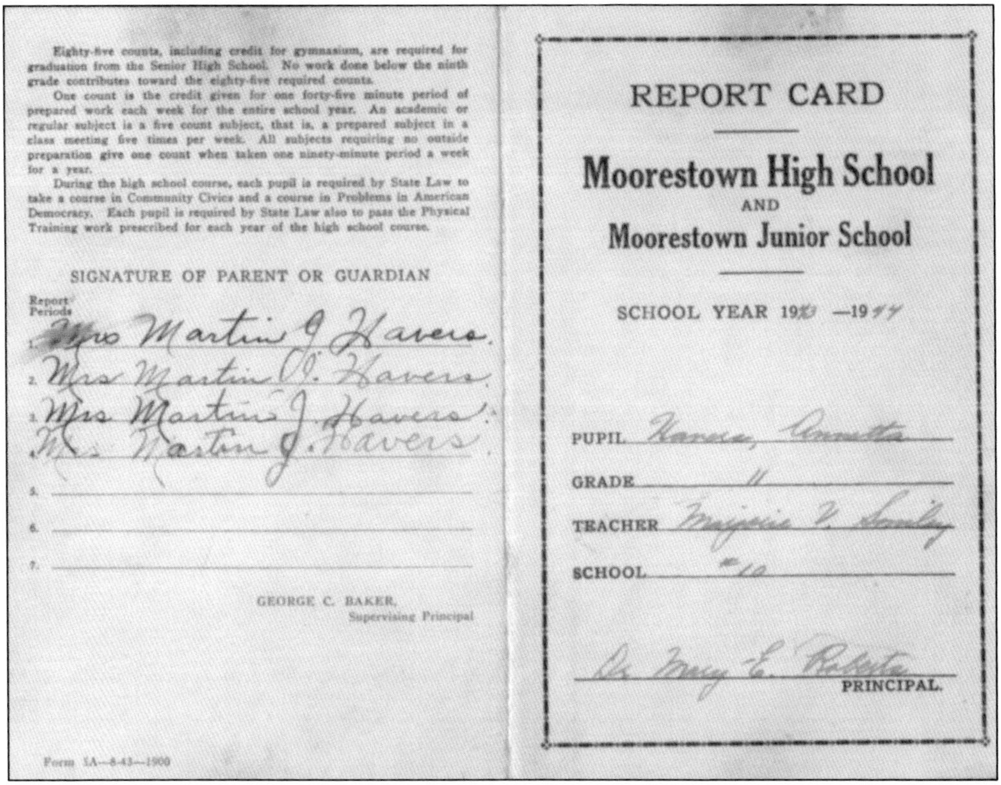

Annetta Havers' report card is typical of those at Moorestown High School. This report card is from 1943, when she was in 11th grade. The Mount Laurel students attended Moorestown High School for many years, until Lenape High School opened in 1958. Previously, Mount Laurel students also went to Moorestown for junior high, but that changed when the Hillside School opened in 1955 as a middle school. (Courtesy of Annetta Verner.)

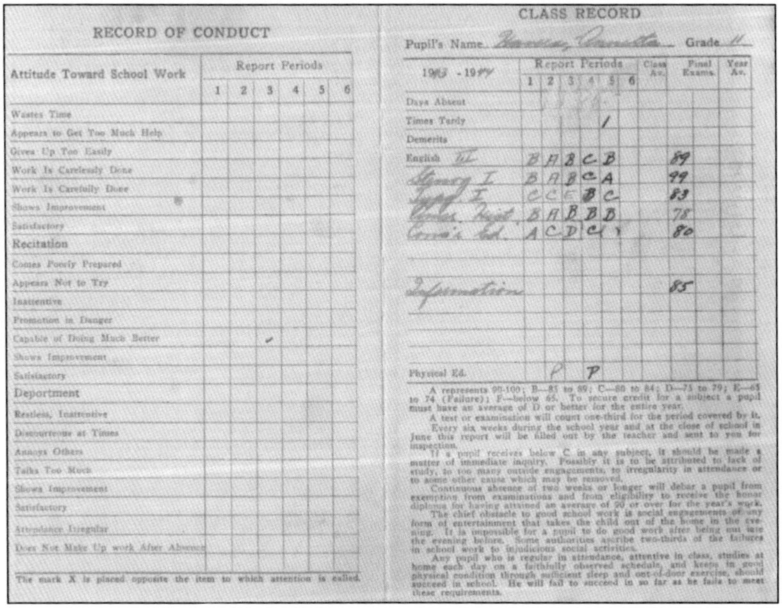

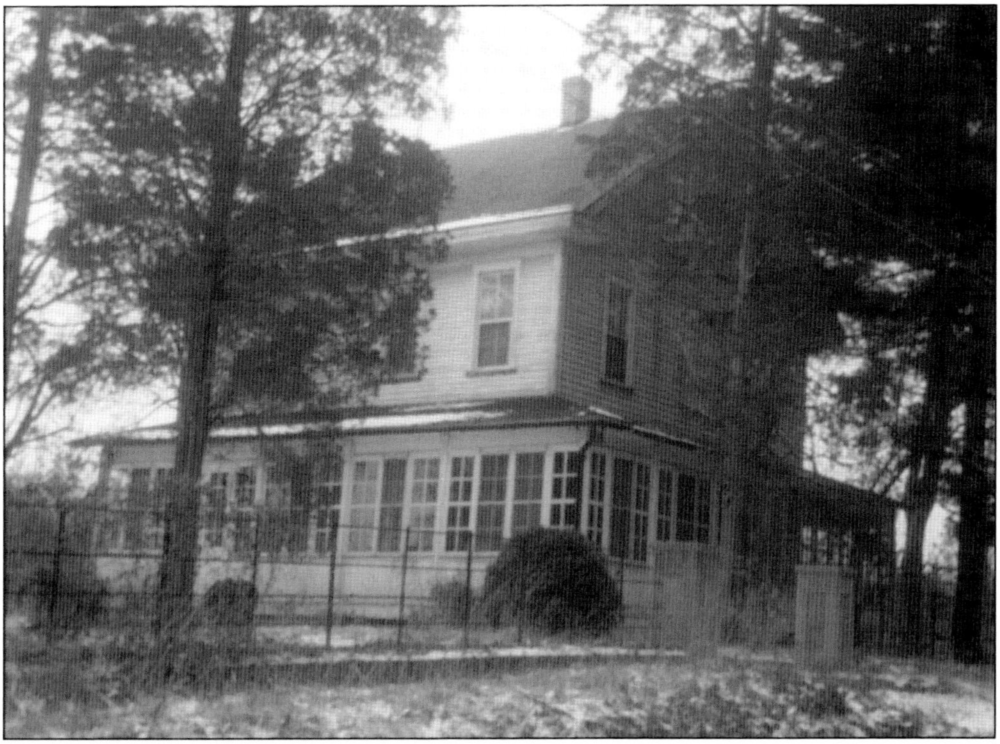

School No. 80, as this building was called, was erected in 1850 near the base of the mount and used as a Friends' School. In 1869, it became a public school for 13 years, then reverted back to being a Friends' School. It was not used as a school for long. After it became a private residence, the porch was added. (Courtesy of Gail Greenberg.)

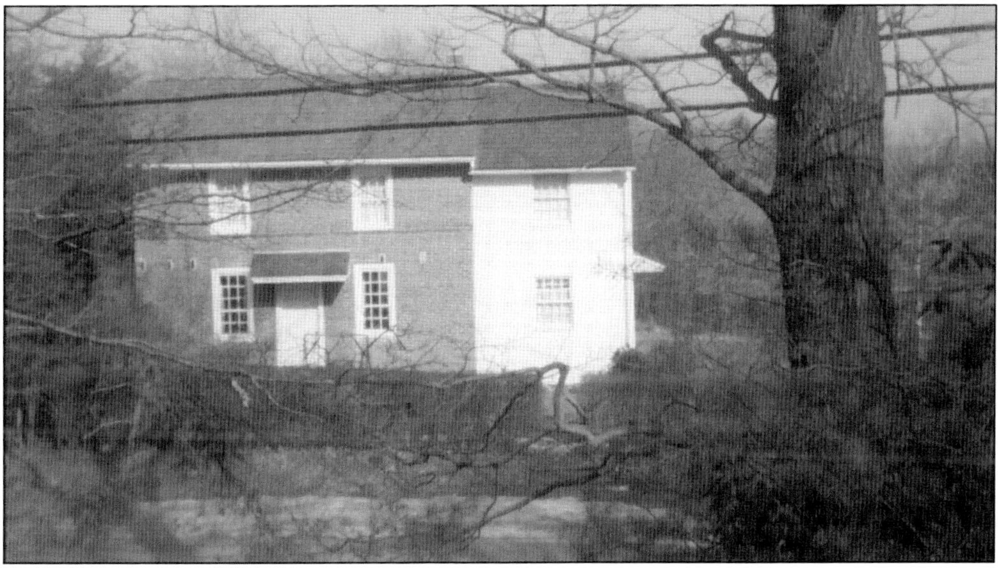

The Evesham Meeting House had a schoolmaster's house next to it, but it had previously been attached to one end of the meetinghouse. The Friends' schoolmaster lived in the original brick portion, which is dated to 1783. This building is now known as the Caretaker's House. (Courtesy of Gail Greenberg.)

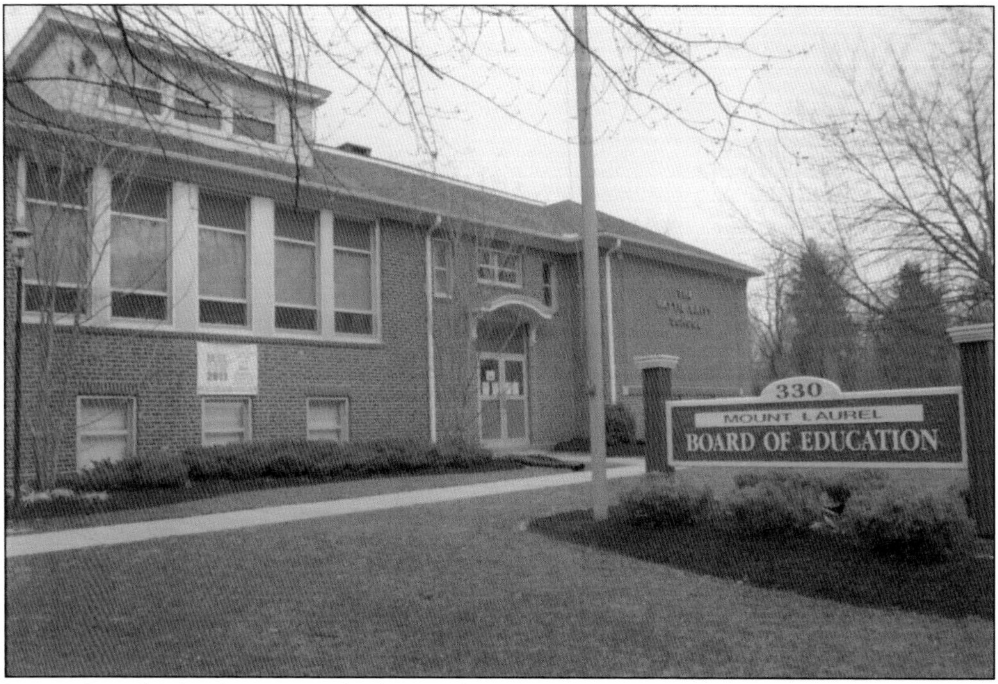

Mount Laurel School No. 1 was built to replace the Colemantown School. It contained grades one through eight. It was named after longtime teacher Hattie Britt in 1964. In 1967, became the administration building for the district. In 1968, the Parkway School used the Hattie Britt building as an annex for its fifth-grade classes. (Courtesy of Mount Laurel Schools.)

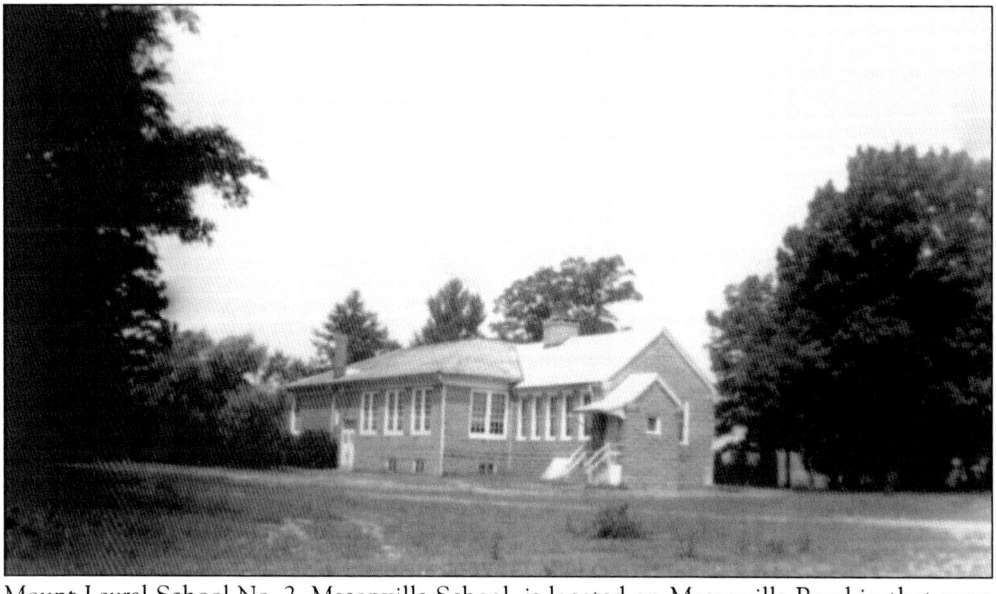

Mount Laurel School No. 2, Masonville School, is located on Masonville Road in that same section of town. It had been enlarged to accommodate the students from Hartford. This building is now the home of the grounds and maintenance departments of the Mount Laurel Schools. (Courtesy of Robert E. DeBolt.)

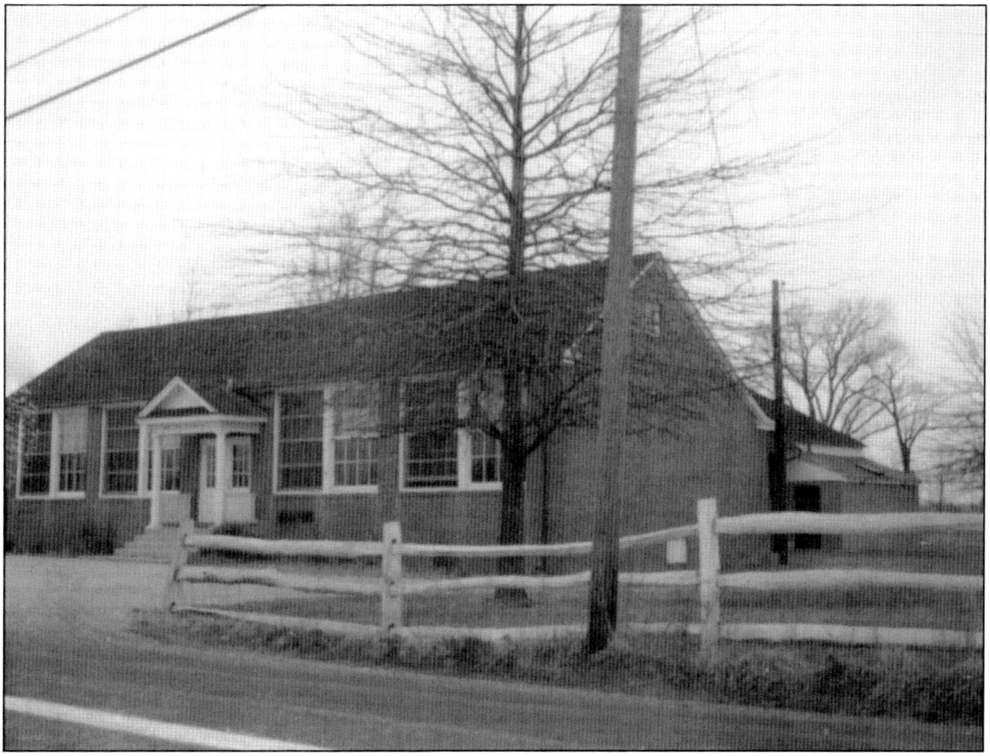

Mount Laurel School No. 3, formerly the Green Grove School, where Hattie Britt began teaching in 1925, is show here in its permanent location on Mount Laurel Road. This building currently houses the transportation department and has classrooms for various uses. During the "separate but equal" phase of education in Mount Laurel, this building served as the segregated black school. (Courtesy of Mount Laurel Schools.)

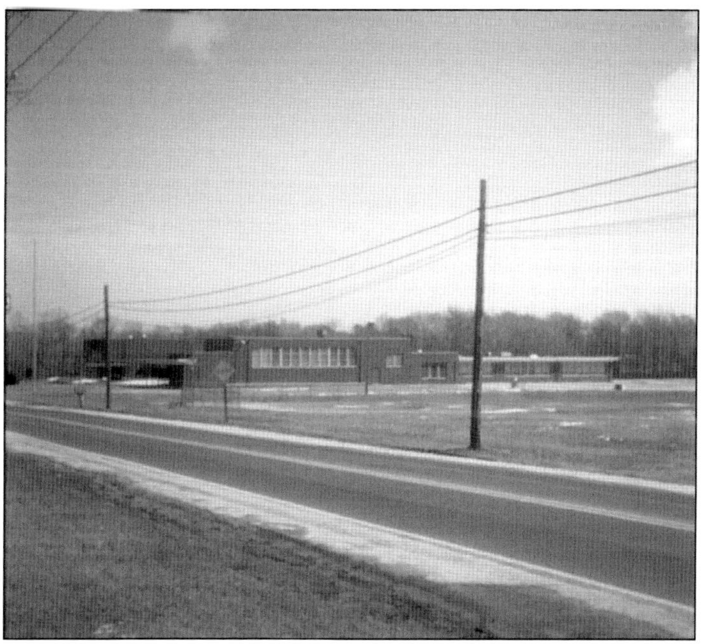

This photograph from the early 1970s shows the Hillside School, which currently accommodates kindergarten through fourth grade classes. Previously, this building was the middle school and served as an alternative to sending Mount Laurel students to Moorestown Junior High. (Courtesy of the Mount Laurel Historical Society.)

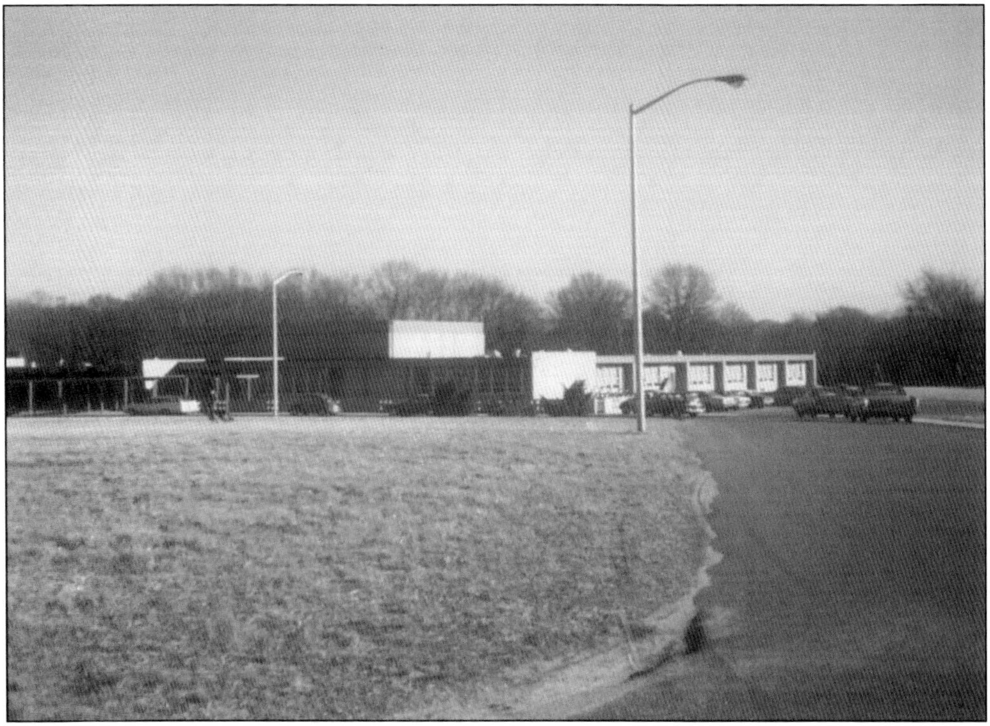

Fleetwood School, built in 1963 and opened in 1964, is shown in the early 1970s. This school is located on Fleetwood Avenue in the Masonville section of town, close to Mount Laurel School No. 2. The classes held at Masonville School were moved to Fleetwood in the early 1980s. (Courtesy of the Mount Laurel Historical Society.)

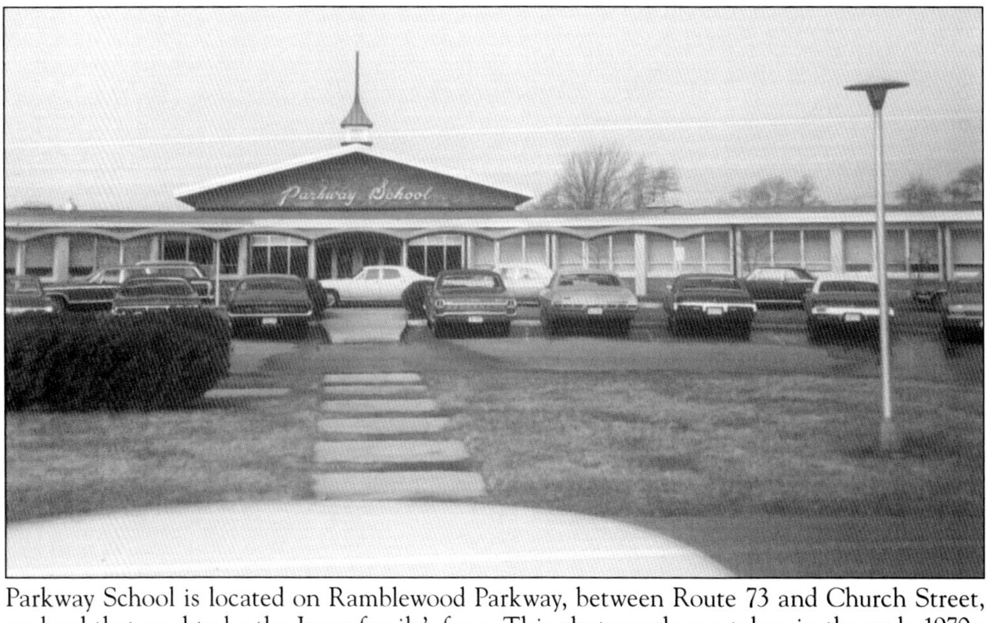

Parkway School is located on Ramblewood Parkway, between Route 73 and Church Street, on land that used to be the Jones family's farm. This photograph was taken in the early 1970s. Parkway School educates children from preschool through fourth grade. (Courtesy of the Mount Laurel Historical Society.)

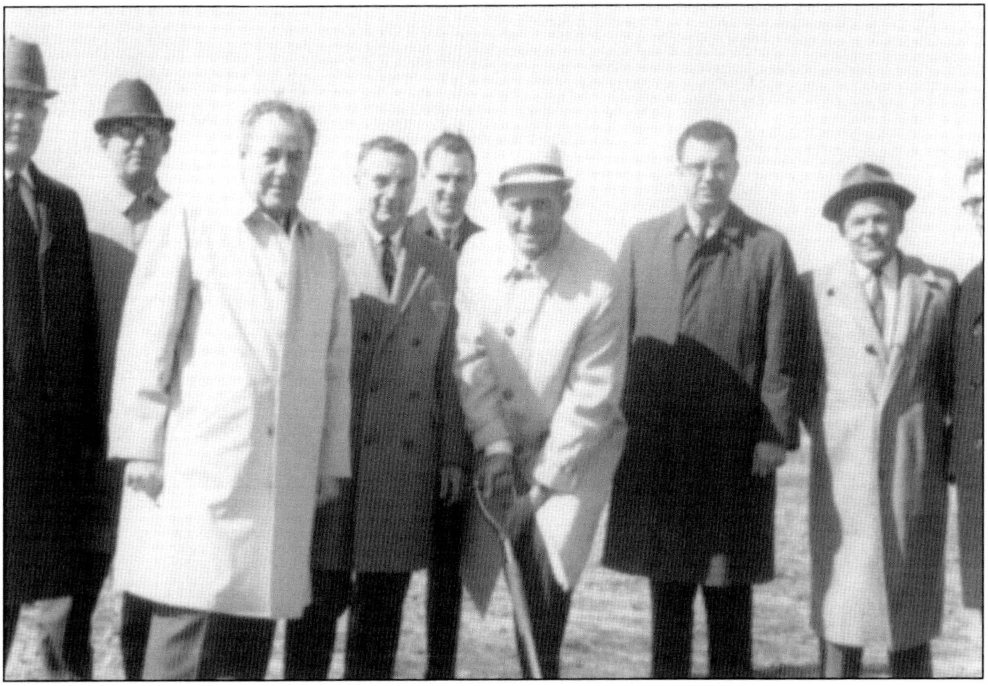

Ground was broken for the new Mount Laurel Middle School in the late 1960s. The building would replace Hillside School as the middle school. Pictured here are, from left to right, Thomas E. Harrington, superintendent; Richard Remington, board president; Thomas Malone, architect; Alfred West, contractor; Robert Hughes, board member; William Breuer, building committee chairman; Robert Keane, school board vice president; Edward Wells, board member; and William Shields, township committee member. (Courtesy of Mount Laurel Schools.)

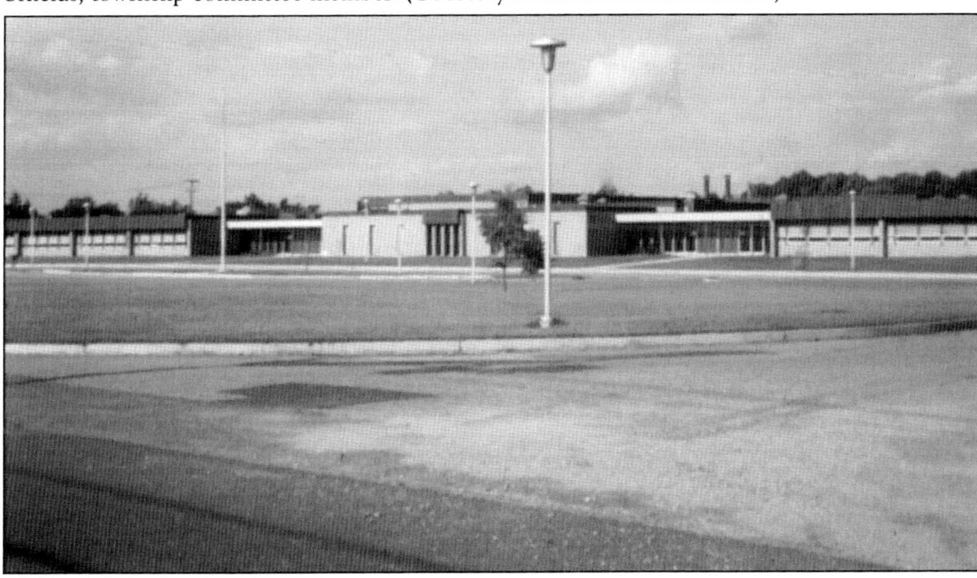

The Mount Laurel Middle School, built in 1969, provided a larger space for the students. With the opening of this facility, Hillside School became an elementary school. This school was renamed in 1982 for the superintendent of schools, Thomas E. Harrington, who was in office at the time it was built. (Courtesy of the Mount Laurel Historical Society.)

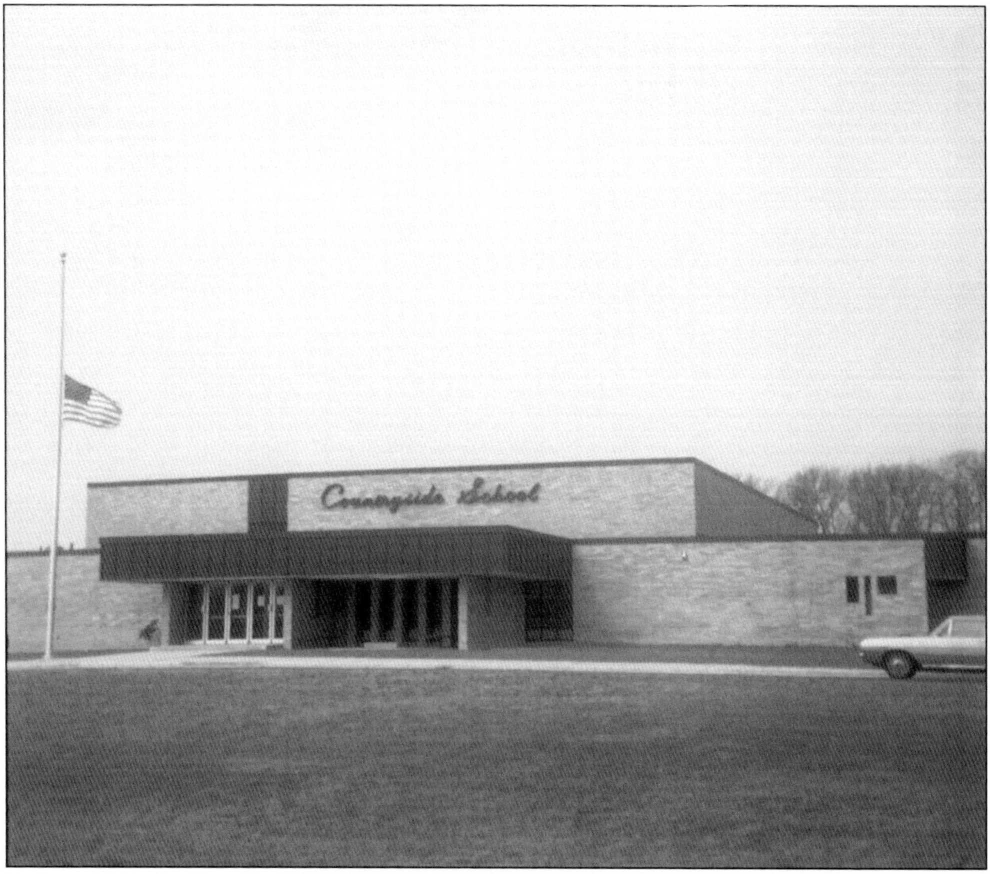

Built in 1971, the Countryside School is located in a residential neighborhood in the Fellowship section of Mount Laurel. This photograph of the elementary school was taken approximately one year after it was built. Most of the Mount Laurel Schools are named for the road on which they are located or for a description of the location. (Courtesy of the Mount Laurel Historical Society.)

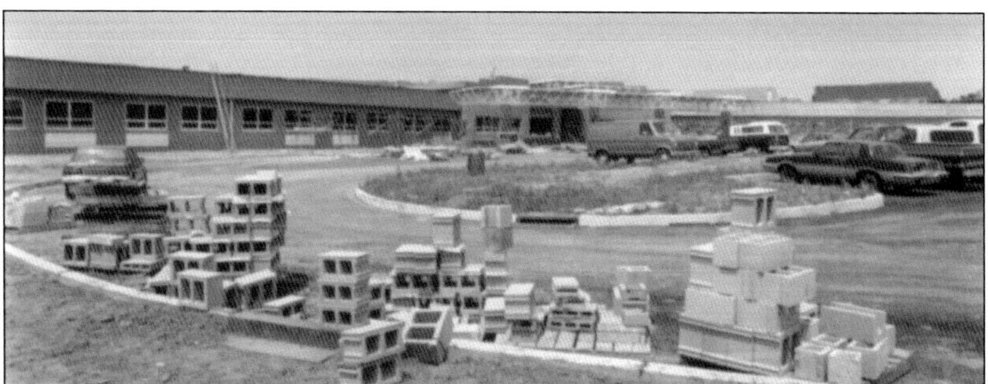

Almost 20 years after the last elementary school was constructed, the township had grown again, and a new school, the Larchmont School, was built. This 1991 photograph shows the school, located on Larchmont Boulevard, under construction. (Courtesy of the *Burlington County Times*.)

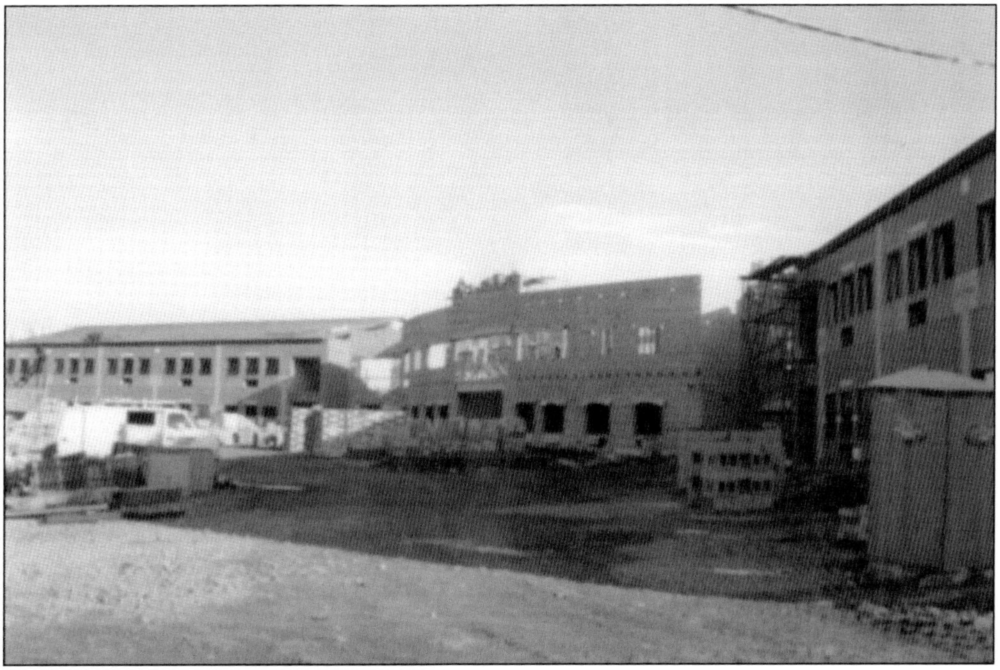

The final two schools that make up the Mount Laurel school system are the Hartford School (above), which was built in 1994, and the Springville School (below), built in 2001. Hartford School is an upper elementary school, and Springville serves students from preschool through fourth grade. Mount Laurel has a total of six elementary schools, one upper elementary school, and one middle school. (Courtesy of the Mount Laurel Schools.)

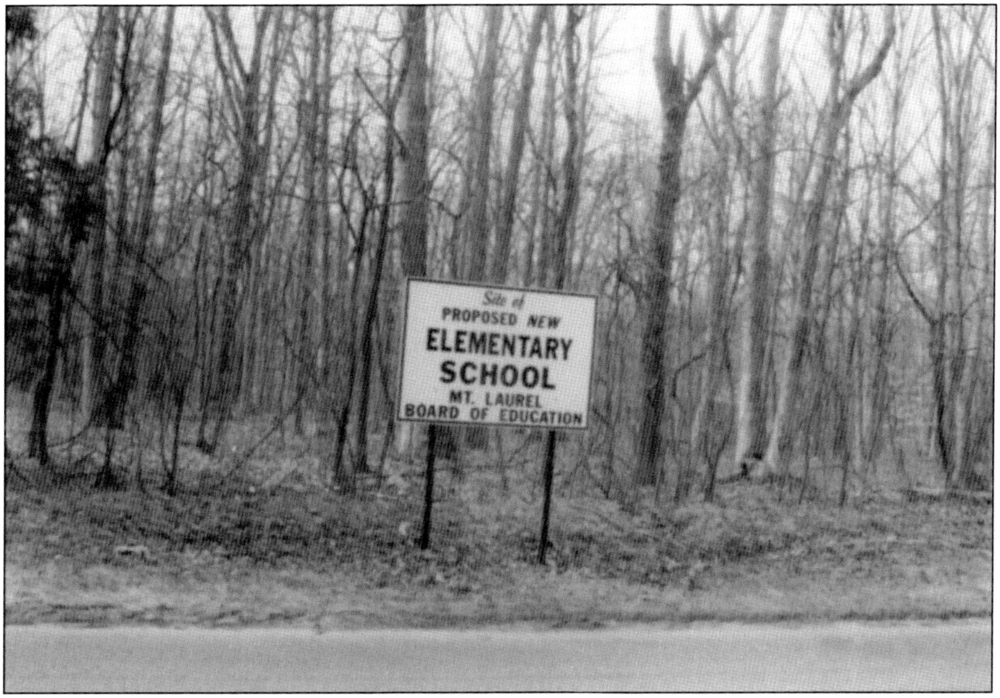

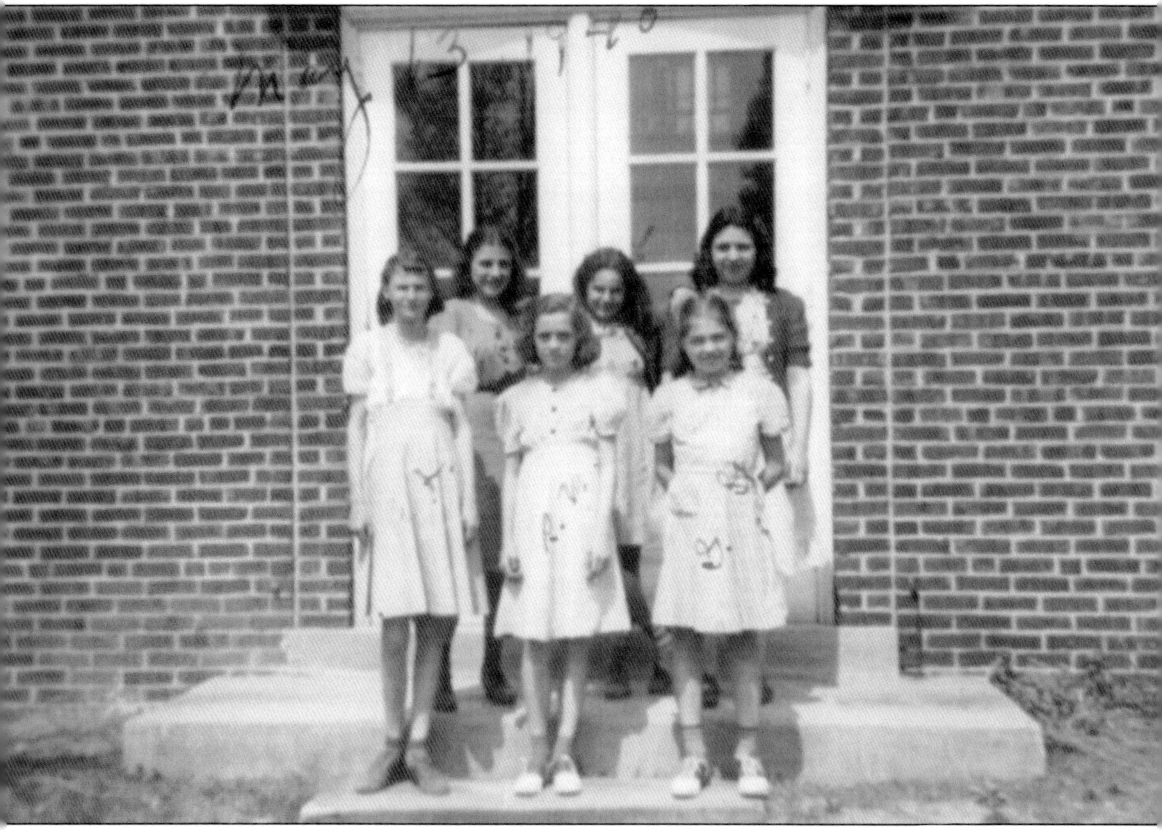

Taken on May 13, 1940, this photograph shows students outside of Mount Laurel School No. 1. According to Annetta Verner (first row, far left), there were 18 students in her 1941 graduating class. She recalls outdoor plumbing for all the years she was at Mount Laurel schools, which was kindergarten through eighth grade. Indoor plumbing was added later, in 1941, when she was attending Moorestown High School. Verner was in the class of 1945. She did not want to go to college, even though her teachers encouraged her. She wanted to start earning her own money, so she worked for a company owned by two of her high school teachers. (Courtesy of Annetta Verner.)

Six

Mount Laurel Police, Masonville Fire Company, and Fellowship Fire Company

The Mount Laurel Police Department was started by William T. Nardin in 1938, and he was made the first director of public safety. Over the next few years, officers were added to the department and were later sent to be trained by the state police in Woodbury. Unfortunately, the township committee disbanded the department in the 1940s, and it was not until 1955 that the force was reorganized. The chief of the department worked out of his home, and the township hired more officers and purchased police cars. The department was relocated to Farmer's Hall, where it had a small office. As the department grew, it hired officers and outgrew the space in Farmer's Hall. In 1972, a new building was erected.

In 1913, residents of Masonville organized the Masonville Fire Company. In the fall of that year, a plot of land was donated, and the fire company built a firehouse that was dedicated in 1914 but burned down in 1915. In 1916, the community built a new firehouse, with a bell tower in the front. This facility was in use until 1960. The next firehouse served the community, with a few additions, until a major renovation was done in 2003.

The Fellowship Fire Company was formed in 1943 to fulfill a need for fire services on the other side of Mount Laurel. Ground and a building were donated, and Masonville Fire Company donated a pumper. The chief of the Masonville company became chief of both companies and trained the new firemen. Fellowship was able to purchase its first truck in 1948. In 1953, ground was broken for a new firehouse on donated land. This building was later razed and reconstructed in 1993. The 1970s brought a need for a substation on Elbo Lane; again, the land was donated and another firehouse was completed in 1976, then later remodeled.

The Masonville and Fellowship Fire Companies were joined in 1983, becoming Mount Laurel Fire District No. 1. This allowed the fire service to be funded by tax dollars.

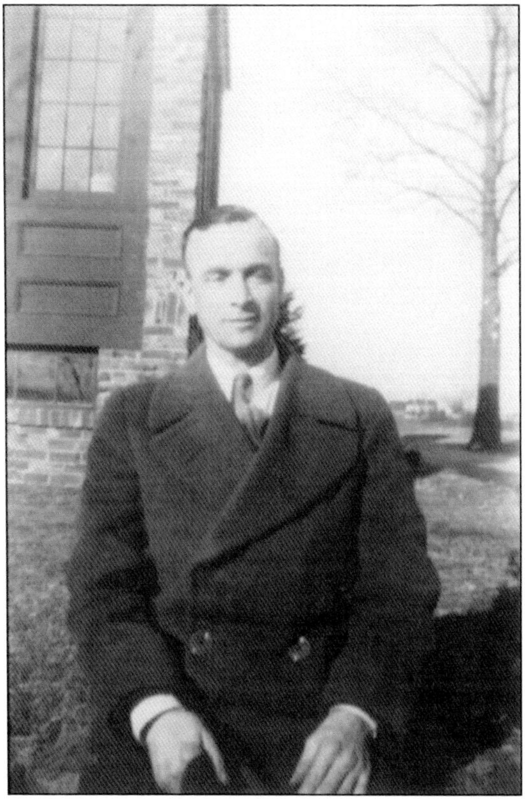

The photograph at left, taken in 1937, shows William Thomas Nardin, who served as the mayor of Mount Laurel. He established the police department on January 1, 1938. On his urging, the township committee created the police force. Nardin was named the first director of public safety. A budget of $1,000 was created for three special officers, so that there was always someone on call. William Nardin lived on Church Road at Fellowship Road, where the current waste facility stands today. (Both images courtesy of Meg Ellis.)

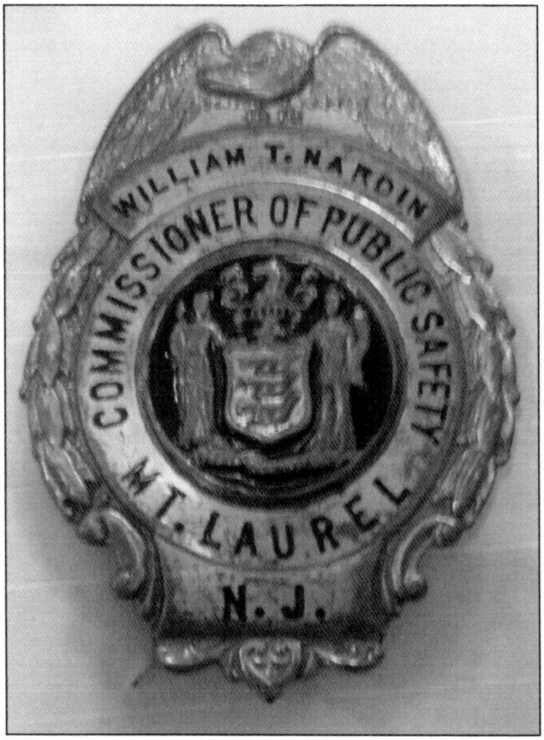

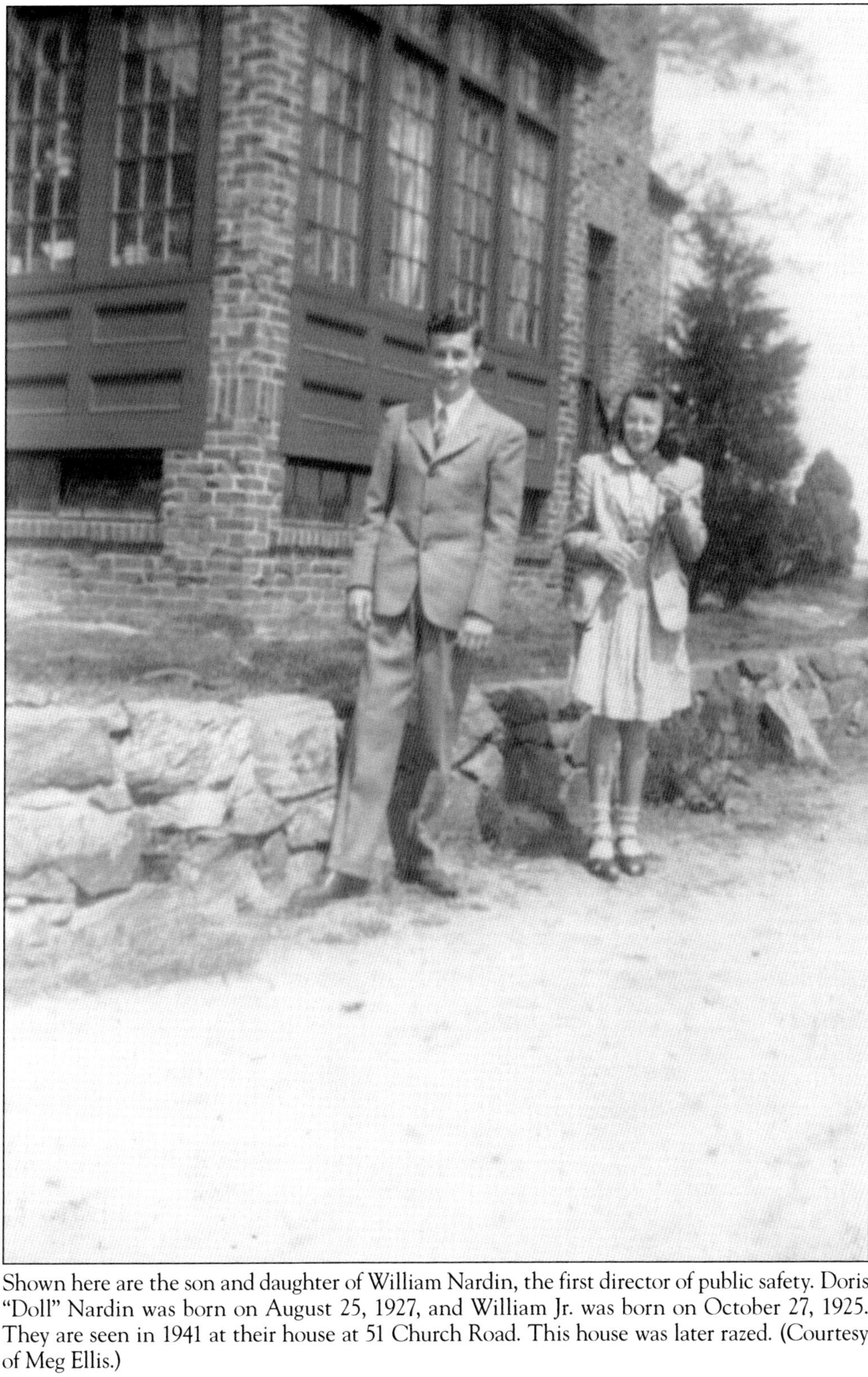

Shown here are the son and daughter of William Nardin, the first director of public safety. Doris "Doll" Nardin was born on August 25, 1927, and William Jr. was born on October 27, 1925. They are seen in 1941 at their house at 51 Church Road. This house was later razed. (Courtesy of Meg Ellis.)

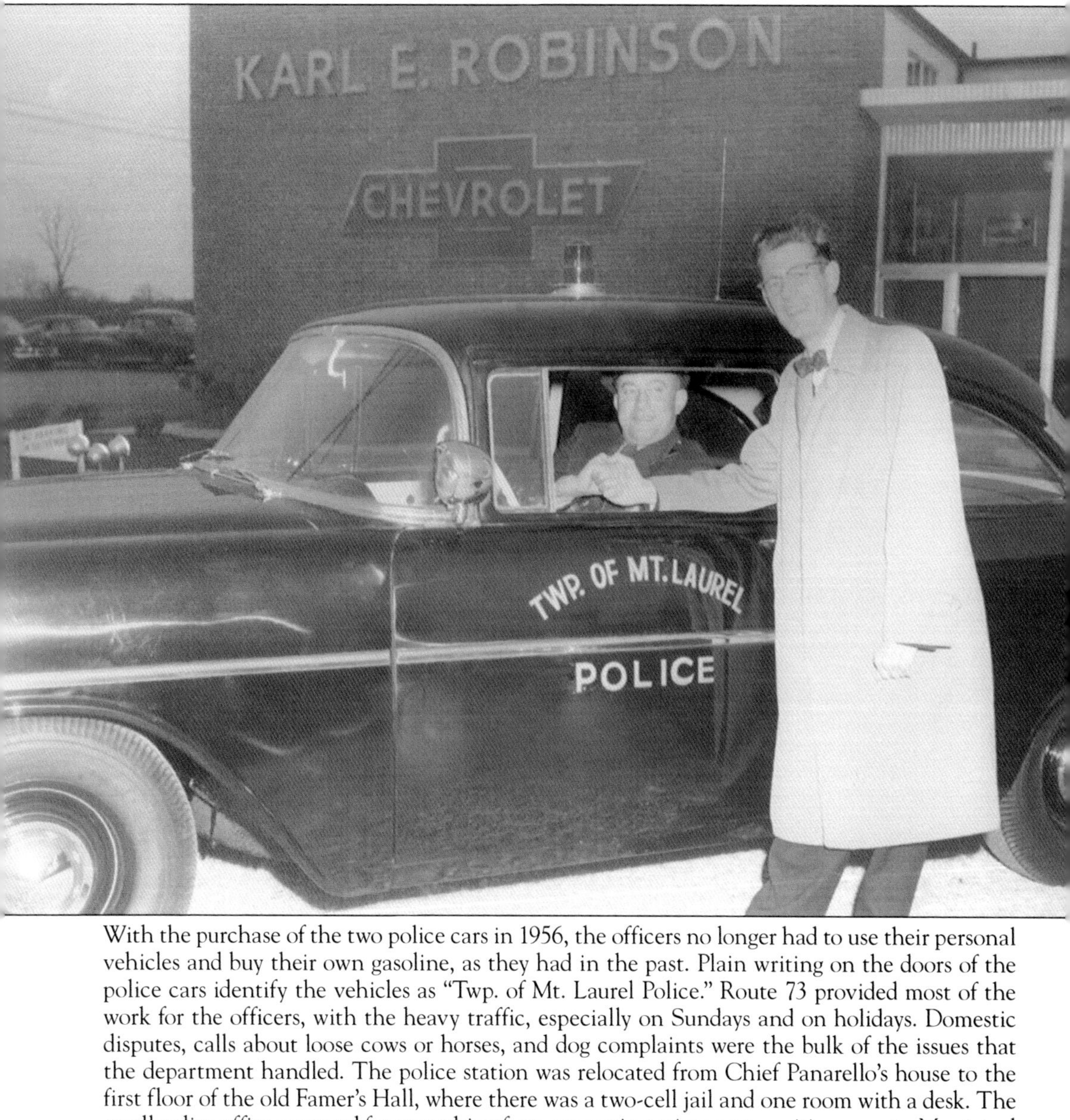

With the purchase of the two police cars in 1956, the officers no longer had to use their personal vehicles and buy their own gasoline, as they had in the past. Plain writing on the doors of the police cars identify the vehicles as "Twp. of Mt. Laurel Police." Route 73 provided most of the work for the officers, with the heavy traffic, especially on Sundays and on holidays. Domestic disputes, calls about loose cows or horses, and dog complaints were the bulk of the issues that the department handled. The police station was relocated from Chief Panarello's house to the first floor of the old Famer's Hall, where there was a two-cell jail and one room with a desk. The small police office was used for everything from processing prisoners to writing reports. Municipal court was held on the second floor of Farmer's Hall. (Courtesy of the Mount Laurel Police and Police Chief Dennis Cribben.)

The police station and the police chief's office were located in Farmer's Hall. The officers came to work in their uniforms and worked a six-day-on, one-day-off rotation. Because the officer on duty would pick up the officer who had the next shift, the officers had to live in town. If the assigned officer was unavailable, the previous officer worked that shift. (Courtesy of the Mount Laurel Police and Police Chief Dennis Cribben.)

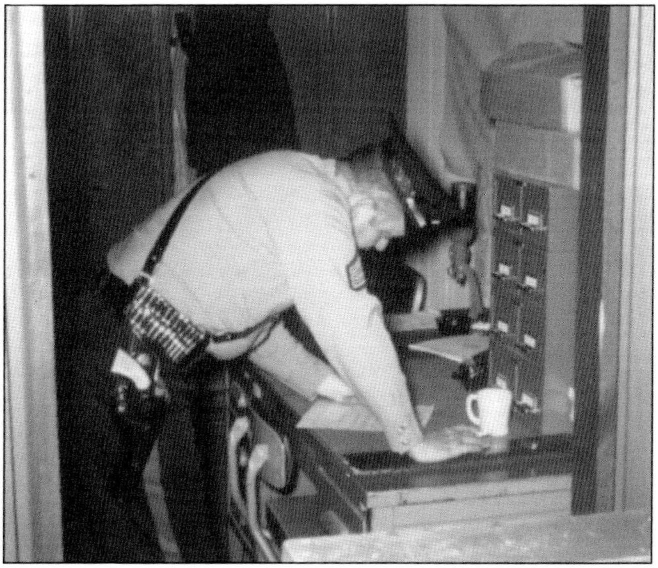

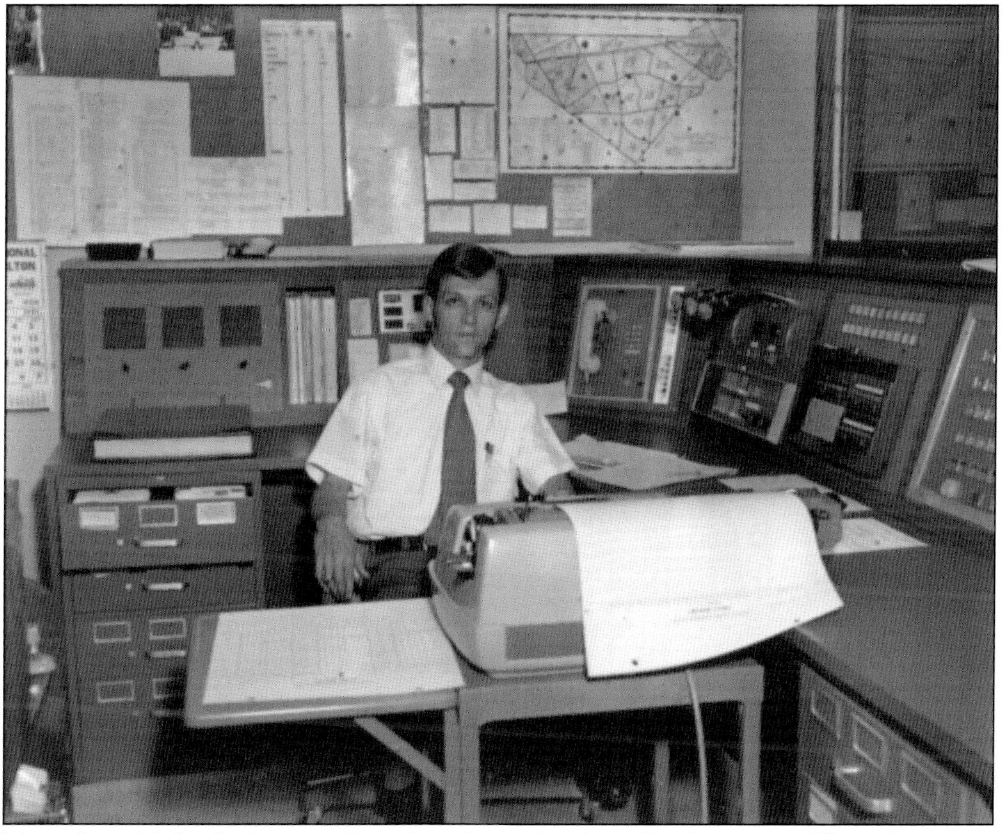

Mount Laurel Police had its own dispatchers, located in the police department. These dispatchers contacted the officers with complaints and issues and maintained a log of what the officers did. The phone was controlled by a toggle switch located at Farmer's Hall, which switched calls to the Moorestown Police Department while the station was unmanned in the 1960s. (Courtesy of the Mount Laurel Police and Police Chief Dennis Cribben.)

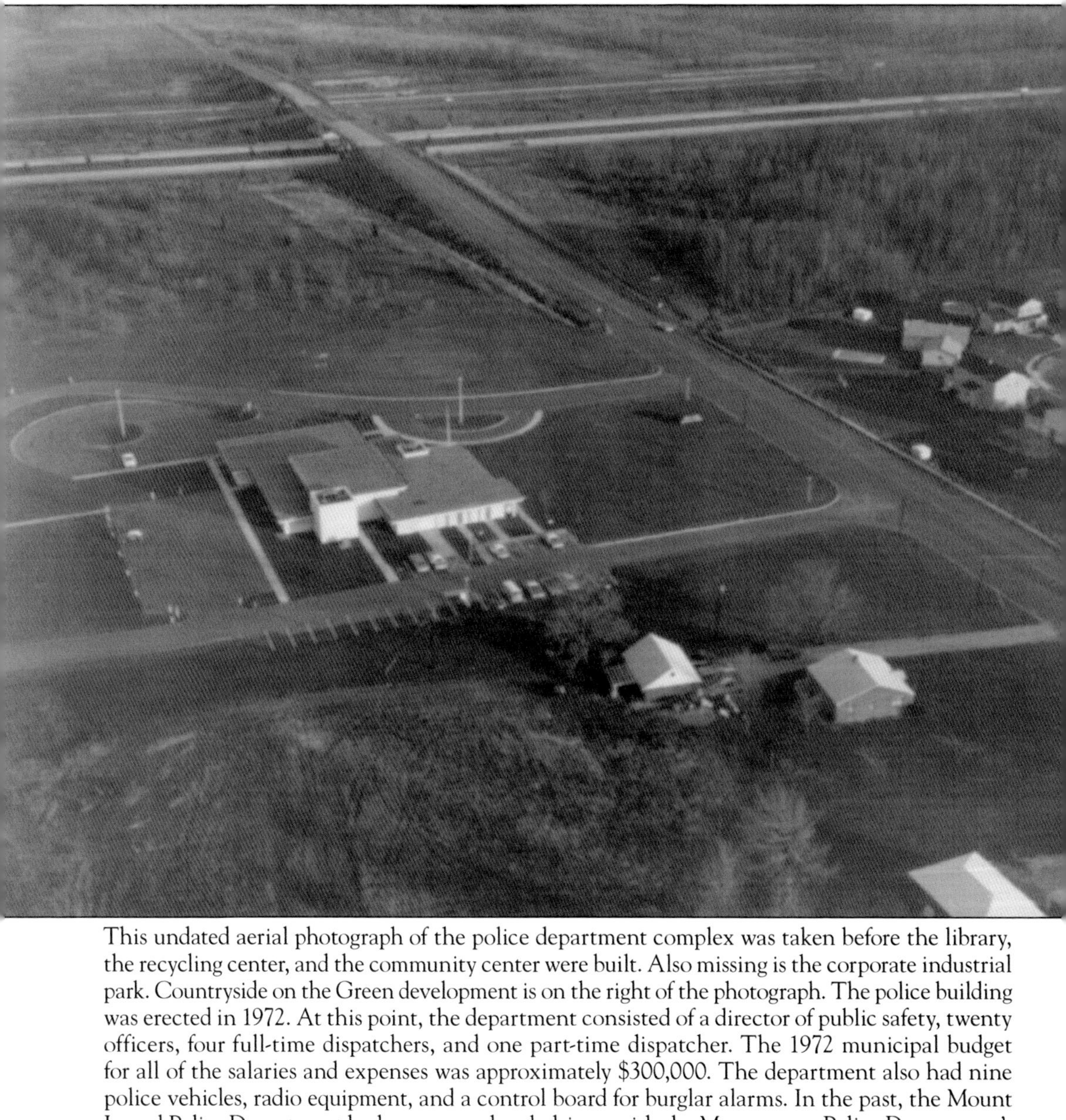

This undated aerial photograph of the police department complex was taken before the library, the recycling center, and the community center were built. Also missing is the corporate industrial park. Countryside on the Green development is on the right of the photograph. The police building was erected in 1972. At this point, the department consisted of a director of public safety, twenty officers, four full-time dispatchers, and one part-time dispatcher. The 1972 municipal budget for all of the salaries and expenses was approximately $300,000. The department also had nine police vehicles, radio equipment, and a control board for burglar alarms. In the past, the Mount Laurel Police Department had to process drunk drivers with the Moorestown Police Department's Drunkometer device. Finally, Mount Laurel purchased a Breathalyzer unit in the early 1970s. (Courtesy of the Mount Laurel Police and Police Chief Dennis Cribben.)

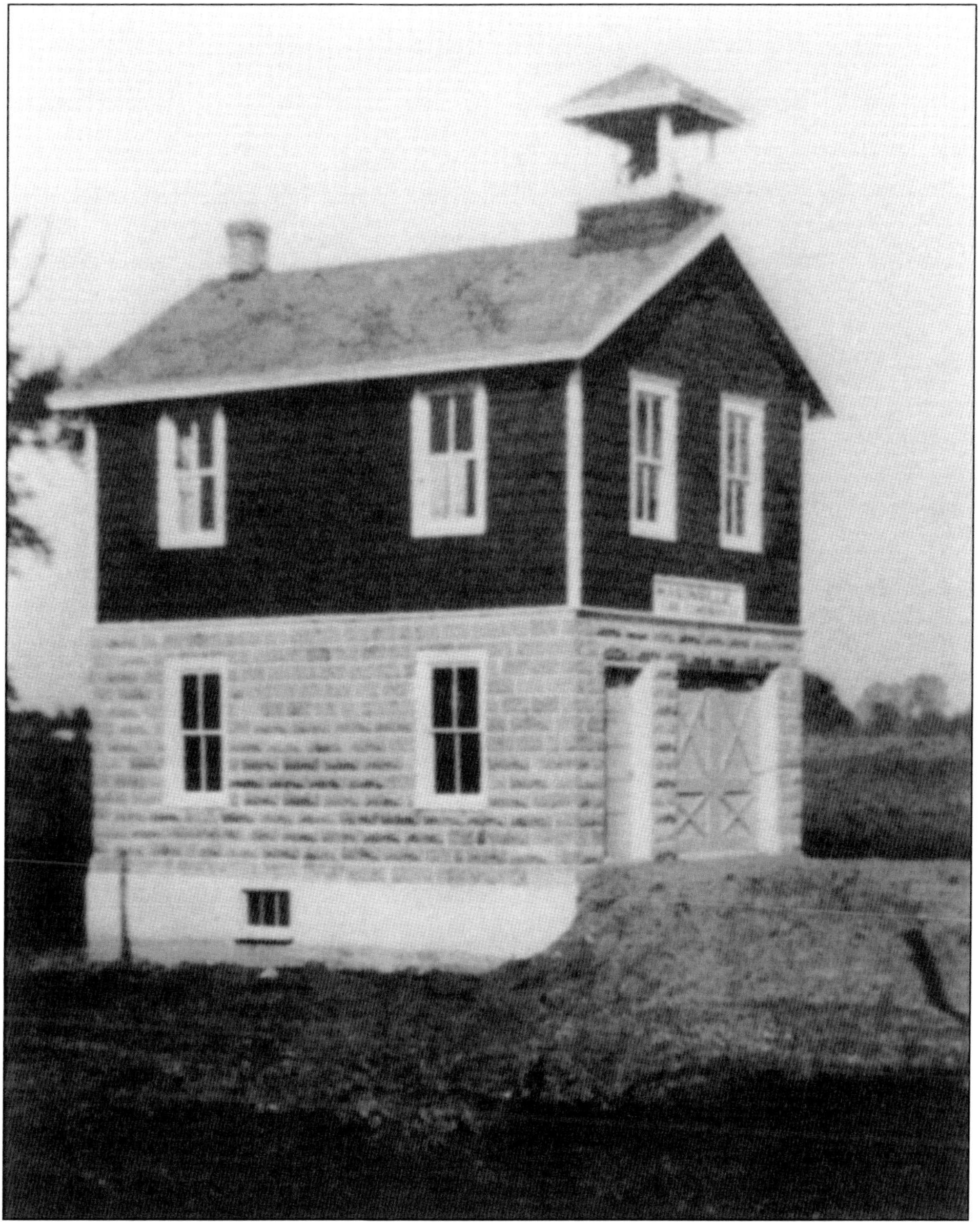

On April 2, 1913, a small group of rural residents met in the Brotherhood of America Hall to discuss the formation of a fire company. The Masonville Fire Company was officially organized on July 1, 1913. The first firehouse was dedicated in 1914 on a plot of land on what was previously called Centerton Road, now Masonville Road. The land was donated to the fire company by the Haines family. The fire company purchased from James Boyd & Brothers in Philadelphia a two-wheeled engine with 35-gallon chemical tanks, which they then outfitted with front wheels. James Boyd & Brothers built fire apparatus from 1908 to 1916. It was thought that a faulty heater pipe caused a fire that destroyed this firehouse one year later, in October 1915. (Courtesy of Richard Tremper and the Masonville Fire Company.)

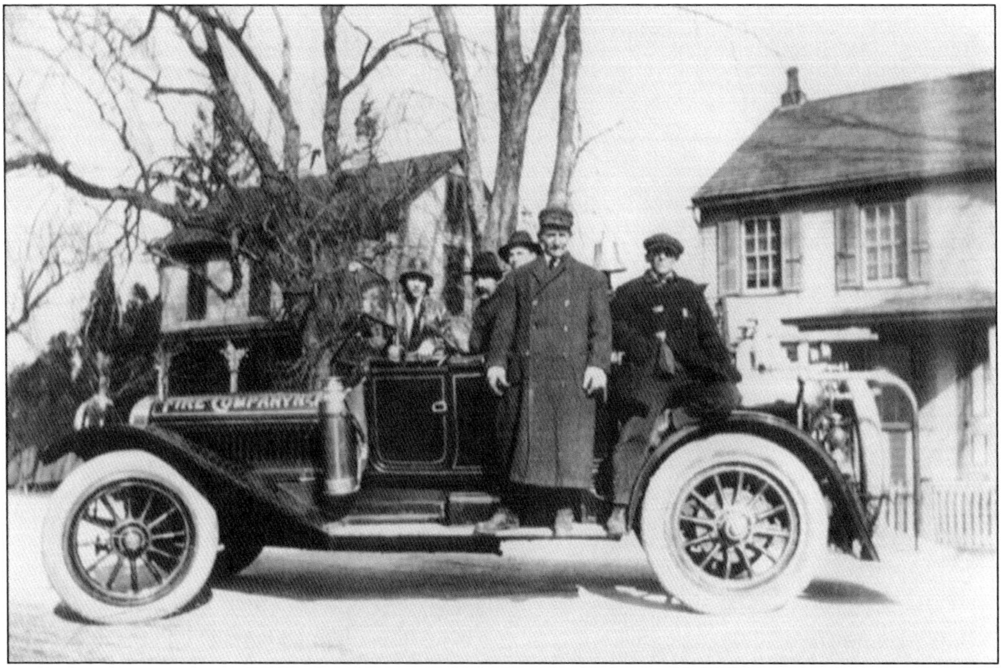

This Winton Touring Car was the first motorized firefighting equipment that the Masonville Fire Company owned. Purchased around 1916, it was converted from a regular automobile with the mounting of chemical tanks on the sides, along with ladders and other firefighting equipment. These photographs show both sides of the chemical engine. The houses in the background stood across the street from the firehouse and are still there. (Courtesy of Richard Tremper and the Masonville Fire Company.)

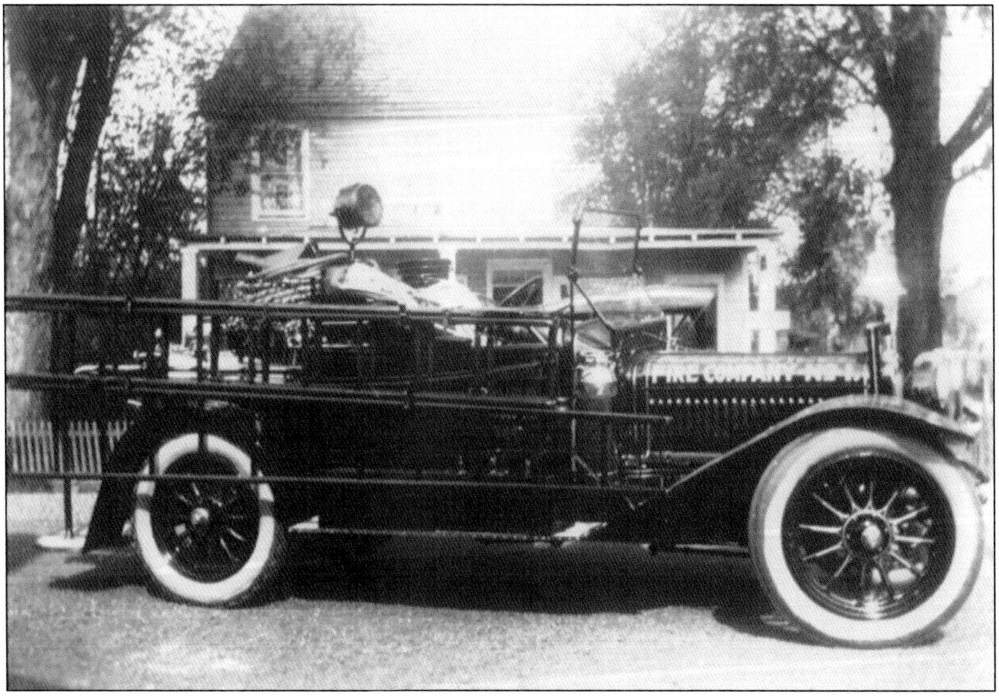

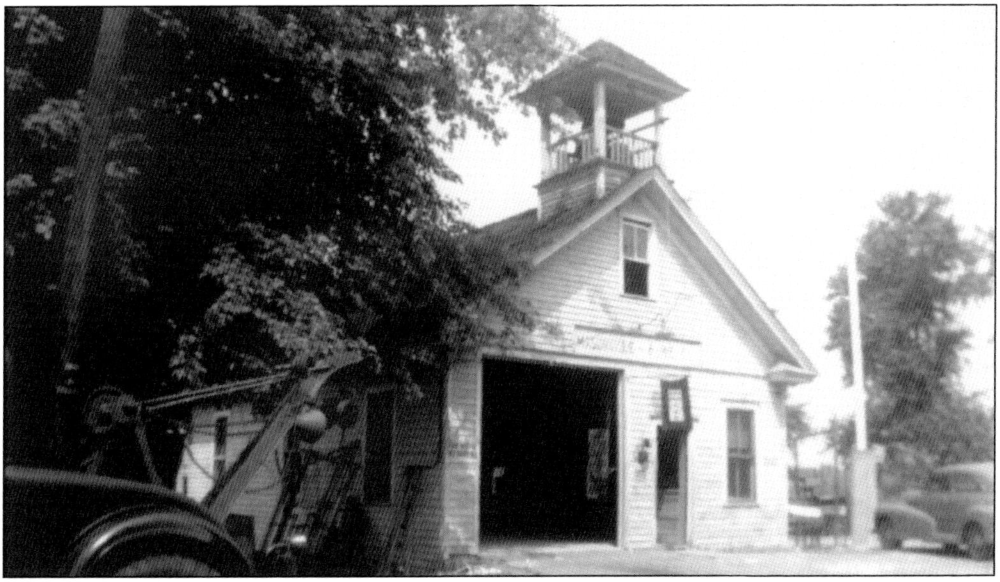

The rebuilt Masonville firehouse was in use and modified many times, with many upgrades, until the 1960s, when the area began to grow, requiring construction of a new firehouse. The firehouse was rebuilt at the same location as the original one. (Courtesy of Richard Tremper and the Masonville Fire Company.)

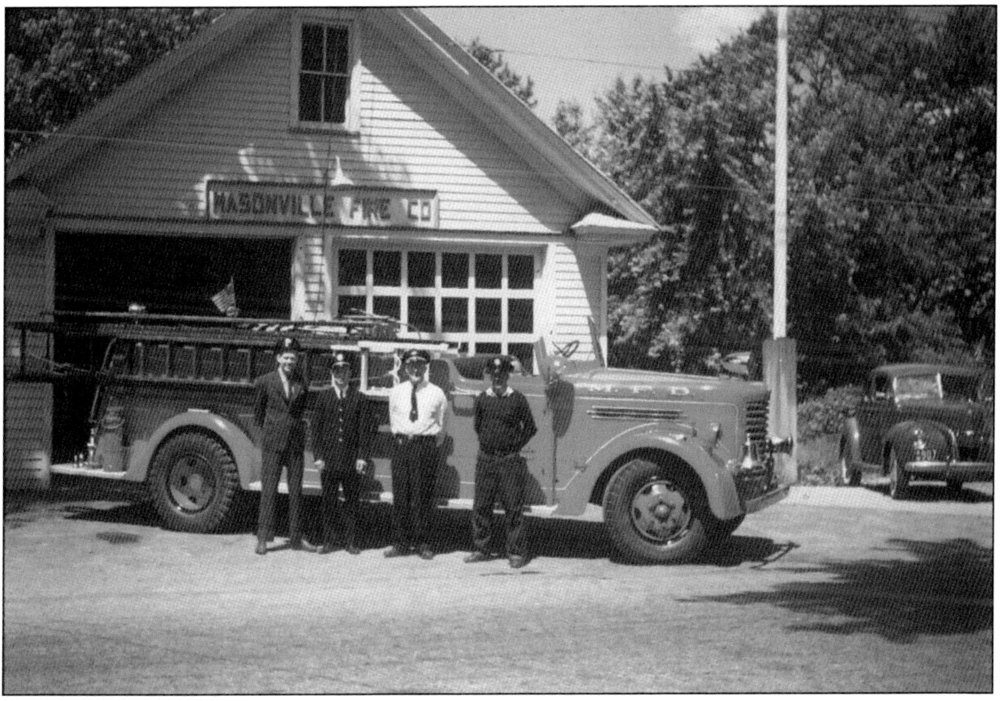

Several unidentified members of the Masonville Fire Company pose at the remodeled firehouse, with its two engine bays. The men are standing in front of a Peter Pirsch engine in the 1950s. At the time, Pirsch, located in Wisconsin, was a leading manufacturer of fire apparatus. The Pirsch company closed in the 1980s. (Courtesy of Richard Tremper and the Masonville Fire Company.)

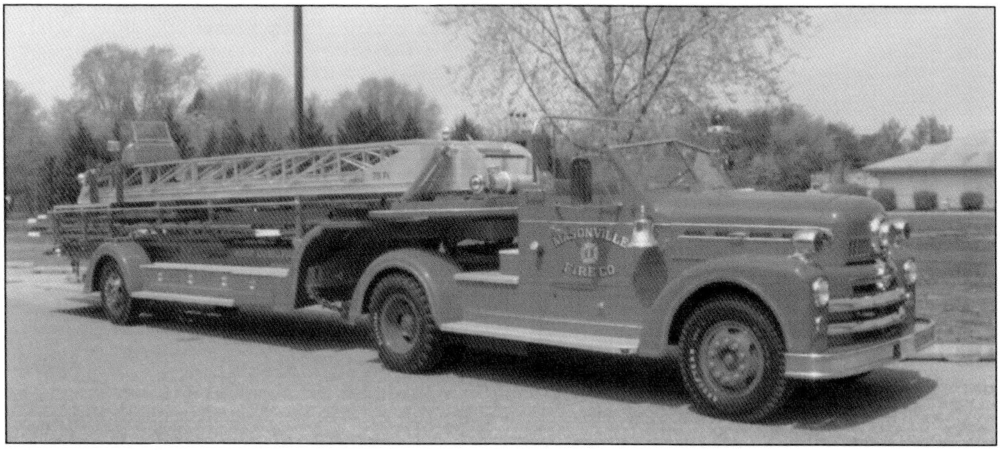

The Masonville Fire Company's 1951 Seagrave Model "66" open cab, 75-foot, tractor-drawn aerial ladder was purchased in 1976 from the Union Fire Company in Mount Holly, where it had served that town for 25 years. It was Mount Laurel Township's first piece of aerial apparatus. The Seagrave was in service for 12 years, until it was retired after a new aerial piece was purchased. The Seagrave became a showpiece for the Masonville Fire Company. (Courtesy of Richard Tremper and the Masonville Fire Company.)

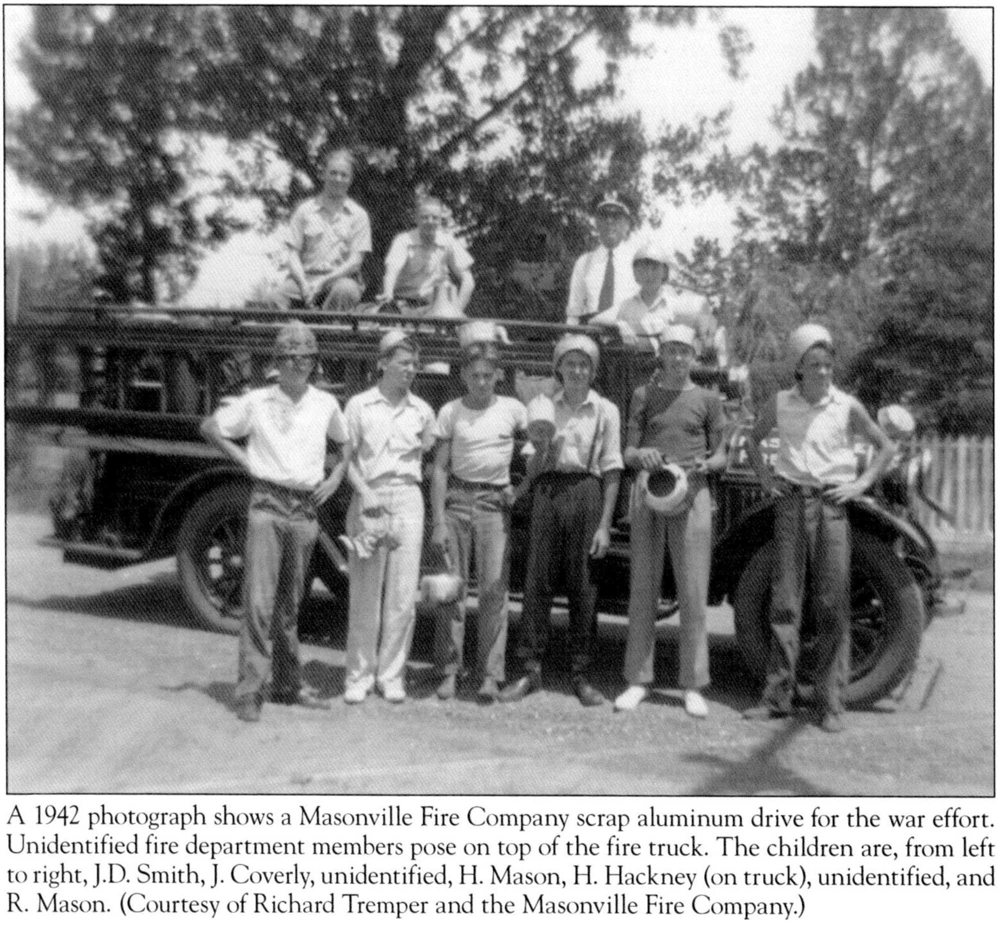

A 1942 photograph shows a Masonville Fire Company scrap aluminum drive for the war effort. Unidentified fire department members pose on top of the fire truck. The children are, from left to right, J.D. Smith, J. Coverly, unidentified, H. Mason, H. Hackney (on truck), unidentified, and R. Mason. (Courtesy of Richard Tremper and the Masonville Fire Company.)

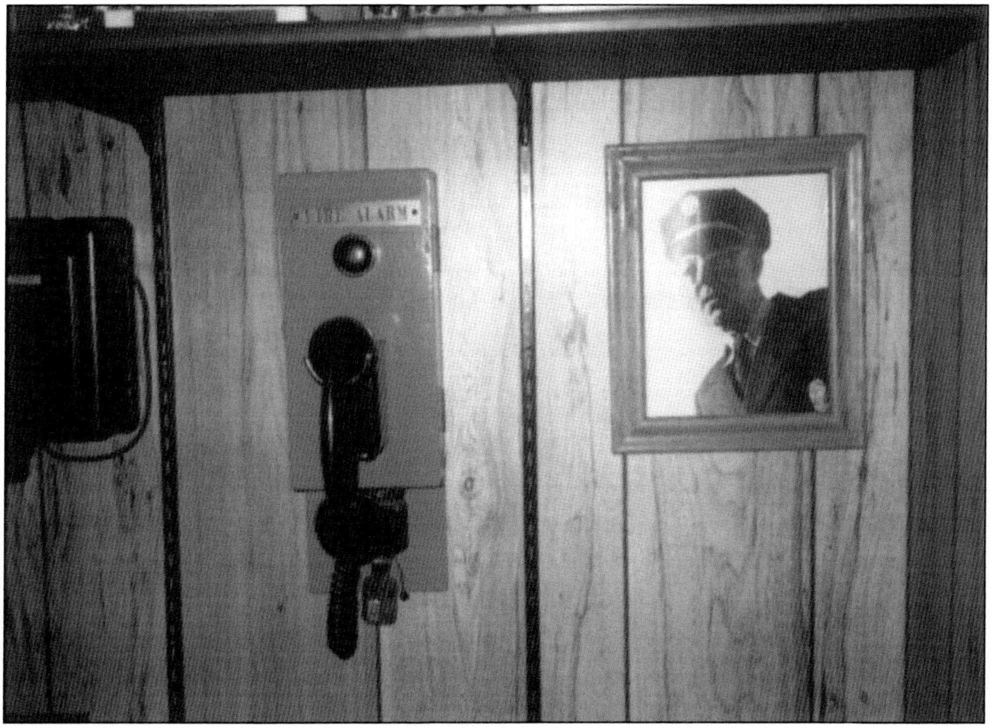

In the 1930s, Chief Arthur Mason designed and installed a phone line in the firehouse and at his home on Centerton Road, about one mile away. Bell Telephone let him run the wire on its cross arms for free, so that he could communicate directly with the firehouse from his home. Chief Mason had been a member of the Philadelphia Fire Department before moving to Masonville. (Courtesy of Richard Tremper and the Masonville Fire Company.)

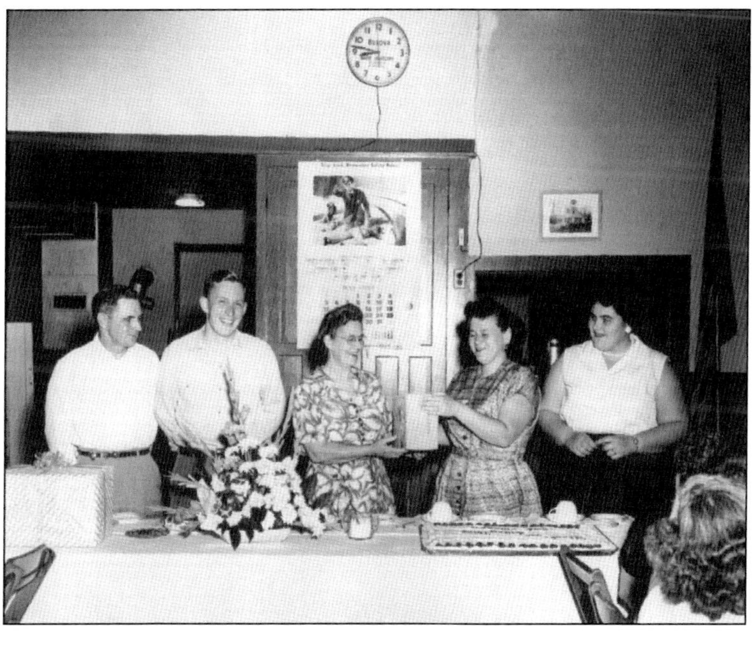

In May 1957, the Masonville Fire Company Ladies' Auxiliary presents a gift and cake to member Mrs. Arthur Mason (center). The cake reads, "Thanks for Everything Mrs. Mason." On the wall in the back is a photograph of the second firehouse. (Courtesy of Richard Tremper and the Masonville Fire Company.)

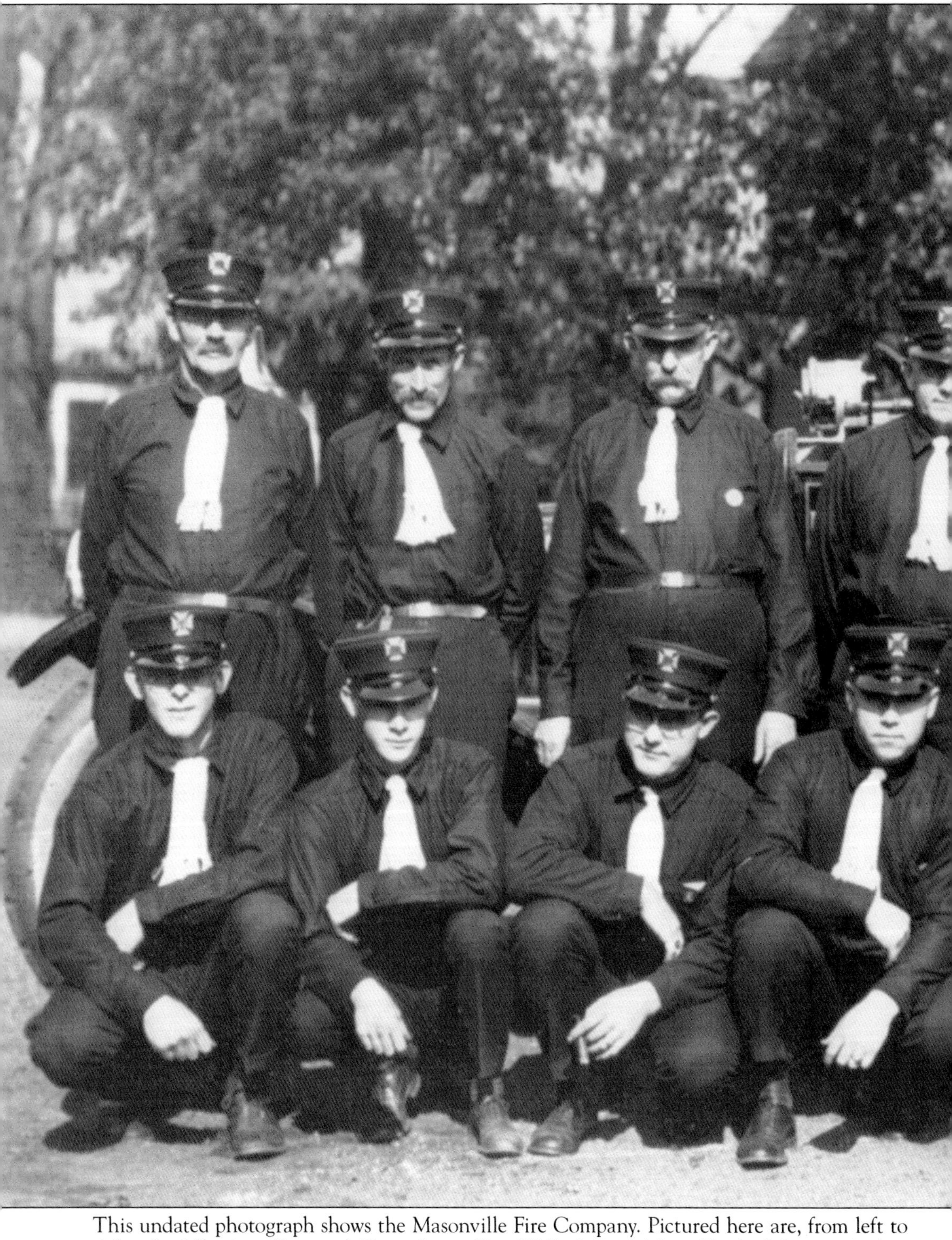

This undated photograph shows the Masonville Fire Company. Pictured here are, from left to right, the following: (first row) Henry Jones, Dan Wells, Julius Melcer, Heisler Johnson, Arthur Mason, Howard Johnson, William H. Mason, George Robinson, and their mascot, Jackie the dog;

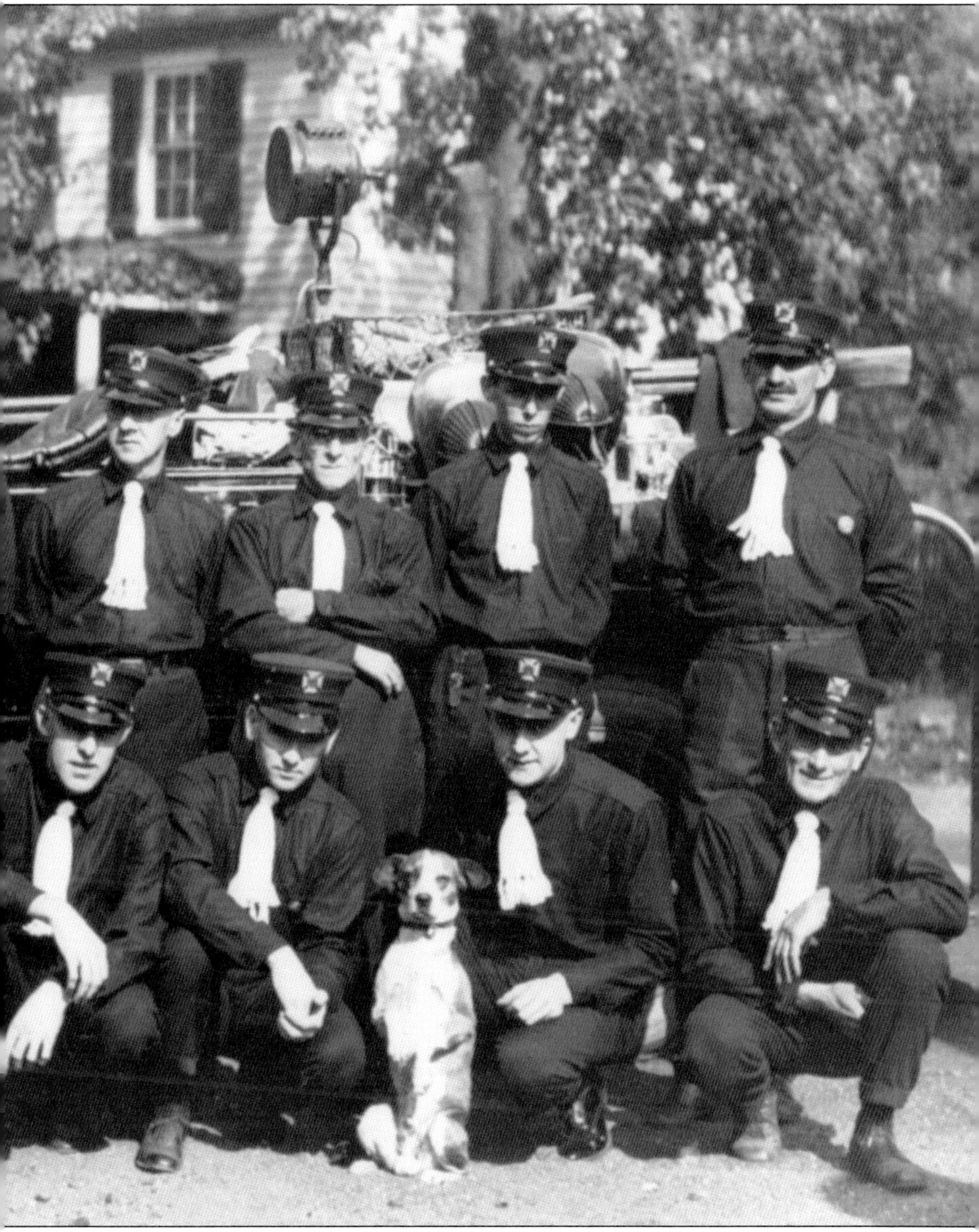

(second row) Chief William A. Lippincott, William Bougher, Squire Aaronson, Raymond Warrick, George LeDent, Fred Gibbs, John Gibbs, and Dave Hunter. (Courtesy of Richard Tremper and the Masonville Fire Company.)

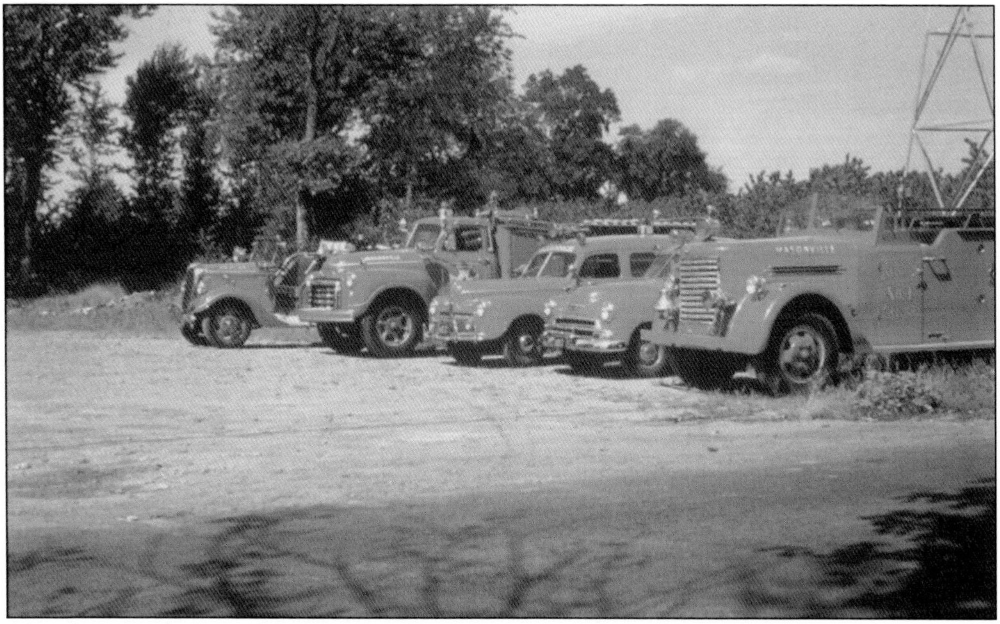

This photograph shows fire apparatus displayed in front of the Larchmont Farms apple orchards. The vehicles are, from back to front, a 1938 Ford AFE engine, a 1953 GMC engine, Masonville Emergency Squad's 1940s Ford-Siebert ambulance, a 1951 Chevrolet ambulance, and a 1942 Pirsch engine. (Courtesy of Richard Tremper and the Masonville Fire Company.)

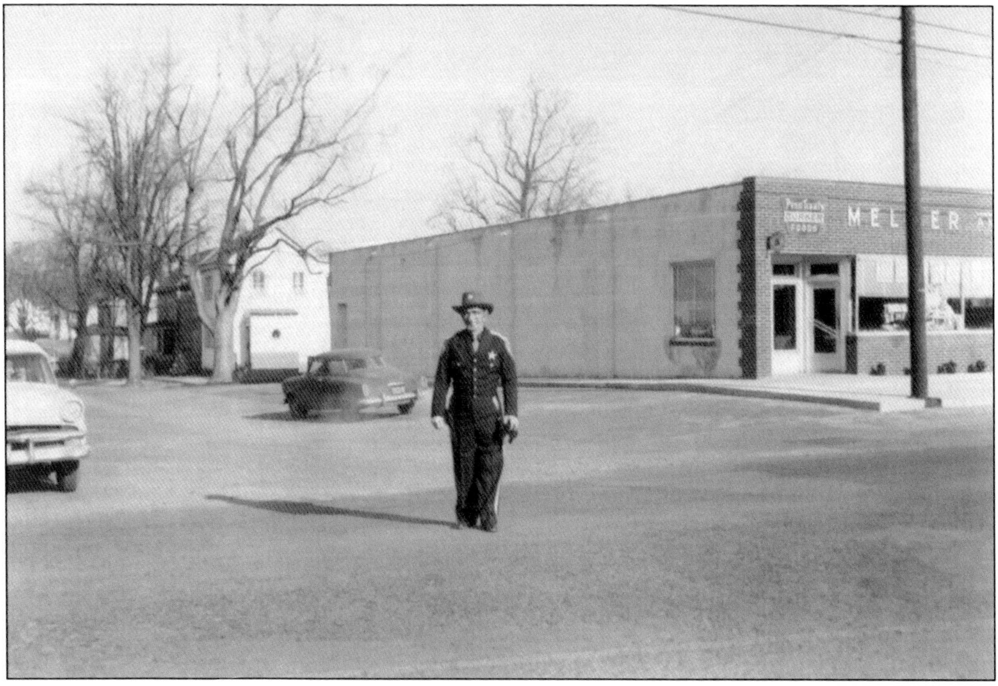

Harry Dolan, standing in the intersection of Masonville Road and Marne Highway, was a Masonville fireman and fire police officer. He also served as a special officer with the Mount Laurel Police. The building behind him is Melcer's Grocery. (Courtesy of Richard Tremper and the Masonville Fire Company.)

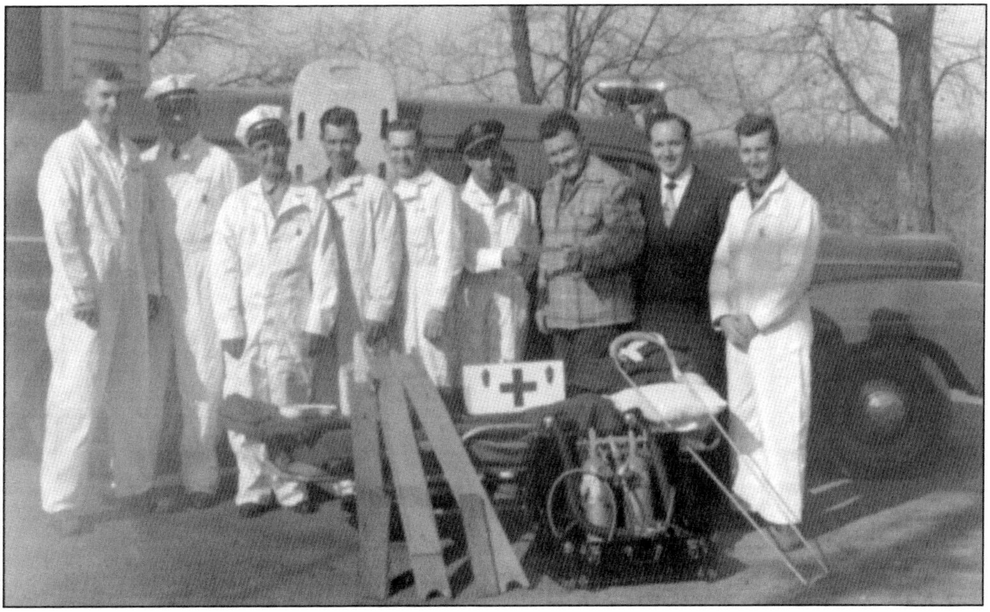

A 1942 Ford Siebert ambulance is shown behind squad members as they receive new ambulance equipment. Shown here are, from left to right, S. Roger Sharp, Walter Janssen, Harry Dolan, Ray Fenimore, Theodore Thomas, Norman Thomas, two representatives from the Lions Club, and John S. Coverly. (Courtesy of Richard Tremper and the Masonville Fire Company.)

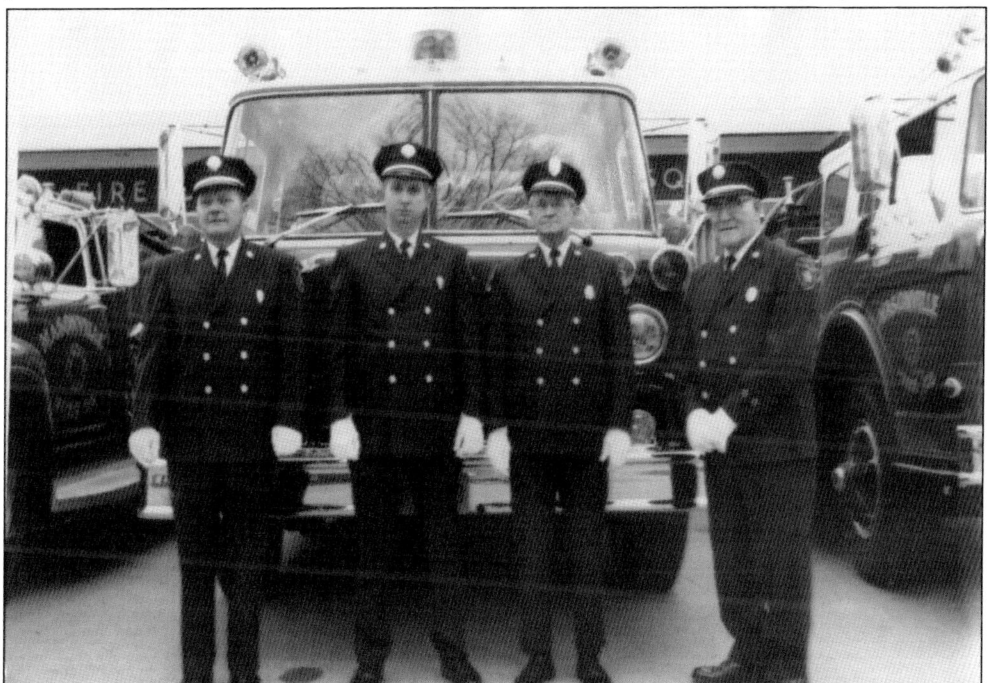

Posing here are, from left to right, G. Willis Graham, S. Roger Sharp, John Peak, and Maurice "Whitey" Forvour. They are standing in front of a 1966 Ford Thibault pumper. On the left is a 1953 GMC pumper, and on the right is a 1968 Ford Thibault pumper. (Courtesy of Richard Tremper and the Masonville Fire Company.)

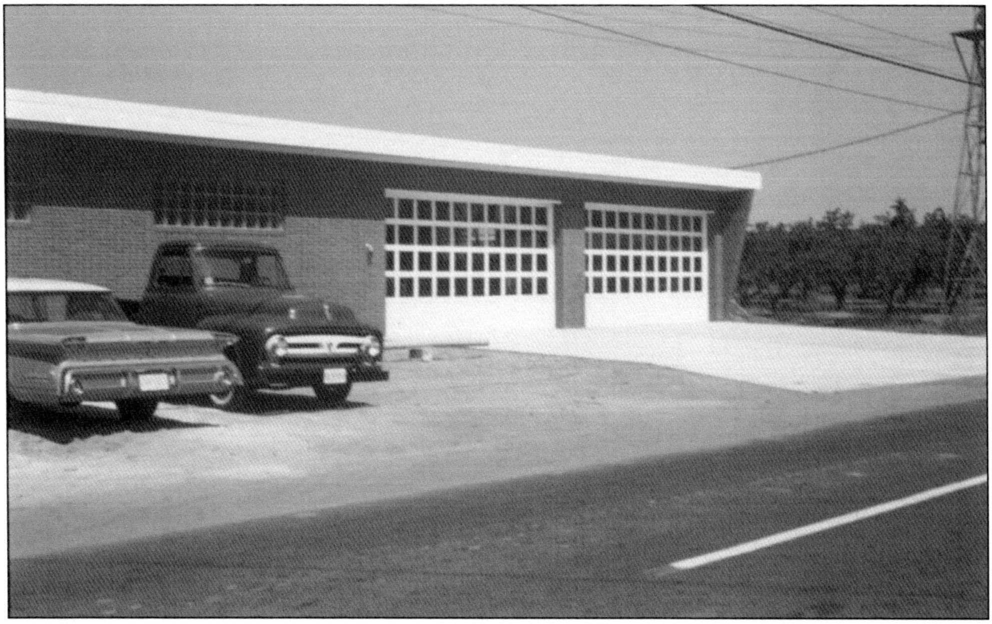

This Masonville firehouse, built in 1961, was among the most modern firehouses in the area. This facility was built at the same location as the previous firehouses. The structure was remodeled several times, including the addition of a bingo/banquet hall in 1976. (Courtesy of Richard Tremper and the Masonville Fire Company.)

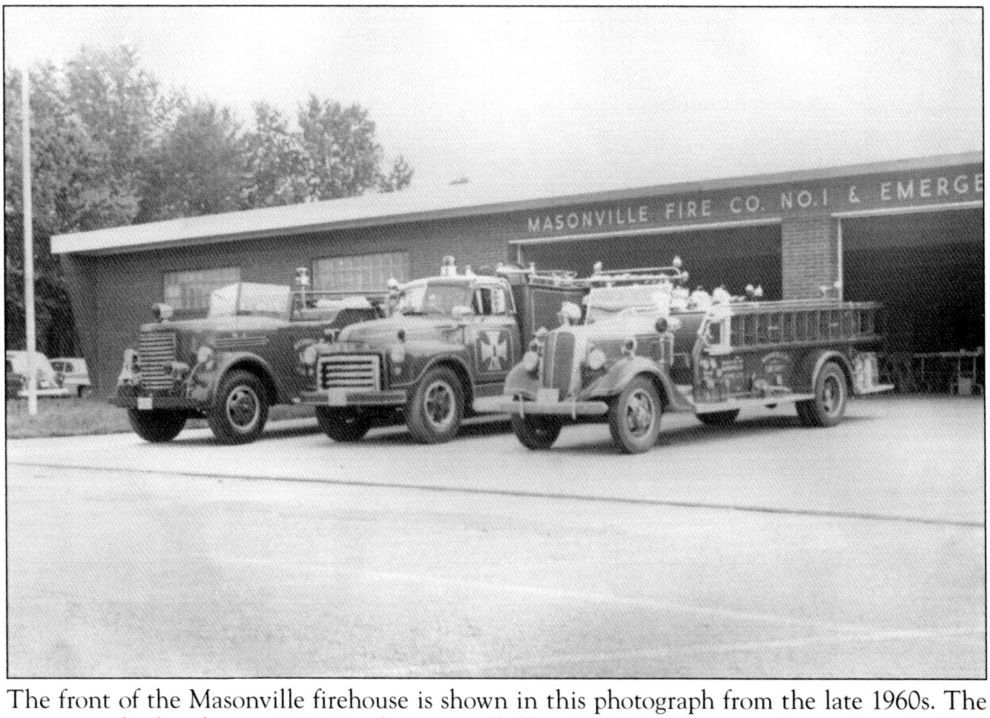

The front of the Masonville firehouse is shown in this photograph from the late 1960s. The apparatus displayed are a 1942 Pirsch pumper (left), a 1953 GMC pumper (center), and a 1938 Ford pumper. At this time, the entire fire company comprised volunteers, who were alerted via a fire siren. (Courtesy of Richard Tremper and the Masonville Fire Company.)

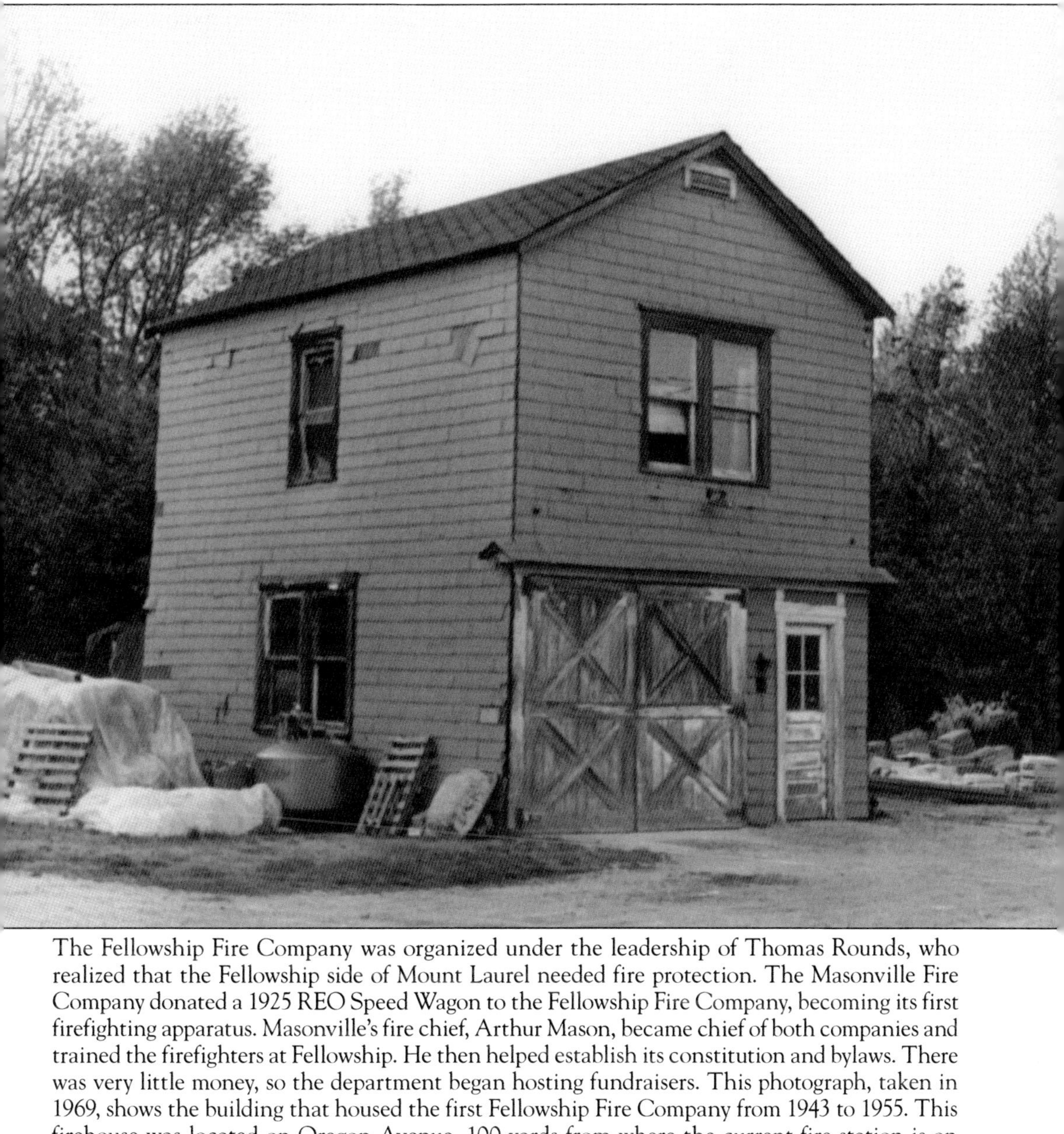

The Fellowship Fire Company was organized under the leadership of Thomas Rounds, who realized that the Fellowship side of Mount Laurel needed fire protection. The Masonville Fire Company donated a 1925 REO Speed Wagon to the Fellowship Fire Company, becoming its first firefighting apparatus. Masonville's fire chief, Arthur Mason, became chief of both companies and trained the firefighters at Fellowship. He then helped establish its constitution and bylaws. There was very little money, so the department began hosting fundraisers. This photograph, taken in 1969, shows the building that housed the first Fellowship Fire Company from 1943 to 1955. This firehouse was located on Oregon Avenue, 100 yards from where the current fire station is on Church Road. The land that was used for the second firehouse was donated by Paul Panarello in 1953. To save money, the firemen built the firehouse themselves, completing it in 1955. (Courtesy of the Fellowship Fire Company.)

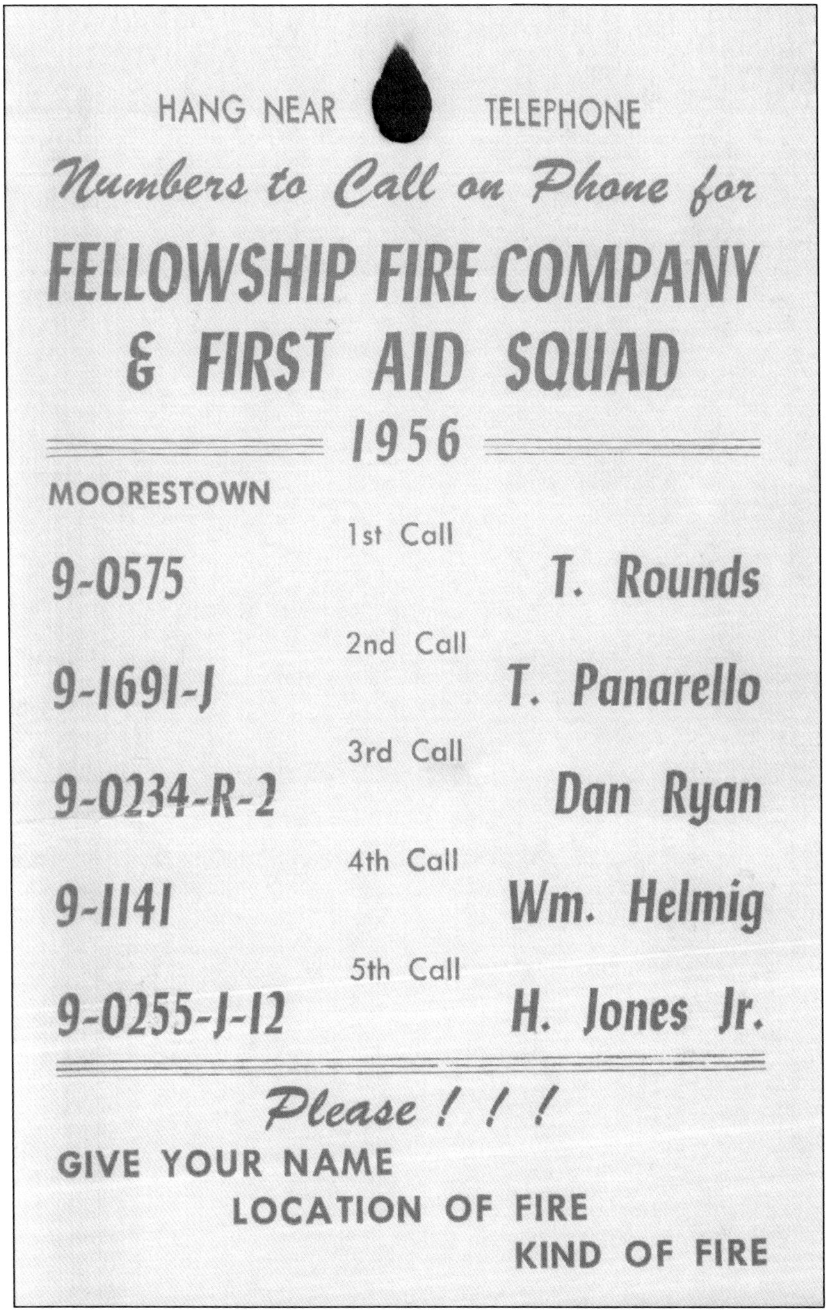
HANG NEAR TELEPHONE

Numbers to Call on Phone for

FELLOWSHIP FIRE COMPANY
& FIRST AID SQUAD

1956

MOORESTOWN

	1st Call	
9-0575		T. Rounds
	2nd Call	
9-1691-J		T. Panarello
	3rd Call	
9-0234-R-2		Dan Ryan
	4th Call	
9-1141		Wm. Helmig
	5th Call	
9-0255-J-12		H. Jones Jr.

Please ! ! !

GIVE YOUR NAME
LOCATION OF FIRE
KIND OF FIRE

Each Mount Laurel resident in the Fellowship area was given a sticker to hang near their telephone. In case of a fire or medical emergency, residents needed to call the first person on the list, Thomas Rounds, who organized the Fellowship Fire Company. If he was not available, Tony Panarello, the chief of police, was the second person to be called, then Dan Ryan, William Helmig, down to the fifth person, Harvey Jones Jr. The resident would continue to call until reaching one of these people. This list is from 1956. Before the 911 system and caller ID, the caller had to give their name, the location of the fire, and the type of fire it was. (Courtesy of the Fellowship Fire Company.)

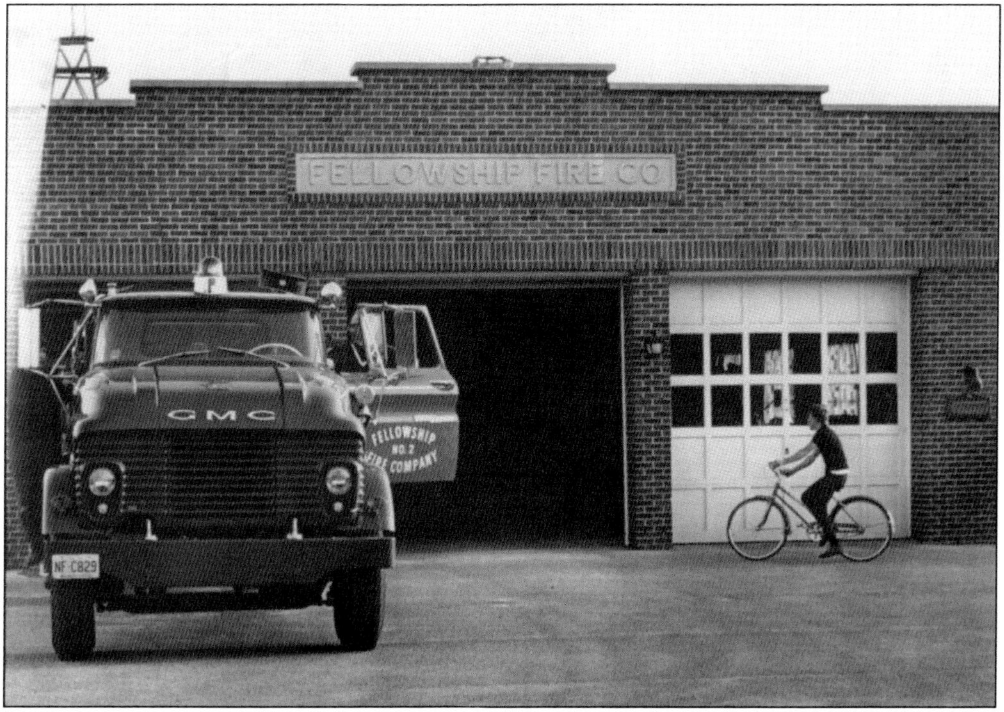

These photographs show a 1960 GMC in front of the Fellowship Firehouse. Clyde Tew is seen riding his bike on the right side in the above photograph. The township supported Fellowship through a small yearly budget, but it was not enough, so they held scrap-metal drives, oyster suppers, and card and bingo events, making enough money to not only sustain the fire company, but also to purchase desperately needed apparatus. (Both images courtesy of the Fellowship Fire Company.)

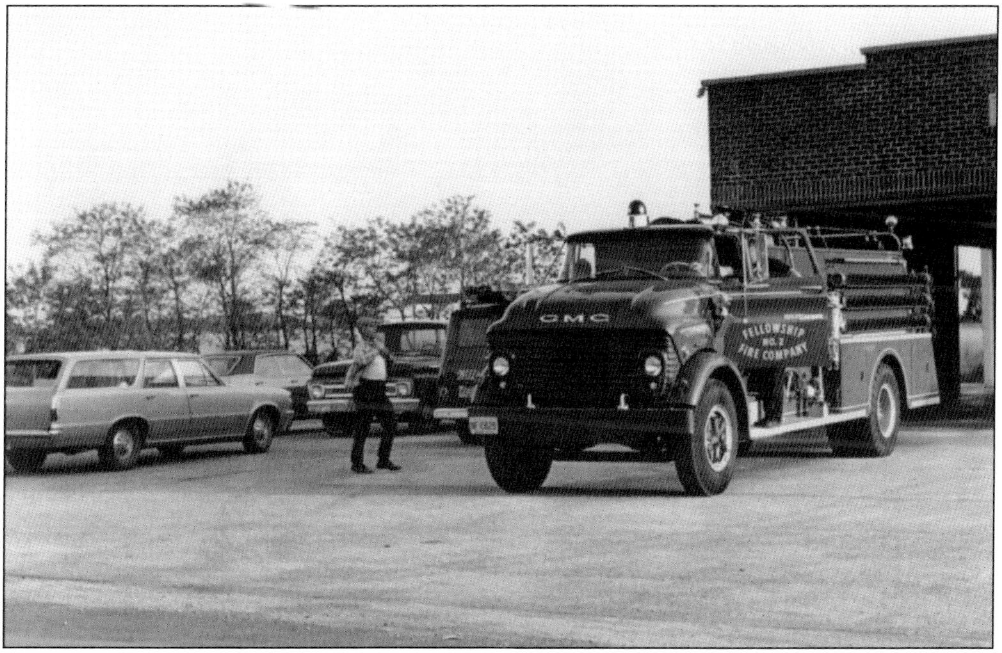

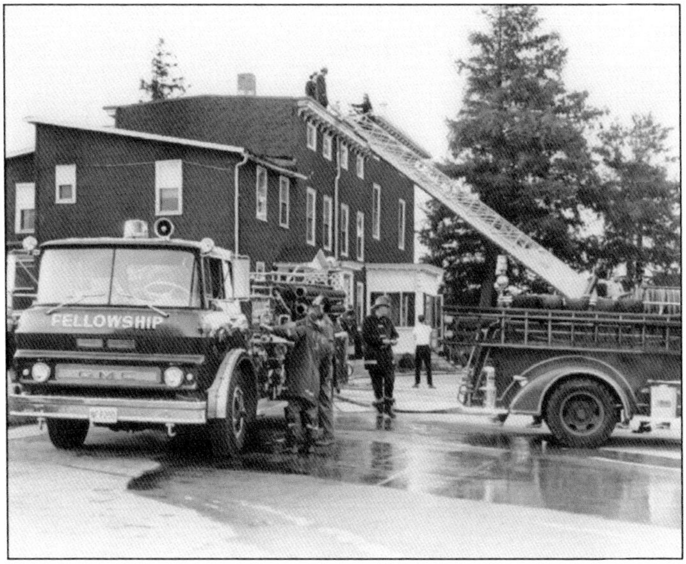

This undated photograph shows the Fellowship Fire Company participating in a drill at the Wiley Mission on Main Street in Marlton, New Jersey. Because volunteers made up the fire companies, they needed to practice their firefighting skills whenever possible. Also, the companies were part of a system of "mutual aid," whereby towns would help each other. It was thus important for each fire company to learn the areas of other towns. (Courtesy of Fellowship Fire Company.)

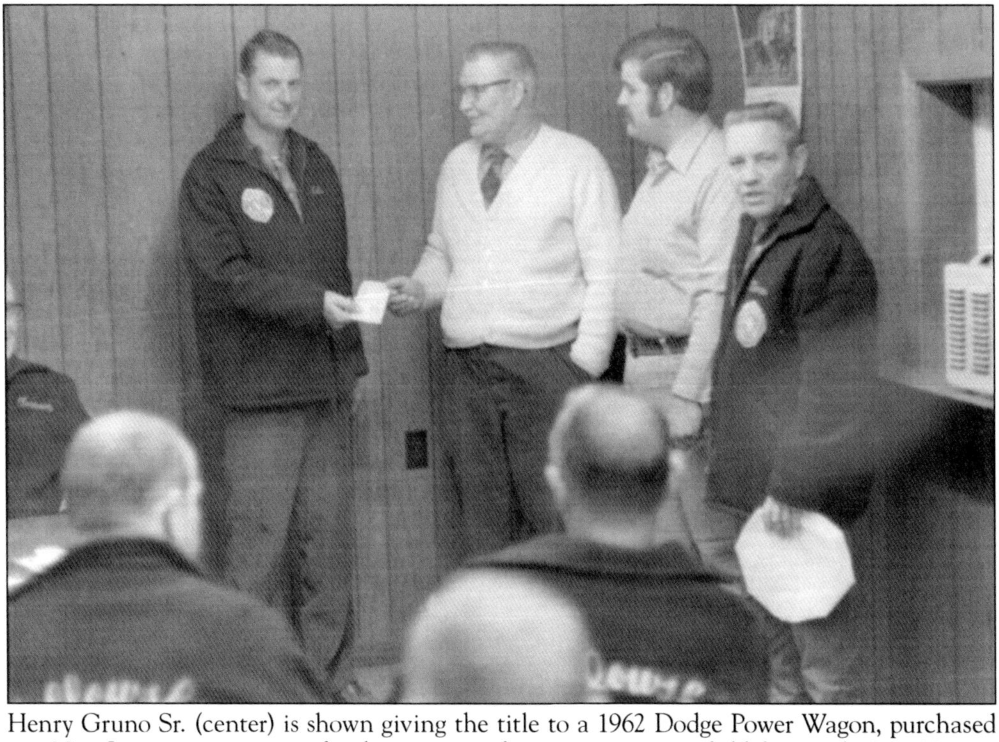

Henry Gruno Sr. (center) is shown giving the title to a 1962 Dodge Power Wagon, purchased at a New Jersey state auction, for the purpose of converting it to a field fire truck. Pete Harvey Jones (left) accepts the title, while Chief M. Norm Tew (far right) and Henry Gruno Jr. of the Fellowship Fire Company watch. Seated at the table at left is Clarence West, treasurer for the fire company. (Courtesy of Fellowship Fire Company.)

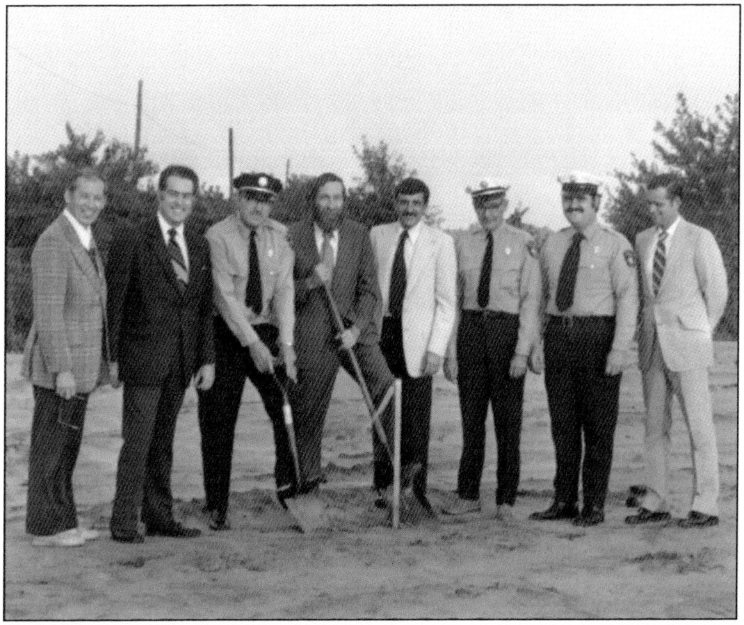

Ground was broken for the Birchfield Firehouse in September 1974. Pictured here are, from left to right, Councilman Massari, Councilman Anderson, Fellowship president Roy Snyder, Mayor Fessler, Councilman Ansaldo, Rich VanHouten, Henry Gruno, and Jarry Jones. (Courtesy of Fellowship Fire Company.)

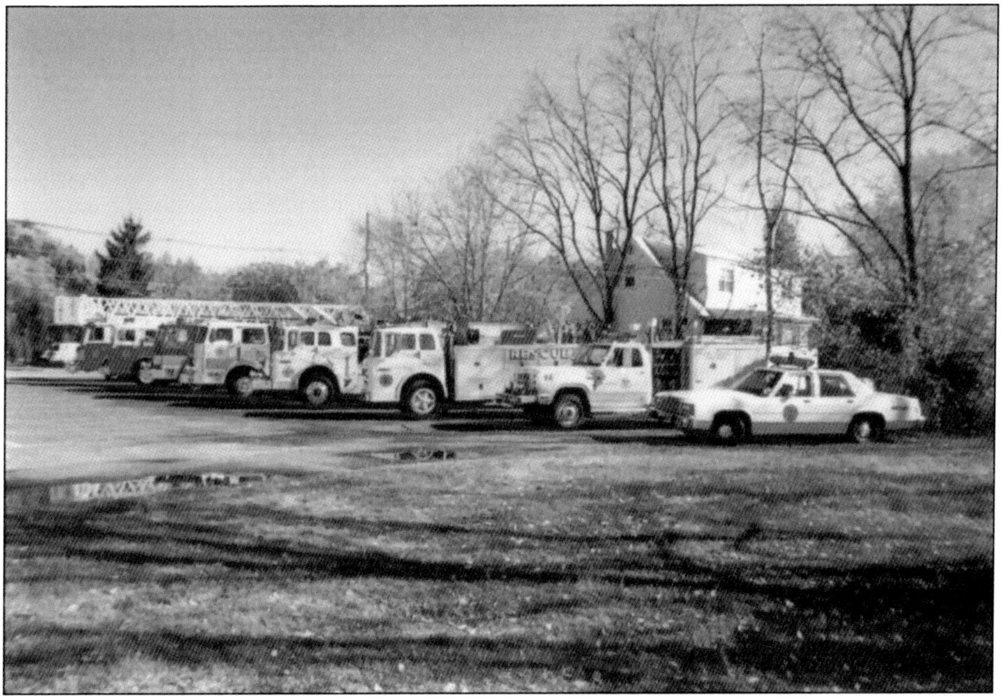

This photograph shows the Fellowship Fire Company's fleet of apparatus in the late 1980s or early 1990s. Pictured here are, from left to right, the following: a 100-foot tower ladder; an unidentified vehicle; a 1976 Hahn pumper; a 1981 Hahn pumper; a Marion Body works pumper; a Ford chassis with utility body, which was purchased secondhand from Holloway Terrace DE; a Dodge Power Wagon "mini pumper," so-called because it was too small to be a pumper and too overloaded with equipment to be a brush truck; and a mid-to-late 1980s Ford LTD chief's car. (Courtesy of the Fellowship Fire Company.)

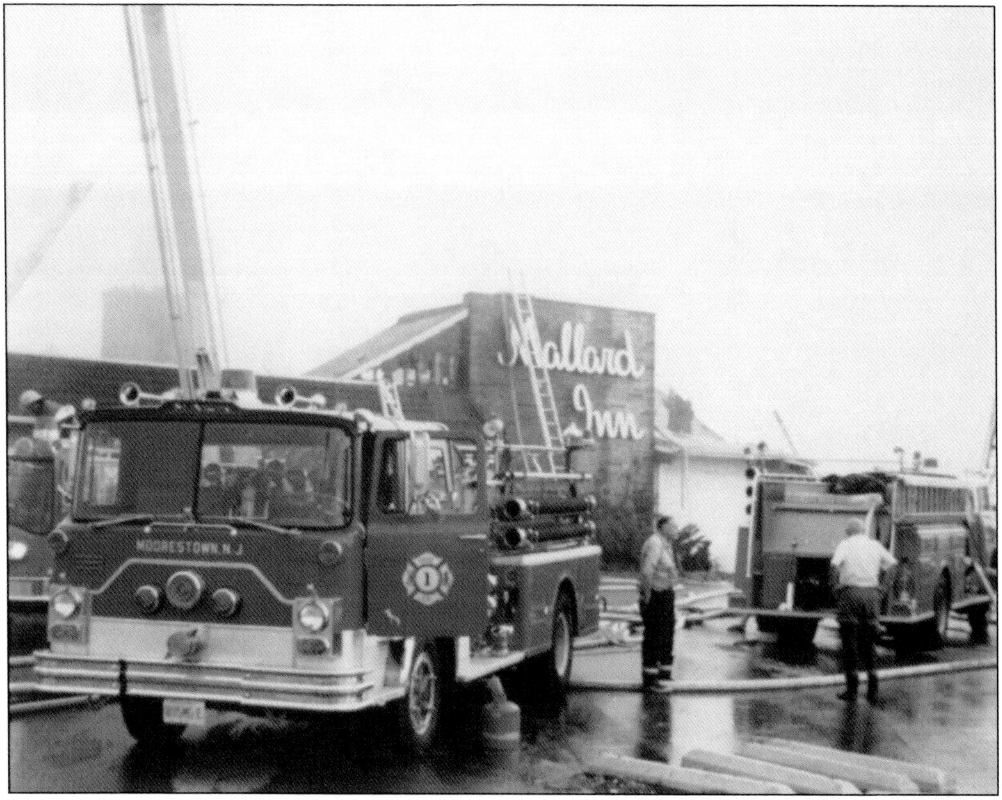

The Mallard Inn stood on Route 73 near the turnpike entrance. It had a dining room, banquet facilities, meeting rooms, and a motor lodge. It caught fire on July 8, 1979, and went to numerous alarms. Clyde Tew, the first one in, reported "light smoke showing." This fire gutted the kitchen, and the roof burned off, but the tables in the dining room were still set like nothing had happened. (Both images courtesy of Fellowship Fire Company.)

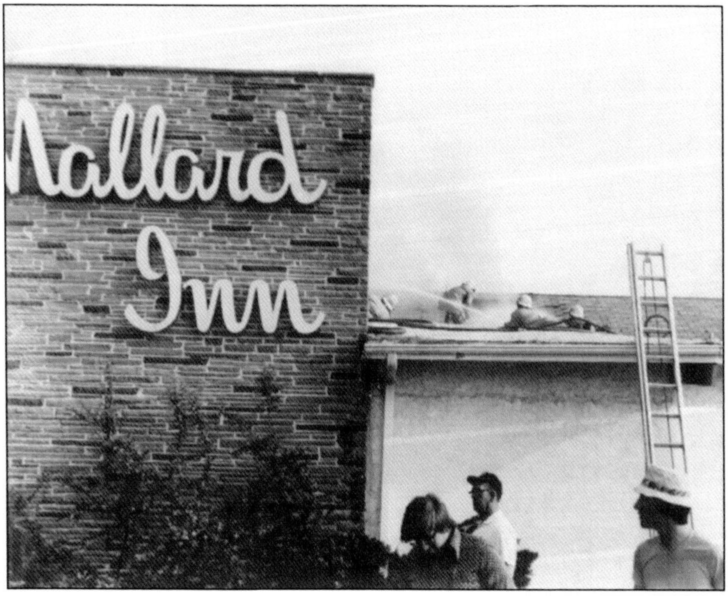

Seven

ALICE PAUL AND PAULSDALE

One of the most influential residents to live in Mount Laurel was Alice Paul. She dedicated her life to the vision that women and men should be equal, an idea her mother fully supported and taught her, and one that her religion endorsed.

Alice Paul was the first child born to William and Tacie Paul, in 1883. The Paul family lived on Hooten Road in Mount Laurel, at what is now called "Paulsdale." Alice's father was a businessman and earned enough to hire labor to handle the necessary daily chores and tasks on a farm. Although the Pauls lived simple lives, Alice and her siblings had responsibilities around the house and farm, which instilled the values of industry and perseverance.

The Paul family was Hicksite Quakers, a group of Quakers that seceded from the more conservative Quakers in 1827 and became more liberal under the leadership of Elias Hicks, thus paving the way for the Paul family to believe in equality for all. Tacie Paul was a member of the National American Woman Suffrage Association and attended meetings, bringing Alice along. Tacie may have had some of these meetings at their home farm, which reinforced the beliefs that Tacie and her fellow suffragettes had.

As Quakers, the Paul family used plain speech. Alice attended a Hicksite Quaker school in Moorestown, to which she walked every day. She was a good student and graduated first in her class in 1901. Alice then left the Mount Laurel area and attended Swarthmore College, just as her mother did. Her grandfather, one of the founders of the school in 1864, also believed in gender equality.

Although many suffragists felt that they had accomplished their mission after the passage of the 19th Amendment in 1920 and then left the crusade, Alice went on to continue the fight for the Equal Rights Amendment.

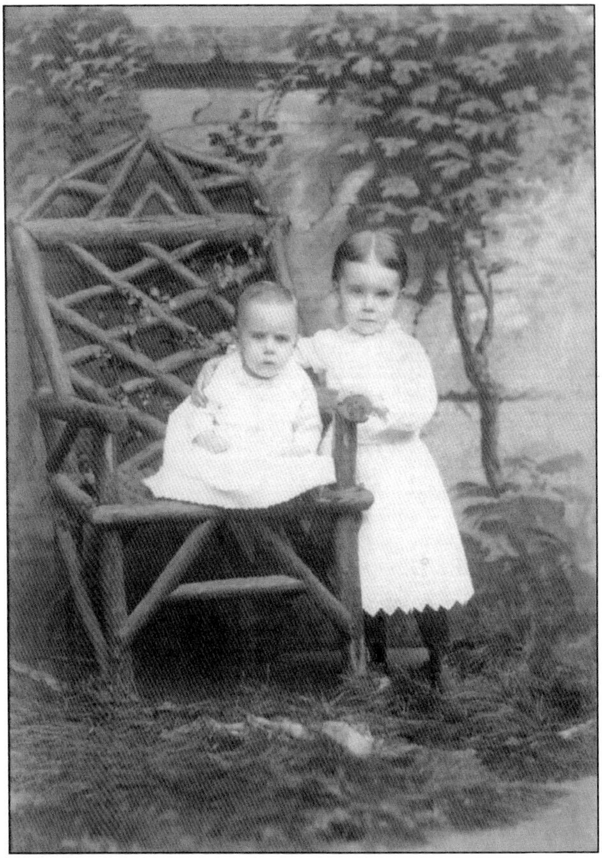

Alice Paul, age two and a half, poses with her brother, William Jr., 10 months old. Alice was born on January 11, 1885, and she died in 1977. She lived in Mount Laurel until she left to attend Swarthmore College in 1901. After college, Alice traveled overseas numerous times. (Courtesy of the Alice Paul Institute.)

Along with Alice, her family included her father, William, mother, Tacie, and three siblings, William Jr., Helen, and Parry. This photograph shows Parry's beagle puppies, which he raised on the home farm. Dating to the 1870s, the Paul's Greek Revival home was listed in the National Register of Historic Places in 1991. (Courtesy of the Alice Paul Institute.)

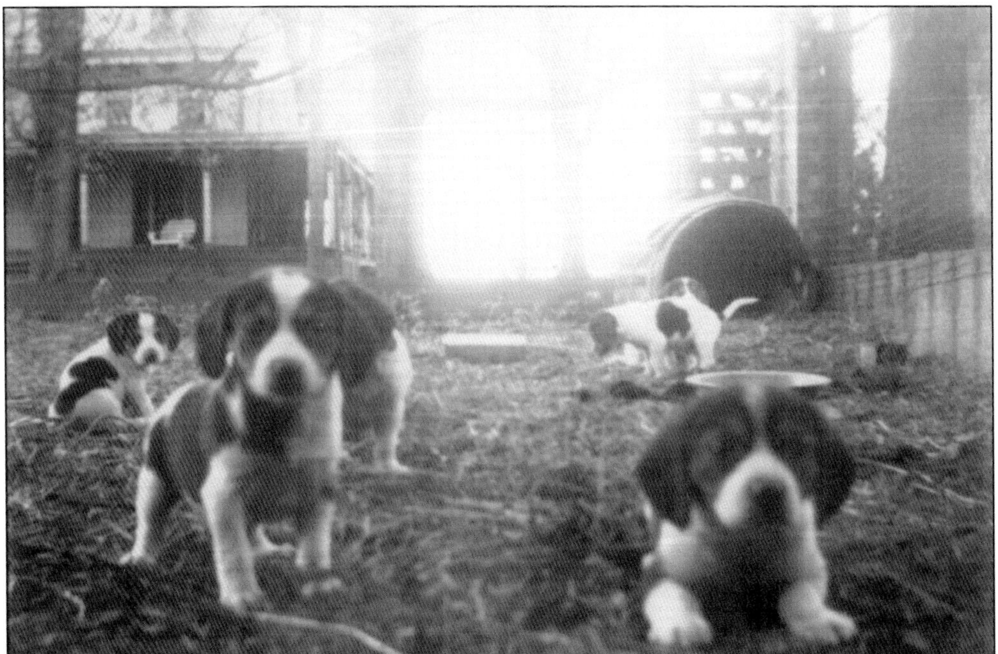

Alice Paul was born at Paulsdale, her family's farm in Mount Laurel. She grew up there and attended a Quaker school in nearby Moorestown. Alice believed, as did her family, that all people should have equal rights. She went on to become a famous suffragette who was integral in getting women the right to vote. (Courtesy of the Alice Paul Institute.)

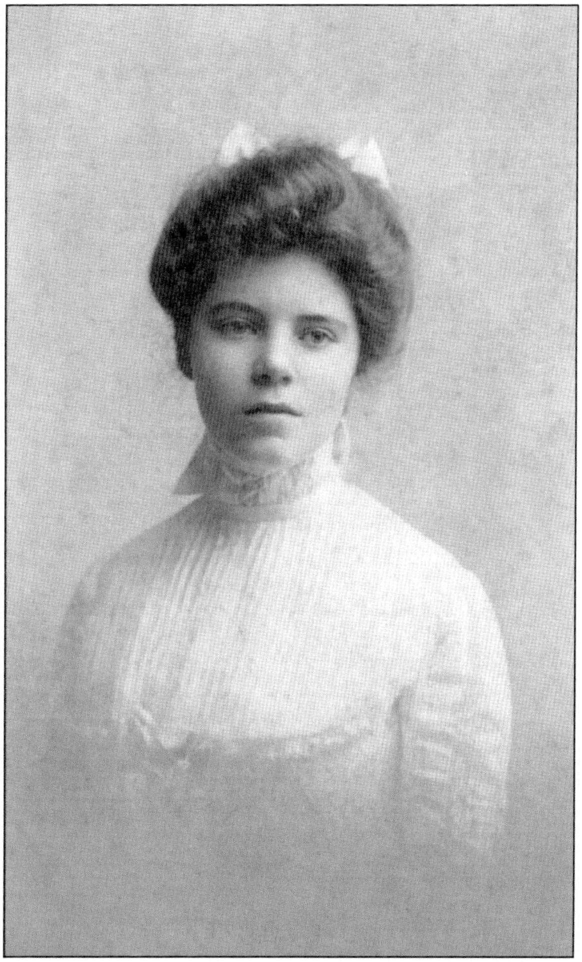

This is the farmhouse, which is the centerpiece of the property where Alice Paul grew up. Today, Paulsdale includes a garage, an icehouse, part of a cow barn and its brick foundation, part of the horse barn and its stone foundation, and two wells. A fire in 1973 consumed many architectural embellishments that had been taken off of the house and stored in the horse barn. (Courtesy of the Alice Paul Institute.)

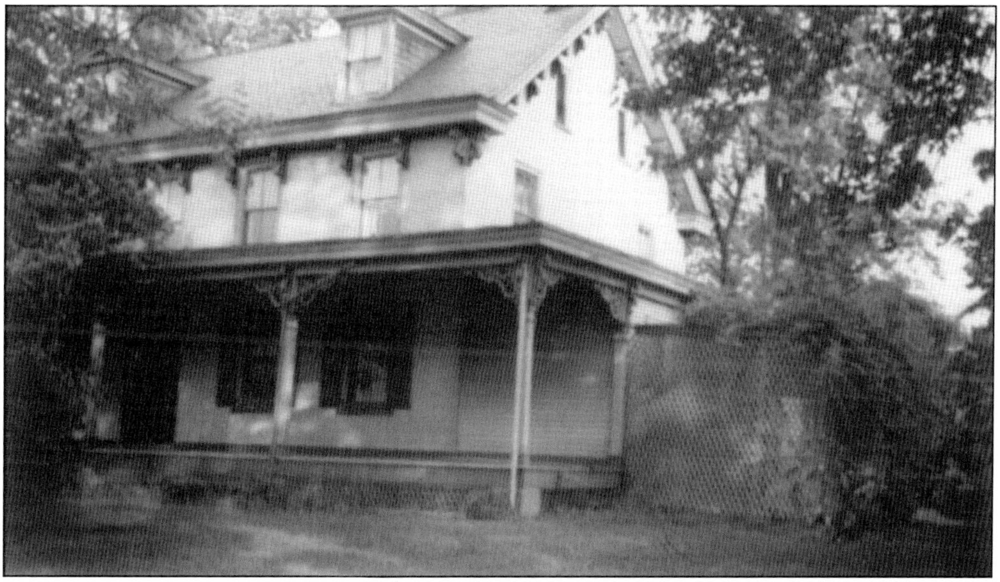

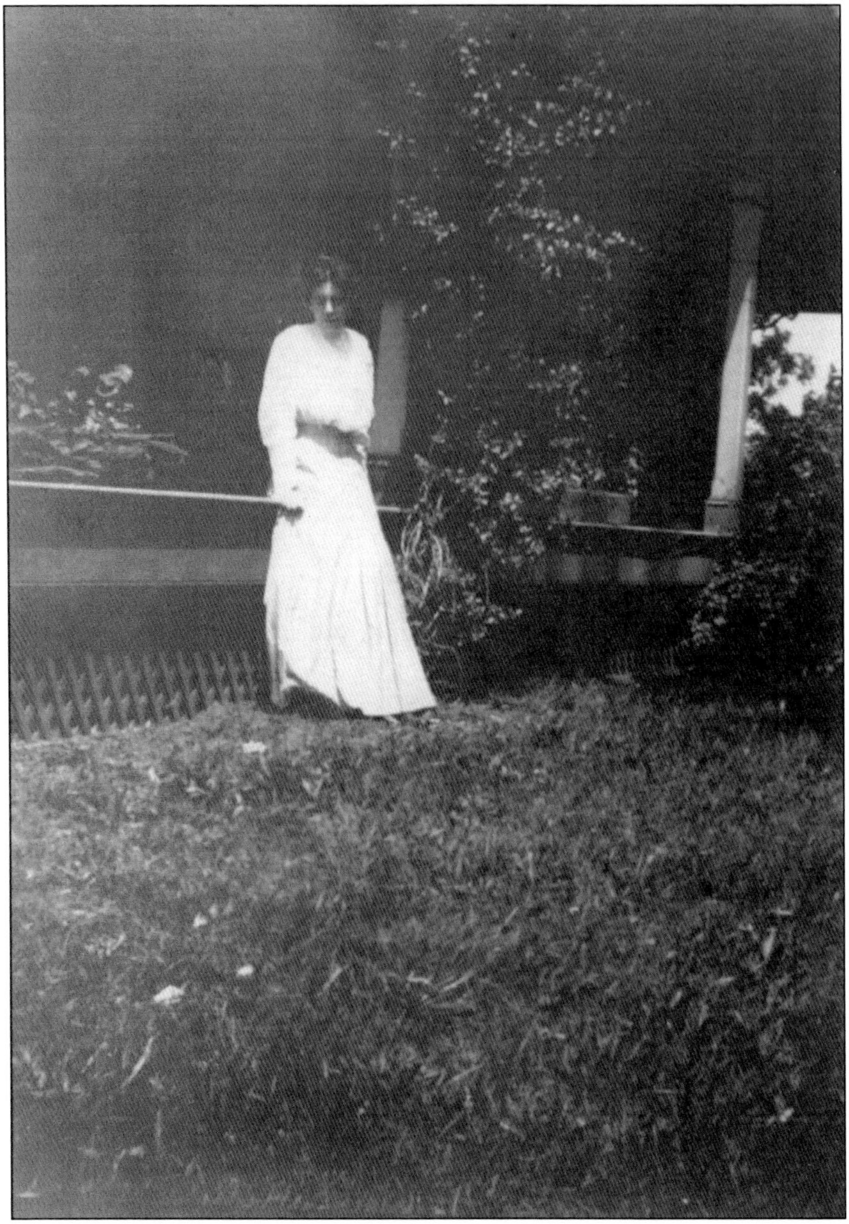

Here, Alice leans on the back porch of her home. There were peach orchards and barns, a henhouse, and an icehouse in the yard that can be seen from the wraparound porch. Paulsdale, her family home, was purchased from John G. Haines and Rebecca P. Haines in 1883 for $17,000. The purchase included the farmhouse, outbuildings, and 166.52 acres. The Paul family lived at Paulsdale from 1883 to 1958. There were Irish maids and other staff that did most of the work, allowing Alice and her family to relax under their copper beech tree, romp with the Beagle puppies, or play tennis on their court. Alice's mother was her biggest influence because of the Quaker values she taught in the home. Growing up, Alice went with her mother to area meetings of women's rights groups. Alice Paul went on to craft the language of the Equal Rights Amendment and first presented it in 1923. Alice led the final campaign to pass the 19th Amendment. (Courtesy of the Alice Paul Institute.)

Bibliography

AOPA *Airport Directory 1968*. Airport Owners and Pilots Association, 1967.
Beck, Henry Charlton. *Forgotten Towns of Southern New Jersey*. New Brunswick, NJ: Rutgers University Press, 1961.
———. *More Forgotten Towns of Southern New Jersey*. New Brunswick, NJ: Rutgers University Press, 1963.
Bisbee, Henry H. *Sign Posts*. Willingboro, NJ: Alexia Press, 1971.
Buck, Watson. *Watson Buck's Presentation: A talk he gave to the Rancocas Women's Club in 1962*. www.rancocasnj.org, accessed on May 20, 2013.
DeCou, George. *Moorestown and Her Neighbors: Historical Sketches*. Philadelphia: Harris & Partridge, 1929.
Flynn, Eileen L. *A History of Mount Laurel*. Mt. Laurel, NJ: Mt. Laurel Board of Education, 2002.
Greenberg, Gail, and Barbara Pickens. *Mt. Laurel: A Centennial History*. New Jersey, 1972.
Griscom, Lloyd E. *Historic County of Burlington*. The Burlington County Cultural and Heritage Commission, 1973.
Lyght, Ernest. *The Black Presence in New Jersey's Burlington County, 1659–1900*. Cherry Hill, NJ: E&E Publishing House, 1978.
Massey, Douglas S., Len Albright, Rebecca Casciano, Elizabeth Derickson, and David N. Kinsey. *Climbing Mount Laurel*. Princeton, NJ: Princeton University Press, 2013.
McMahon, William. *South Jersey Towns*. New Brunswick, NJ: Rutgers University Press, 1973.
Rizzo, Dennis. *Parallel Communities: The Underground Railroad in South Jersey*. Charleston, SC: History Press, 2008.
Spurr, O. Kirk. *Dorothy's Dream*. North Andover, MA: Persimmon Press.